A Short History of
Presidential Elections

Eugene H. Roseboom

A SHORT HISTORY
OF
PRESIDENTIAL
ELECTIONS

Collier Books / New York
Collier-Macmillan / London

First Collier Books Edition 1967

A History of Presidential Elections
was published in a hardcover edition
by The Macmillan Company

The Macmillan Company, New York
Collier-Macmillan Canada Ltd., Toronto, Ontario
Printed in the United States of America

CONTENTS

PREFACE

This book is largely a condensation of the author's *A History of Presidential Elections* (2nd ed., Macmillan, New York, 1964). The pages covering the campaigns have been taken from the larger volume and incorporated in the abridgment with only minor changes and omissions. The chapter on the election of 1964 is new as the older work ended with the beginning of that campaign. The background and transitional sections and the accounts of nominations have been replaced with shortened versions, but with enough of the essential facts retained to make the story of the campaigns intelligible, it is hoped, even to those readers who may have forgotten most of the American history they learned in school or college.

The selective bibliography includes several books that were not available when the original volume was in preparation. I have changed slightly the totals of popular votes—always a headache for the meticulous researcher—to conform to figures of the most recent compilations.

I am deeply indebted, as in the case of the earlier work, to my wife, Thelma Matheny Roseboom, for many hours of careful typing, as well as for clarifying my foggy sentences and for insuring that pronouns had proper antecedents, hyphens were inserted in the right places, and spelling conformed to the best usage.

Eugene H. Roseboom

CHAPTER I

THE ELECTORAL SYSTEM
AND THE FIRST ELECTIONS

1789–1800

AMERICANS HAD BEEN accustomed to politics, but without organized parties, almost from the time of the first elections for assemblies in the early years of British rule. National divisions first appeared when colonial Americans revolted in 1775. The term Whig was used for patriots (rebels, in British eyes) and the term Tory for loyalists (traitors, to Americans). The success of independence eliminated the Tories, and politics resumed its local character with vague radical-conservative connotations attached to the alignments in the different states during the post-Revolution years.

The conservative groups, moving for a stronger central government, produced the Philadelphia convention of 1787 which wrote the Constitution of the United States. The struggle over its ratification became a national one but fought out in each state with differing circumstances affecting the results. Supporters of ratification called themselves Federalists (avoiding the more accurate "nationalists") and dubbed their opponents Antifederalists. With some exceptions, the wealthy, more thickly populated areas of the seaboard were Federalist; the small farmer inland, Antifederalist. With the success of ratification and the fortunate return of prosperity after the hard times of the 1780's, antifederalism could make but a feeble gesture in the first Presidential and Congressional elections.

The framers of the Constitution of the United States did not rely on precedents in setting up the electoral system for nominating and electing the President. Theirs was an original contribution to American political processes. Their crystal ball failed them here, for it did not reveal the emergence of national political parties, which made their carefully wrought piece of eighteenth-century machinery a nineteenth-century anachronism. They had hammered out a method of nominating and electing the chief executive which, they believed, would not let in too much democracy, would sift out the less fit among the possible choices, would let Congress have a restricted share in the final selection, and would satisfy the states by leaving to them a good deal of leeway in the initial stages of the process.

Except for the changes in the Twelfth Amendment, the old machinery is still with us. It is cranked up quadrennially for what is generally regarded as a meaningless performance, for it has been made to fit, after a fashion, the operations of a party system that had no place in the thinking of its creators. But its rusty gears are dangerously defective and might, under certain circumstances, be manipulated to subvert the democratic process of electing a President long accepted by the descendants of the framers. The old electoral machine needs a complete overhaul or a relegation to the scrap heap.

The original system provided that each state should choose electors equal in number to the state's Senators and Representatives in Congress. The state legislature was free to set up the method of election. It could elect them itself; it could use some form of popular vote; or it could adopt a hybrid arrangement, as Massachusetts and New Hampshire did in the first elections. These electors were to meet in their respective states on the same day, and each elector was to vote for two persons for President, one not a resident of the state. The two houses of Congress, in joint session, were to tabulate the votes. If one person had a majority of the whole number of electors, he became President; the second high man became Vice President. A tie in majority votes would be settled by the House of Representatives, each state casting one vote. If no one had a majority, the House would decide from the five highest. The authors of the system seemed to have assumed that support for local favorites would mean a wide scattering of votes and that, normally, no one would have a majority.

The first Presidential election did conform in a way to the intent of the founding fathers. No primaries, no nominating conventions, no campaigning, no national balloting, and no prognosticating opinion polls—this was the happy state of the nation when George Washington was elected. But all the paraphernalia of present-day elections would not have affected the outcome when the electors, chosen a month earlier in a variety of ways, met to cast their votes on the first Wednesday of February, 1789. Washington had no rival in the hearts of his countrymen and every one of the sixty-nine electors voted for him. But this was an exceptional situation not likely to recur, although Monroe came within one vote of unanimity in 1820.

In registering their second choices the electors performed more nearly according to the norm expected of them. Rotund, snappish John Adams, respected for his scholarly writings on governments, ancient and modern, and for his contributions to the American cause as legislator and diplomat during and after the Revolution, was a logical choice for the second office. But he received only thirty-four electoral votes while thirty-five were divided among ten other worthies. He accepted the office but wrote afterward to a friend: "Is not my election to this office in the scurvy manner in which it was done, a curse rather than a blessing? Is there Gratitude? Is there Justice?" Only his fears of "great mischief" and "the final failure of the government from my refusal" prevented him from spurning it.

Adams did not know that Alexander Hamilton influenced some of the electors so not to couple him with Washington. Hamilton did this to make certain that the New Englander's total did not pass Washington's vote and give the former the first office, an unnecessary stratagem to guard against an unlikely contingency. He regarded Adams as a potential malcontent who had to be mollified with some high office—and the Vice Presidency would serve. The first Vice President called his position "the most insignificant . . . that ever invention of man contrived, or his imagination conceived."

National political parties under the Constitution started not in the grass roots but in cabinet and Congress and spread from the top downward. Alexander Hamilton, first Secretary of the Treasury, offered a financial program that quickly aroused strong opposition. He recommended to Congress the refunding of the depreciated Continental securities at par value, the assumption of state debts by the federal government, the creation of a United States Bank, the levying of an excise tax on distilled liquors, and a protective tariff. All but the last were enacted. These measures were designed to put the government on a sound financial basis, and they won the approval of the seaboard's business and financial centers. But representatives of rural constituencies, angry at the activities of speculators in securities and fearing that the measures meant heavy taxes, debt increases, and the rule of the rich, drew together to oppose the Treasury cohorts.

James Madison, who had worked with Hamilton in the struggle for ratification of the Constitution, fought the Hamilton measures in Congress and soon had the ear of Thomas Jefferson, Secretary of State. Jefferson had helped Hamilton get the assumption proposal through the House in return for support for a future national capital on the Potomac. But he opposed the bill for a United States Bank as unconstitutional and urged Washington to veto it. The President gave the Treasury the benefit of the doubt and signed it. Thereafter the two Secretaries opposed each other on major issues.

Hamilton's philosophy of statecraft involved the use of the power of the new federal government to advance the interests of the business and financial classes, which would form a bulwark to protect the government against the turbulent and changing masses who "seldom judge or determine right." His following kept the name Federalist for themselves and gave their opponents the now unpopular designation of Antifederalist.

Thomas Jefferson's politico-economic philosophy was primarily agrarian. He saw the United States as still a nation of farmers and he would keep it so. Every man could be a landowner and every landowner a voter. He assailed Hamilton's policies as in the interest of "paper capitalists," and he opposed the extension of federal power, particularly in the executive branch, as a threat to states' rights and individual liberties. Later he was to use that power when it benefited his nation of farmers. The Jeffersonians called themselves Republicans as opposed to the monarchists, or "Monocrats," entrenched in the Treasury Department.

A newspaper war between Hamilton's organ, the *Gazette of the United States*, edited by John Fenno, which enjoyed the public printing plums, and the *National Gazette* of Philip Freneau, who received a part-time clerkship in the State Department, worried the President who wanted harmony in the national councils.

1792

Upon one point the rivals were in complete agreement. This was that Washington should accept a second term. Jefferson was insistent. "Your being at the helm will be more than an answer to every argument which can be used to alarm and lead the people in any quarter, into violence and secession. North and South will hang together if they have you to hang on." Washington, now sixty and afflicted with deafness and bad dentistry, as well as the cares of state, reluctantly accepted as a matter of duty, though he longed for the peace and freedom of neglected Mount Vernon. But the Republicans regarded the second office in the government as fair prey, and they set to work to get rid of John Adams.

The Federalists accepted Adams as their Vice Presidential choice without any formal action. Hamilton, at heart more of a monarchist than Adams, nevertheless thought the latter too indiscreet; but he made no attempt to offer another candidate. His efforts were centered on defeating the original opposition choice, New York's Governor George Clinton, an old enemy. The governor's chances were dimmed, however, by a bitter state election in the spring of 1792. Although Chief Justice John Jay, the Federalist candidate for governor, actually had more votes, the state canvassing board threw out the returns from three counties on technical grounds and counted Clinton in. This aroused intense feeling in the state, and there was some doubt as to the wisdom of supporting the veteran governor for the Vice Presidency. In the fall an under-cover project to make Senator Aaron Burr the Republican choice was launched from New York. He was stronger than Clinton in New York City but less well known elsewhere. A Philadelphia conference of middle-state politicians on October 16 indorsed Clinton, and Burr gracefully acquiesced, perhaps with the hope of future support. He was only thirty-six and could wait. Hamilton, alarmed at the possible candidacy of Burr, an "embryo Caesar," now discovered virtues in Clinton, "a man of property, and in private life, as far as I know, of probity"; but his opinion had no influence on the Republican decision.

This campaign, though only the Vice Presidency was involved, at least proved the existence of two embryonic parties. Neither had a formal organization, but the degree of unity achieved by private correspondence and through the newspapers was surprising. The advantages lay with the Federalists, but the Virginia–New-York alliance did yeoman work in creating a Republican opposition. In almost every state little groups of Jeffersonians were active in nominating Congressional candidates and laying the foundations for a powerful party. Adams, sulking in Massachusetts when Congress met in November, bore the brunt of their assaults. He was antirepublican, an aristocrat, a monarchist at heart, they charged, and the Federalists were corrupt speculators and a moneyed aristocracy. In retaliation the Adams men brought up Clinton's opposition to the Constitution and referred to their opponents as the "mobocracy."

Congress had changed the dates for elections to make the first Wednesday in December the day for the Presidential electors to cast their votes, and the second Wednesday in February for Congress to tabulate the result. The electors were to be chosen in each state any time within thirty-four days preceding the first Wednesday in December.[1] This spread the election period over the first two weeks of November. As in the first election there was no uniform method. Legislatures chose the electors in ten states; the voters, in three; and the Massachusetts and New Hampshire legislatures selected the electors only when candidates lacked a majority of the popular vote.

Most of the excitement over the election seems to have been confined to a few newspapers, for the popular vote was light. The choice of a Vice President was not a matter to arouse widespread interest. Nevertheless, the electoral vote reflected sharply the growing party solidarity. Adams had all of New England, New Jersey, Delaware, Maryland, 14 of Pennsylvania's 15, and 7 of South Carolina's 8—a total of 77 electoral votes. Clinton had 50, carrying New York, Virginia, North Carolina, and Georgia, and receiving 1 vote from Pennsylvania. Newly admitted Kentucky gave 4 to Jefferson, while a South Carolina elector cast a vote for Burr. Every elector gave Washington one of his votes, making a total of 132.

The Republicans might have elected Clinton but for Pennsylvania. Below the Potomac they had all the states except South Carolina; in the North, only New York. The victorious Federalists had good reason to be alarmed at the rapid growth of the opposition. Adams had won; but Jefferson believed that his personal worth and past services were responsible, not his political creed. The House, where the popular will was better expressed, seemed to be almost under Republican control. The "monocrats" had been checkmated there.

1796

In Washington's second term the problems of foreign relations became party issues. The French Revolution, with

[1] This was changed in 1845 to the Tuesday after the first Monday in November. In 1887 the day for the electors to meet was changed to the second Monday in January. In 1934, as a result of the Twentieth Amendment, this was shifted to the Monday after the second Wednesday in December.

which Americans generally were sympathetic, whirled off on a radical course culminating in the Reign of Terror, and in 1793 involving France in a great European War.

Washington's policy of neutrality was assented to by Jefferson, but pro-French Republicans enthusiastically welcomed the new French minister, Citizen Genêt, formed Jacobin clubs in imitation of the Parisian radicals, and protested against British infringement of neutral rights on the Atlantic.

The Federalists, alarmed at the excesses of the Revolution and fearing the spread of jacobinism in this country, upheld Washington's neutral course. Close business relations with England made them overlook her one-sided rule of the waves, her retention of Canadian border posts on American soil in violation of the treaty of 1783, and some other old sores.

The indiscretions of Genêt and his insolence toward the President brought on his recall and hurt his and the Republican cause. On the other hand, British seizures of American merchant ships led to demands for retaliation which Washington held back by sending Chief Justice John Jay to England in an attempt to secure a peaceful solution of all problems between the two powers. Jay brought back a treaty that settled several old issues and did relieve tensions, but it was damned as a sell-out to the British by the Republicans. Even Hamilton had difficulty defending its limited trade and neutrality concessions. It became a major issue in the national election of 1796.

The election of 1796, with Washington eliminating himself,[2] soon became a struggle between Adams and Jefferson. Members of Congress from both parties and some outsiders apparently discussed the problem of candidates informally

---

[2] He did not consciously set a precedent against a third term. He would have retired after one term if circumstances had permitted it. Now, disgusted with party bitterness and eager to enjoy the peace of Mount Vernon, he refused to consider another term. At the time of the adoption of the Constitution he had written to Jefferson defending the re-eligibility of the President and opposing any restriction on the number of terms.

and reached an agreement as to their choices for first place. But there was no formal meeting of the "caucus," as in later elections, and there was nothing to bind the electors. Hamilton, doubtful about the wisdom of supporting Adams, had considered Patrick Henry; but that old Antifederalist, now a conservative, showed no interest. The need for a southern running mate for Adams pointed toward South Carolina, and Thomas Pinckney, negotiator of a popular treaty with Spain, was selected. Since there was no separate vote for Vice President, Pinckney's southern friends chose to regard him as a Presidential candidate. He was expected to take votes from Jefferson in the South and thus insure a Federalist victory for both offices. In this situation Hamilton took a hand. His plan was innocence itself. All he asked was that the northern electors should be loyal to their party and give an equal support to both Federalist candidates, ostensibly to keep Jefferson from finishing first or second. Behind this plausible appeal was the possibility that Pinckney might do better than Adams in the South. Thus the New Englander would end up in second place—an outcome which Hamilton admitted afterward "would not have been disagreeable to me." The Adams electors in New England, however, took care of the scheme, as the electoral vote reveals.

Burr's nomination for second place on the ticket with Jefferson seems to have been taken for granted, certainly in the North and West; but if the Virginia leaders favored him they failed to inform their electors. Perhaps the fact that the New York legislature, which would choose the state's electors, was Federalist made Burr's candidacy of little value to the Virginians, as he had proved unable to control his home state.

The campaign raged up to the day in December when the electors were to meet. Though elected on partisan tickets, there were no binding pledges to prevent the exercise of individual judgment by an elector. Consequently, the party newspapers continued the battle until the results were known. While Jefferson and Adams remained in bucolic retirement far from the seat of government, their ardent supporters used every weapon of propaganda, from poisoned arrows to mud.

Adams was traduced as a monarchist, a lover of titles, an enemy of liberty; Jefferson, as an atheist, a coward in the Revolution, a tool of France, and an enemy of the Constitution. The French Minister, Adet, meddled in the campaign by supplying the Republican *Aurora* with copies of his notes to Secretary of State Pickering for immediate publication. His praise of Jefferson and his hostile tone toward the administration were obviously intended for public consumption. His actions proved more embarrassing than helpful to the Republicans.

With legislatures choosing electors in ten of the sixteen states, it is difficult to estimate the influence of campaign propaganda. Federalist electors were chosen from New England, New York, New Jersey, and Delaware, and the majority of Maryland's districts. One Maryland elector judiciously voted for both Adams and Jefferson. The Republicans carried Georgia, Tennessee, Kentucky, North Carolina, Virginia and Pennsylvania, though each of the last three had a solitary Adams elector. A second Pennsylvania elector, reputedly a Federalist, voted for Pinckney and Jefferson. The South Carolina electors also coupled these men as their choices. A bipartisan deal in the legislature was responsible for this all-southern ticket. This might have made Pinckney President had the Adams electors supported him equally with Adams elsewhere, as Hamilton had hoped; but 18 votes were thrown to other Federalists, and Pinckney lost even the Vice Presidency. Adams had 71 votes; Jefferson, 68; Pinckney, 59; and Burr, 30. Nine others received votes. Republican newspapers charged the Federalists with fraudulent voting in Pennsylvania, where the popular vote was very close, and in one Maryland district where four votes separated the two parties; but their protests were unheeded.

On the Republican side, Burr's poor showing was a surprise. The southern Republican electors from Virginia, North Carolina, and Georgia had given Jefferson 35 votes to Burr's 7. The alliance of the Old Dominion and New York had been dissolved without notice to the junior partner. Burr said nothing but was to be more canny when the Virginians looked northward for support in 1800.

Jefferson's defeat had its compensations. In the Vice Presidential chair he could see and hear much, keep in touch with his friends in Congress, and yet preserve a discreet silence in public. Votes and speeches are not required of Vice Presidents.

1800

The story of John Adams's administration largely revolves around the difficulties with France, including the "XYZ Affair," which led to the undeclared French War of 1798. Martial fever caused Congress to make preparations for war and to pass a series of repressive measures, the Alien and Sedition Acts. Hamilton, field commander of the army newly created at Washington's insistence, found his visions of military glory dispelled when Adams, unexpectedly, renewed negotiations with France, now under Napoleon Bonaparte, and arranged a peaceful solution of the issues at stake. The President also purged his cabinet of two of Hamilton's satellites.

Adams was nominated for a second term, with C. C. Pinckney of South Carolina for Vice President, by a caucus of Federalist Congressmen. Hamilton, unable to uncover a suitable candidate, proceeded to attack Adams in a pamphlet intended for secret distribution among leading Federalists. It soon became public, damaging its author more than its subject.

The Alien and Sedition Acts, enforced against Republican editors and other critics of the government, many of them foreign-born, caused Jefferson and Madison to prepare the Virginia and Kentucky Resolutions of 1798–99 attacking the constitutionality of the laws. Their purpose was to arouse public opinion and influence elections, but the Resolutions were used years later as a justification of state sovereignty and the idea of nullification.

As the war fever subsided and the Federalists fell to fighting among themselves, Republican hopes rose. Working quietly through conferences with small groups and through a wide range of correspondence, Jefferson, Madison, Gallatin,

Burr, and other key leaders welded together a powerful party. Newspapers were financed, pamphlets were printed and circulated, Congressmen wrote letters to their constituents, and the propaganda mills ground steadily through the campaign. New York, Pennsylvania, and South Carolina were the key states that must be won, though the Jeffersonians refused to concede even New England to the enemy without a battle.

In New York the election of the legislature, which was to choose the Presidential electors, was held in the spring of 1800. Colonel Aaron Burr, whom Jefferson had been courting since 1797, became the Republican man of the hour. His task was to make Federalist New York City Republican, swinging the balance of power in the legislature to the Jeffersonians. The arrest and harsh treatment of Jedediah Peck for circulating petitions for the repeal of the Sedition Act helped upstate; but in the city the clever tactics of Burr accounted for the result. The Society of St. Tammany proved to be a useful ally. Organized in 1789 by William Mooney on the foundations of earlier groups of the Revolutionary period, it was at first a fraternal order with a membership of mechanics, artisans, and laborers. Its democratic personnel caused it to evolve into a Republican club, which met in Martling's Tavern in a room the scoffing Federalists called the "Pig Pen." It was soon playing an important part in local elections, and Burr, though not a member, worked with it.

In order to draw the widest possible popular support, Burr drafted an assembly ticket of big-name Republicans including Clinton, General Gates, and a Livingston, and offered it to the voters in opposition to a group of Federalist mediocrities whom Hamilton had named to insure control of the city delegation. Burr also created some new voters by a clever legal device which made them landowners. The polls, open for four days, were scenes of great excitement as the two rivals electioneered in person, though Burr depended more upon his disciplined organization to get results. The county voted Republican, and its assemblymen furnished the margin by which the new legislature chose Jeffersonian electors. An average majority of 490 votes was the balance of power in the county, and indirectly in state and nation.

One last card remained for the stunned Federalists to play. After conferring with friends, Hamilton proposed to Governor Jay that he call the old assembly into special session at once to enact a law providing for the choice of Presidential electors by popular vote under a district system. This would give the Federalists a second chance and would insure them at least a part of the New York electors. "It is easy to sacrifice the substantial interests of society by a strict adherence to ordinary rules," he wrote, urging the governor not to be "over-scrupulous." But austere John Jay had none of the arts of the political manipulator. He filed away the letter after inscribing on it, "Proposing a measure for party purposes which it would not become me to adopt."

The outcome of the spring election in New York made it certain that the Vice Presidential candidate would come from that state. But would it be Clinton or Burr? Gallatin asked his father-in-law, Commodore James Nicholson, to sound out the New York Republicans and let him know their preference for the benefit of the Republican Congressional caucus. The details of the negotiations were later a matter of controversy. At least Clinton seemed unenthusiastic toward the nomination while Burr's friends were quite insistent. Burr agreed to take the nomination provided assurances were given that the southern Republicans would act fairly toward him. He had not forgotten their treatment of his candidacy four years earlier. The party Congressional caucus met on May 11 and unanimously agreed to support Burr for Vice President.

In Pennsylvania the Senate, containing a number of holdover members, was Federalist, but the House of Representatives, elected in October, 1800, was strongly Republican. Had a state-wide popular vote been permitted for Presidential electors, as in past elections, all fifteen would have been Republican. But the Federalist Senate blocked all attempts in this direction, refused to vote by joint ballot, and forced a compromise which gave the Federalists seven electors, the Republicans eight. The outcome in no sense represented public opinion, for the state elected ten Republican Congressmen to three Federalists.

In South Carolina, which also elected through its legislature, the Republicans carried the assembly in October, though the city of Charleston, as usual, was Federalist. The energetic Charles Pinckney, breaking completely with his Federalist kinsmen,[3] had organized the Republican cause upcountry and stirred up planters and farmers against Federalist tax burdens on lands and slaves. He wrote to Jefferson that the "Federal interest" at Charleston voted "the lame, crippled, diseased and blind," whether taxpayers or not, and used colored ballots as a check on how their underlings voted.

While only four states permitted a popular vote, even the indirect choice through the legislatures reflected the swing toward Jefferson. The Republicans had found plenty of fuel for their propaganda in the record of the Adams administration. Militarism, high taxes, debt increases, and unconstitutional measures were played up along with the old refrains of aristocratic rule, the dangers of monarchy, and the power of the "monied interest." Republican journals joyfully quoted from Hamilton's pamphlet on the defects of John Adams.

The Federalists, thrown on the defensive by the effectiveness of the Republican appeal, resorted to a campaign of fear and smear in a vain attempt to save the day. Jefferson, they thundered, was an infidel, a fanatic, a believer in French revolutionary doctrines, who would destroy religion, set up agriculture over commerce, repudiate the public debt, and lead the country into bloodshed and anarchy. "Tremble then in case of Jefferson's election, all ye holders of public funds, for your ruin is at hand," wrote "Decius" in a Federalist newspaper. "Old men who have retired to spend the evening of life upon the fruits of the industry of their youth. Widows and orphans with their scanty pittances. Public banks, insurance companies, literary and charitable institu-

---

[3] Charles Cotesworth Pinckney, Federalist Vice Presidential candidate, and Thomas Pinckney.

tions . . . will be involved in one common, certain, and not very distant ruin." A pamphlet addressed to "Religious Republicans" charged that Jefferson, looking at a church building in a ruined condition, had said, "It is good enough for Him that was born in a manger." A Connecticut Federalist wrote in his diary: "I do not believe that the Most High will permit a howling atheist to sit at the head of this nation."

The electoral count gave Jefferson and Burr 73 votes each, Adams 65, Pinckney 64, and Jay one. At last party discipline had been made completely effective. Only one Rhode Island elector, fearful that Pinckney might lead Adams, refused to support both Federalist candidates. Adams had all the votes of New England, New Jersey, and Delaware, five of Maryland's ten, four of North Carolina's twelve, and seven of Pennsylvania's fifteen; Jefferson had all the rest.[4]

With Jefferson and Burr in a tie, the House of Representatives had to choose between them, though everyone understood that the latter was intended for second place. Burr, in a letter to General Samuel Smith before the final results were known, made it clear that he "would utterly disclaim all competition." A little later he was equally positive, in a letter to Jefferson, that his friends would not think of "diverting a single vote from you."

Nevertheless, Federalist leaders, bitterly disappointed over their defeat, turned hopeful eyes toward Burr. He might prove to be the lesser evil. He was a northerner, a lawyer and not a farmer, a practical politician rather than a Jacobin fanatic, and he was on friendly terms with many of his opponents. His election by the House would disorganize the Republicans and might destroy the leadership of the man the Federalists hated most, Thomas Jefferson. These opinions were well summed up by one Federalist: Burr's "ambition and interest will direct his conduct—and his own state is commercial and largely interested in the funded debt. If he will honorably support the government for which he has undoubted talents, he will have support of the federalists and

[4] Only Virginia, Rhode Island, Maryland, and North Carolina chose their electors by popular vote, the last two using a district system.

some of the Jacobins whom he may detach—and his election will disorganize and embarrass the party who have given him their votes."

But Hamilton, in the unhappy role of choosing between two men he thoroughly disliked, differed with his party colleagues. There was for him but one choice. Burr was the "Catiline of America," a man devoid of scruples and possessed of an inordinate ambition and the "boldness and daring necessary to give success to the Jacobin system." Jefferson at least had "pretensions to character," though he was unscrupulous, not very mindful of truth, and was a "contemptible hypocrite." "Nor is it true that Jefferson is zealot enough to do anything in pursuance of his principles which will contravene his popularity or his interest. He is as likely as any man I know to temporize—to calculate what will be likely to promote his own reputation and advantage; and the probable result of such a temper is the preservation of systems, though originally opposed, which, being once established, could not be overturned without danger to the person who did it." To Representative James A. Bayard of Delaware and others Hamilton wrote in the above strain. But his pleas fell on deaf ears. The Federalist members of the House held a caucus, and though some dissented, the majority voted to support Burr.

Voting as individuals the Federalists controlled the House, for this was a lame-duck Congress, elected when the war fever was mounting; but the Constitutional requirement that the members vote by states in choosing the President placed them at a disadvantage. Their strength was too heavily concentrated in New England, while the vote of the Republicans was better distributed and gave them control of more states. In addition, there were enough Federalist defections to deprive Burr of two states, New Jersey and Georgia, and to divide Maryland. Vermont was also evenly divided. Burr had four New England states, Delaware, and South Carolina; Jefferson was supported by New York, Pennsylvania, New Jersey, Virginia, North Carolina, Georgia, Tennessee, and Kentucky, eight in all. In the case of the last three, four members cast three votes for Jefferson, while twenty-five

Federalists in New England could give Burr but four votes, voting by states. The vote by individuals gave Jefferson 55, Burr 49.

From the 11th through the 17th of February the House balloted with the result always the same: eight states for Jefferson, six for Burr, and two divided. The New Yorker needed three changes of votes—in New Jersey, Maryland, and Vermont—to get nine states. Maryland would have been his if Joseph Nicholson had let illness and a raging fever keep him away. Through a heavy snowstorm he came to the House to cast his vote for Jefferson from a bed fixed up in a committee room. This kept Maryland evenly divided. Gallatin, the cool-headed, was the floor leader of the Jeffersonians, carefully holding his lines intact while he waited for a break in the Federalist ranks.

The balloting started on Wednesday, but not until the week-end were there signs that the Federalists were weakening. Burr was apparently doing nothing to get the three Republican votes necessary to win, and some of his supporters were losing heart. Fears of what might happen if the 4th of March came with the deadlock unbroken had some effect on the sober-minded. The Republican governors of Pennsylvania and Virginia were reported as ready to call out their militia to prevent a Federalist usurpation of the Presidency. Bayard of Delaware, sole representative of that little state, was now prepared to shift it to Jefferson. Hamilton's importunities or Burr's failure to act or fears of a civil war or some other factors may have determined his course. In any case, he announced in the Federalist caucus that the deadlock must end. The die-hards from New England denounced him, but had to yield. On the thirty-sixth ballot a Vermont Federalist was purposely absent, Bayard and the Maryland and South Carolina Federalists voted blanks, and Jefferson had ten of the sixteen states. Four New England states still voted for Burr on this final trial.

The whole plot—for it was hardly more than that—to elect Burr and frustrate the popular will had finally broken down. The good sense of the moderates had at least prevented the supreme blunder, a prolongation of the struggle until Adams's term expired. Without a constitutionally elected President or Vice President, the nation might have found itself plunged into civil strife. Before the next election the Twelfth Amendment was added to the Constitution. This provided that the electors should vote separately for President and Vice President. The original purpose of the electoral college had been altered by the development of parties.

Rumors of an understanding or even a bargain between the Federalists and Jefferson were circulated at the time of the election; but not until Bayard of Delaware lifted the curtain several years later was the nature of the negotiations revealed. Denials promptly followed from Jefferson and his henchmen, and a sharp controversy ensued. Bayard insisted that he had received assurances about Jefferson's policies on such points as support of the public credit, maintenance of the navy, the protection and encouragement of commerce, and the retention of subordinate officials in office, including a particular Delaware officeholder. General Samuel Smith, who lodged at Conrad's boardinghouse with Jefferson and was in his confidence, had acted as a self-appointed intermediary to confer with Bayard and other Federalists. Smith's explanation, made years later, was that he had sounded out Jefferson on these points to quiet Federalist fears "without his having the remotest idea of my object." Then the busy go-between had let Bayard believe that he was authorized to speak for the Republican candidate. Jefferson's emphatic denial of any understanding or bargain still leaves unanswered the question whether he knew that he was being pumped when he expounded his views to General Smith.

Poor Burr was roundly denounced by the Federalists for his failure to give them pledges and to render aid in securing his election. "The means existed of electing Burr," wrote Bayard to Hamilton, "but this required his co-operation. By deceiving one man (a great blockhead) and tempting two (not incorruptible), he might have secured a majority of the States. He will never have another chance of being President of the United States; and the little use he has made of the one which has occurred gives me but an humble opinion of the talents of an unprincipled man." This remarkable left-handed compliment to Burr certainly exonerates him from any charge of activity in his own interest. The Machiavelli of the Republicans had behaved like an honorable man! The archintriguer had refused to use his base talents, and the Federalists were confounded in their efforts to help him. The humor of the situation was utterly lost upon them, for Thomas Jefferson had been elected President. The leaders of the party of "the wise and the good" had dug themselves a pit of their own misdeeds and follies and had fallen into it never to emerge.

CHAPTER II

THE VIRGINIA PRESIDENTS AND THE SECOND ADAMS

1804–1828

1804

JEFFERSON, although putting the ship "on her republican tack," did nothing very revolutionary. Rigid economy and simplicity in government, drastic reductions in the military establishment, repeal of the excise tax, and reduction of the national debt constituted a popular program. He did not disturb Hamilton's financial structure, and business benefited from an expanding foreign trade. A brief period of peace in Europe disposed of the problems of neutral rights for the moment. It was in this breathing spell in the Napoleonic wars that fortune favored Jefferson with the purchase of Louisiana.

Nor did the Republican President let his theories stand in the way of accomplishing his aims. He exercised a control over Congress that few Presidents have achieved. Strict construction of the Constitution went by the boards with the Louisiana purchase.

As Jefferson's popularity zoomed, a few die-hard New England Federalists in Congress talked of the possibility of dismemberment of the Union. They tried to draw Aaron Burr into a secession plot which would set up a northern confederacy. The Vice President, disgruntled at his treatment by the administration, ran for governor of New York, without, however, committing himself to the scheme. He was defeated by an administration candidate. Angry at Hamilton for casting aspersions on his character, he challenged him to a duel and the founder of Federalism went to his death on the field at Weehawken. Burr's political career was blasted, and presently he embarked on his western schemes whose purposes are still a matter of conjecture.

Jefferson was renominated at a formal caucus of Republican Senators and Representatives on February 25, 1804. George Clinton of New York received 67 of the 108 votes cast on the one ballot for Vice President. An informal understanding among Federalist leaders made Charles Cotesworth Pinckney and Rufus King their choices.

Republican national victory was conceded, but New England Federalists fought desperately to save their states from democratic defilement. The Massachusetts legislature enacted a law for popular election of Presidential electors but required that all nineteen be chosen by a state-wide vote. The Republicans had demanded a return to the old district system, used before 1800, which would insure them a share of the electoral vote. To the chagrin of the Federalists, the state went Republican by over four thousand votes and Jefferson secured all nineteen electors. In Connecticut, Abraham Bishop led a Republican assault against the ruling Federalist-Congregational oligarchy. He denied the validity of the old royal charter, which had been used as a state constitution, and demanded a reform constitution with a simple taxpaying requirement for voters and an end of high property qualifications. Denunciations from press and pulpit and the power of the ruling hierarchy were too much for the reformers, and Connecticut voted Federalist as usual.

Where the Federalists campaigned at all, they were hard put to find issues. Peace, prosperity, the repeal of internal taxes, economy and the acquisition of Louisiana were too much for them. Old issues and old prejudices were dusted off but made little impression. The godless, pro-French President had disappointed his detractors. On the more solid grounds of his attack upon the judiciary, his reduction of the navy, and the expense of Louisiana, it was difficult to arouse the voters. Even the charge that Louisiana cost every person in Massachusetts four dollars fell flat. The benefits were too obvious.

Seven states chose electors through their legislatures; seven used state-wide popular vote; and three had a district system. Jefferson had 162 votes; Pinckney, 14. Connecticut, Delaware, and two of Maryland's nine went to the loser. Federalism was almost extinct.

1808

Jefferson's second term was troubled by insurgency in the party and mounting difficulties with Europe's warring powers over paper blockades and impressment of American sailors. John Randolph, a brilliant, caustic tongued, erratic Virginia member of the House of Representatives, feuded with Secretary of State Madison and won the support of a small group of old-fashioned, strict construction Republicans in opposing administration policies. Jefferson was able, however, by skillful tactics to reduce their power for mischief except for Randolph's tongue.

Jefferson was confronted with a war crisis with Great Britain in June, 1807, over an impressment outrage—the Chesapeake-Leopard affair—in which several Americans were killed and wounded, and four seamen impressed. But he preferred economic sanctions and in December secured the passage by Congress of an act laying an embargo on American shipping. This drastic measure was a severe blow to the commercial interests, proved difficult to enforce, brought no concessions from the European belligerents, and put new life into the Federalist party. Jefferson gave in to its repeal just before he went out of office.

James Madison had long been regarded as Jefferson's successor. Their harmony of views and Madison's services made him the logical choice. Accordingly, a caucus of Republican members of Congress in January, 1808, named him for the Presidency and renominated George Clinton for second place. The action was almost unanimous, for the friends of Randolph and some other dissenters were absent. A group of them denounced the caucus system of nominations as a violation of the Constitution. The arrogant, acid-tongued Randolph hoped to create a diversion for Monroe in the Old Dominion and destroy Madison's prestige at home. Curiously enough, although Clinton was the administration candidate for Vice President, he was also the Presidential candidate of certain northern Republicans who were opposed to the succession of another Virginian. His ambitious and aggressive nephew DeWitt Clinton was the real force behind the candidacy of the cheerful old gentleman of sixty-nine, who found even the duties of Vice President too arduous and was manifestly unfit for the office of chief executive. He told the diarist Plumer that "the sitting three hours in the Chair at a time was extremely fatiguing to him." His chances depended on the amount of insurgency in Pennsylvania and New York and the possible support of the Federalists.

Monroe, despite Jefferson's efforts to reconcile him to Madison, lent himself to Randolph's schemes. He had acted as a kind of diplomatic errand boy for the administration to the courts of France, Spain, and England with little to show for it. The Louisiana Purchase had been largely settled before he arrived in France, and his work elsewhere was unsatisfactory. He had faced difficult situations in both Spain and England, but the treaty he and William Pinckney had arranged with England went beyond his instructions and was not even sent to the Senate. As a result Monroe felt that Jefferson had repudiated him.

The Virginia legislature divided between the two native sons, 124 members holding a caucus in January to name Madison electors, while 57 indorsed Monroe. John Taylor of Caroline, an old-fashioned agrarian Republican, favored Monroe but tried to induce him to withdraw so as not to disrupt the party. The anti-administration men—the Quids —used the embargo as an argument against Madison and expressed fears that war would soon result. Monroe's candidacy probably was not helped by the indorsement of a group of Virginia Federalists, while the possibility of victory for Clinton as a result of the Virginia split drew support to Madison. Before the election it was clear that Monroe had no chance.

Some twenty-five or thirty Federalist leaders from seven states north of the Potomac plus South Carolina, taking heart from the unpopularity of the embargo, held a secret conference at New York in August. The chief question at issue was whether the conference should support Clinton as the best means of defeating Madison. The majority accepted Rufus King's view and decided in favor of separate Federalist candidates. C. C. Pinckney and King were then named.

Fortunately for Madison, a bad factional fight in Pennsylvania—where Simon Snyder, Michael Leib, and William Duane, editor of the powerful *Aurora*, a radical trio, and Governor Thomas McKean, a conservative, had been at swords' points—was compromised sufficiently to unite Republican support for him. In New York DeWitt Clinton failed to control the legislature, and it chose six electors for his uncle to thirteen for Madison. Largely as a result of these developments in Virginia, Pennsylvania, and New York, the key states of the Republicans, Madison won with 122 electoral votes to 47 for Pinckney and 6 for George Clinton.[1] Clinton was re-elected Vice President with 113 votes to 9 for John Langdon of New Hampshire and 3 each for Monroe and Madison.

Jefferson had passed his scepter to his closet friend, but his joy was far from complete. The embargo had failed and now had to be repealed. Federalism, apparently defunct in 1804, had revived and was in control of New England. Its powerful business leaders, quiescent in times of prosperity, were aroused against a President who, they believed, aimed at the destruction of commerce and the dominance of agriculture. They continued hostile to the Republicans for many years.

Yet Jefferson had laid the solid foundations on which American liberalism was to build. He had demonstrated the falsity of the Federalist dogma that the propertied few alone were fitted to govern and that democracy meant mob rule. He had shown the possibilities in wise, patient, skillful political

---

[1] One Kentucky elector was absent. Pinckney added to all the New England electors except those from Vermont three each from Delaware and North Carolina, and two from Maryland.

leadership and—surprisingly, in view of his earlier predilections—had established the pattern of Presidential direction of the party majority in Congress, which came to be the mark of reformer chief executives. He had secured an empire for his country that would give future generations of farmers the room they needed and would strengthen and prolong frontier democracy's influence. He was the master political architect of his day and few have equaled him.

1812

In his grasp of governmental problems and in his experience in public life, James Madison was excelled by none of his contemporaries. But little Jeemy lacked Jefferson's skill in political manipulation and his ability to appraise and use men. Concessions to factional pressure affected his cabinet choices, and eventually he had to replace his first Secretary of State with his old rival, James Monroe, with whom he made peace.

Madison tried diplomacy and a weaker version of Jefferson's peaceable coercion policy in attempting to protect neutral rights but made no headway with either belligerent. The Congressional elections of 1810 took matters out of his hands. From the West and South came the War Hawks, young men like Henry Clay of Kentucky and John C. Calhoun of South Carolina, who were eager to defend the national honor and who would solve the western Indian problem by seizing Canada as a hostage. Westerners attributed Tecumseh's activities and Indian unrest to British encouragement.

Clay became Speaker of the House of Representatives and filled important committee posts with War Hawk colleagues. Federalists and old-fashioned Republicans like John Randolph opposed these young bloods and blocked some of their preparedness measures.

Fortunately for the majority group, a Presidential election was at hand. Here was their opportunity, for the Congressional caucus was under their control. The power to nominate lay in their hands. There has been no proof that

Madison bargained with the war party; but no bargain was necessary. He knew that only an aggressive attitude toward Great Britain would win him War Hawk support. In the spring of 1812 his actions foreshadowed a war message; in May the Congressional caucus renominated him; in June war was declared. The caucus met much later than had been the custom. Was the war party waiting to see what the President would do?

John Langdon, a New Hampshire Revolutionary War patriot and a successful businessman, who had served as United States Senator and as governor of his state, was named for the Vice Presidency. He declined, perhaps because he was past seventy, and a second meeting of the caucus named Elbridge Gerry, "Gentleman-Democrat," governor of Massachusetts and leader of his party in New England. Formerly an independent and a friend of Adams, he had been ostracized by the Federalists for his part in the X Y Z affair. While he was governor, his party had used redistricting to deprive the Federalists of control of the Massachusetts Senate. The device was not new, but it had lacked a name. The governor's enemies called it "gerrymandering," and the name has stuck.

The Virginia–New-York alliance, which had monopolized Republican nominations for national office since 1796, was now at an end, killed by George Clinton's death and DeWitt Clinton's insurgency. The younger Clinton's friends had not attended the caucus. With New York's backing he intended to try for the Presidency as an anti-administration Republican, appealing especially to northern jealousy of Virginia domination and New England antiwar bitterness. He was too shrewd to carry the peace banner, as this would hurt him where the war was popular. In his calculations the Federalists might be won without definite pledges because of their eagerness to divide the Republicans and defeat Madison.

The elder statesmen of Federalism, after consultation and correspondence, held a conference at New York in September to which the dwindling remnant of the party in South Carolina sent delegates; otherwise the region south of the Potomac was unrepresented. Rufus King proved to be the stumbling block in the way of outright indorsement of DeWitt Clinton. Accompanied by John Jay and Gouverneur Morris, he had conferred earlier with Clinton and found him ready to promise much in private but unwilling to make public commitments. Dissatisfied, King bluntly told the assembled Federalists that an alliance with the Clintonians might place a "Caesar Borgia" in the Presidency, and he favored a separate Federalist ticket. The majority, however, influenced by Harrison Gray Otis of Massachusetts, turned down this proposal; and, without formally indorsing Clinton, the conference adjourned, understanding that the shrewd New Yorker would get Federalist support in each state.

Publicity was avoided, and this suited Clinton well enough as he had no desire to appear openly as the Federalist-Peace candidate and thus offend his war following. The Federalist-Clinton understanding included support of Jared Ingersoll, a moderate Pennsylvania Federalist, for the Vice Presidency. Although the term "Federalist" was dropped in some places in favor of "Friends of Peace," Clinton was pictured as a war supporter wherever it meant votes.

Some dissatisfaction with Clinton developed in the Federalist ranks. A Virginia convention put forward King and William R. Davie of North Carolina, and Federalist members of the New York legislature refused to support the Clinton electors; but these defections were not serious. Far more important was Clinton's failure to draw Republican votes, notably in Pennsylvania. The factionalism characteristic of the Republicans of that state did not prevent united support for Madison, and this was fatal to the hopes of Clinton. He had 89 electoral votes to Madison's 128. The West and the South alone could not have elected Madison, but Pennsylvania's 25 saved the day. To all New England except Vermont, Clinton added New York, New Jersey, Delaware, and 5 of Maryland's 11. His coalition had come very near to success.

The election was a weak vote of confidence in the administration. Even this was hardly warranted by the course of the war. Failures on the battlefield and maladministration plagued the American effort, and only the successful defenses against invasion in 1814 created the military stalemate that the Treaty of Ghent fortunately recognized.

Antiwar discontents in Federalist New England produced a movement for a northern confederacy, which led to the Hartford Convention of late 1814. This body, not controlled by the extremists, offered a moderate report for certain constitutional changes to strengthen New England's minority position in the Union. But the news of peace coupled with Jackson's victory at New Orleans produced a belated outburst of patriotism that lumped together all war critics as Federalist plotters and disunionists. Federalism sank under the leaden load of the discredited Hartford Convention, which became a symbol of treason in wartime.

But Federalism was no longer needed. It had become too narrowly sectionalized, and its Hamiltonian principles were now attaining fruition under the Young Republican leadership of Clay, Calhoun, and their associates. Taught by the lessons of the war, Congress passed measures for a larger peacetime army and navy, for the creation of a second United States Bank, and for the continuance of high war tariff rates with some increases, while John Marshall's Supreme Court gave the new nationalism its blessings in a series of notable decisions. Madison accepted this Hamiltonian victory because of the great change of circumstances.

1816–1820

Monroe received the Republican nomination for President in 1816 after a sharp contest. William H. Crawford of Georgia, who had worked with the Young Republicans in Congress, had fifty-four votes in the caucus to Monroe's sixty-five—a very narrow margin for the Virginian, who had been regarded generally as the heir apparent to Madison from the time of his acceptance of the primacy of the cabinet. Daniel D. Tompkins, the energetic governor of New York, favored at first to head the ticket by that state, was named for the Vice Presidency, thus restoring the old Virginia–New-York alliance of earlier years. No Federalist nominations were made, but the electors of Massachusetts, Connecticut, and Delaware, chosen by the legislatures, cast thirty-four votes for Rufus King. Three Maryland Federalists and one from Delaware did not vote. Monroe had one hundred and eighty-three. The only spark of interest in the campaign was provided by critics of the caucus system, and these accepted its choices.

Fortunately the decline of Federalism and the sweep of nationalistic feeling eliminated party rancor and gave Monroe a political security that no other President except the "Father of His Country" has ever enjoyed. As a mark of his desire to appear as the head of a united nation, the new President set out on a triumphal tour of the North and West. The acclaim with which he was received caused his administration to be termed the "Era of Good Feelings"—a phrase first used by the Boston *Centinel* in describing his visit to that city. New England, which had never looked upon the faces of Presidents Jefferson and Madison, outdid itself to honor their successor.

When Monroe was re-elected in 1820 without opposition, the venerable John Adams served as a Massachusetts elector, and only William Plumer of New Hampshire cast a dissenting vote (for John Quincy Adams). Monroe had not been formally nominated. A poorly attended Congressional caucus decided against any action. That he survived the disastrous financial Panic of 1819 and a bitter sectional struggle over the admission of Missouri as a slave state without apparent loss of popularity is one of the anomalies of American political history. Yet Monroe himself was in part responsible for this. In his desire to blot out party differences he followed a course entirely compatible with his temperament, accepting Congressional solutions to perplexing problems. Fortunately for the country, his immediate successors had more positive qualities, and the power of the President was not allowed to slip into the hands of Congressional politicians. Monroe had achieved the miracle of a partyless administration, but it was an abnormality. American political life was too vigorous to endure long an "Era of Good Feelings."

1824

The Missouri Compromise of 1820 removed the slavery question as a political issue in the 1820's, but a different kind of sectionalism, mostly involving protective tariff and internal improvements, was breaking down the one-party system and creating serious problems for ambitious political leaders.

New England, the Middle States, the Old South, and the Mississippi Valley West were pulling in different directions on these economic issues. Yankeedom was shifting its capital from foreign trade to manufacturing, but the textile manufacturers were not yet dominant and its votes in Congress on the tariff were divided. It opposed federal spending for roads and canals. The Middle States, Pennsylvania in particular, were pro-tariff and pro-internal improvements, although New York, with its Erie Canal nearing completion, was less inclined to favor federal aid for such projects in other states. The South was anti-tariff and anti-internal improvements. Both meant burdens on its cotton-slave economy, as its chief markets were across the Atlantic. The West, especially the Ohio Valley, opposed the South. It needed to develop a home market for its surplus food and raw materials and to obtain federal aid for transportation projects to end its isolation.

Five candidates, all Republicans, were in the Presidential race soon after Monroe's second election. Robust, genial William H. Crawford of Georgia, Secretary of the Treasury, was the politician's candidate. He had the backing of old-line party leaders, New York's Albany Regency headed by Martin Van Buren, and a considerable federal officeholder support. He avoided commitments on the tariff but his southern connections created the impression that he accepted that section's viewpoint. Henry Clay, Speaker of the House, was the voice of the West, in arguing for protective tariff and internal improvements—his "American System." But this destroyed him in the Old South and other obstacles appeared in his path in the East.

John Quincy Adams, in the State Department, confided his

opinions of men and issues to his diary, but this lonely states-man drew the support of New England and the areas where transplanted Yankees lived, and where the slavery issue mattered, as he was the only northern candidate. His silence on tariff and internal improvements was used against him in the West. Secretary of War John C. Calhoun, with a past record of favoring both the controversial issues, had only his home state in the South but had high hopes of northern support, especially Pennsylvania, where he had cultivated party leaders.

Andrew Jackson, offered by the Tennessee legislature, was not taken seriously as a Presidential candidate at first, even by Old Hickory himself. His early backers sought to use him to advance their own interests and weaken a rival fac-tion, and were surprised to find they had a "people's candi-date" on their hands who was winning widespread grass roots support. Jackson held western views on tariff and internal improvements, as his Senate votes showed in 1823–24, but it was the man, not the issues, that mattered to his mushrooming following. In his West, he was soon a dangerous rival to Clay, and he took Pennsylvania from Cal-houn when a state convention indorsed him, as the Scotch-Irish and Germans were reported as "Jackson-mad." Cal-houn then retired as a Presidential candidate.

DeWitt Clinton was out of power in New York or he might have been a formidable contender, for "the Father of the Erie Canal" was highly regarded in states with canal projects.

In 1822 Crawford had seemed to be far in the lead. But two factors combined to wreck his candidacy before the electors were chosen. The first was a stroke of paralysis, in September, 1823. Despite efforts to conceal his condition, it became evident that his health was seriously impaired. For months he could not attend cabinet meetings and was unable to sign official papers. When he reappeared at Wash-ington he was but a shadow of his former self. "He walks slowly like a blind man," wrote an observer. "His feet were wrapped up with two or three thicknesses over his shoes and he told me that they were cold and numb. His recollection seems to be good, and he conversed freely. But it is the general impression that a slight return of his disorder would prove fatal to him." This was in April, 1824. He seemed to improve gradually, but Adams recorded in November that his articulation was still much affected and his eyesight impaired.

The second factor was not an unkind Providence but the blundering of Crawford's friends. In spite of every indication that the move would be unpopular, they called a Congressional caucus to make him the official nominee. Of the 216 Republican members, only sixty-six attended, two others voting by proxy. New York, Virginia, Georgia, and North Carolina sent forty-eight members. Crawford was formally nominated, receiving sixty-four votes, while Albert Gallatin, close to him for many years and coming from the important state of Pennsylvania, was named for the Vice Presidency. The holding of the caucus was a strategic mistake. The friends of the other candidates stayed away, making it appear as a rump affair with no authority to voice the will of the old Republican party. The chief effect was to direct against Crawford the guns of all his rivals, who eagerly presented the caucus as proof that he was an intriguer and a political manipulator who would achieve the Presidency through the machinations of Congressional politicians. Their charge was especially effective in the West, where the new democracy regarded party machinery as a means of perverting the popular will. Jackson probably was the chief gainer, as he appeared to be most removed from party politics, and the Tennessee legislature had been the first to oppose the holding of a caucus. Clay, Jackson, Adams, and Calhoun had been nominated by state legislatures, though popular conventions had been held in some instances, as in Pennsylvania and Ohio.

Foreseeing that the election would go to the House unless the field could be further reduced, friends of the rival candidates tried to use the Vice Presidency as a bait to eliminate an opponent. The Jackson and Calhoun men did arrange a joint ticket. Adams earlier had expressed approval of Jackson as his running mate, thinking that the second office would afford "an easy and dignified retirement to his old age."[2] The rapid growth of the Jackson movement ended such a scheme, and with no other possibility for second place, the Adams electors generally voted for Calhoun, thus giving him an easy victory. The Crawford men, seeing that Gallatin's name brought no strength to their ticket, induced him to withdraw in favor of Clay and intimated to the Kentuckian that Crawford might not live out his term, if elected. Clay thought too much of his own chances in the probable event of a House election to listen. In the end, Clay and Crawford electors scattered their votes for the second office.

Eighteen of the twenty-four states chose electors by popular vote; but among the six using the legislative method was vitally important New York. A clean sweep here would give the successful candidate a block of thirty-six electoral votes, insure him at least second place in the national total, and add to his chances in the House of Representatives. The Albany Regency, refusing to permit a popular choice, expected to control the legislature for Crawford; but the popular uprising which elected Clinton governor weakened their hold and offered an opportunity for Clay and Adams. Thurlow Weed, a young Rochester newspaperman just winning his political spurs as an Adams strategist, outwitted the veteran politicians of the Regency and made a secret deal with some of the Clay men. When the vote was taken in the joint session of the two houses, in an atmosphere murky with duplicity and intrigue, Adams emerged with twenty-six electors; Crawford had five, Clay had four, while one preferred Jackson.

Weed had promised the Clay men enough electors to place their candidate among the three highest before the House but was unable to make good. Even so, Clay would have achieved that goal had he secured Louisiana. But a combination of Adams and Jackson men got control of the legislature of that state and divided the five electoral votes

---

[2] Adams was about four months younger than Jackson.

between them. The Kentuckian finished with only thirty-seven electoral votes in all, four below Crawford, and was eliminated from consideration by the House.

The New York result was almost equally fatal to Crawford. Had he received the entire vote of that state, as Van Buren and the Regency expected, he would have finished well ahead of Adams and in a strong position to bargain for the support in the House of Representatives necessary to elect him. With but forty-one electoral votes the odds were very much against him. Adams with eighty-four and Jackson with ninety-nine votes were the logical contenders for the House majority when the balloting began.[3]

Henry Clay had the hard choice of throwing his influence to one or the other of the two rivals he most cordially disliked, Adams and Jackson (Crawford, because of the state of his health and his reputed hostility toward the economic policies favored by the West, was out of the question). He had to choose either the cold, suspicious New Englander, with whom he had crossed swords in negotiating the Treaty of Ghent, or the frontier military idol, who had wrecked the Speaker's chances in the West with his own ambitions. While he delayed any public pronouncement, Clay actually had little difficulty in making up his mind. There was in reality but one possibility. That was Adams.

Clay had long regarded Jackson as utterly unfit for the Presidency. How could a hot-tempered, dictatorial military chieftain with so little experience in civil office be seriously considered? He had seen Jackson's star rise with mingled anger and disgust, and, it is possible, with no small amount of jealousy. What did Jackson know or care about tariff and internal improvements and other western measures? Yet Clay's friends saw another problem in the elevation of Jackson: Would the country give the West a President soon again? He might have to wait many years for his turn.

[3] Edward Stanwood, *History of the Presidency*, gives the popular vote as follows: Jackson, 152,901; Adams, 114,023; Crawford, 46,979; Clay, 47,217. But six states elected through legislatures, and in most of the others a light vote was cast. Not much significance can be given to the popular vote.

Adams, the impulsive, warmhearted Kentuckian respected, even though the strait-laced, aloof Puritan was as unlike him as any man could be. "Clay is essentially a gamester," Adams had confided to his diary on one occasion; and again, "His morals public and private, are loose, but he has all the virtues indispensable to a popular man"; and more fairly, "Clay has large and liberal views of public affairs, and that sort of generosity which attaches individuals to his person." The "large and liberal views of public affairs" proved to be the bridge between the former rivals.

Yet Clay was not willing to walk into the Adams camp without pledges. He must inform himself as to the good intentions of his former rival and have at least some assurances as to the recognition he might receive from the new President. Intermediaries—Washington was full of busy-bodies trotting from one candidate to another—helped to arrange the preliminaries. But, by chance, Clay and Adams were seated in adjacent chairs at the great Lafayette dinner given by the members of Congress on New Year's Day. When Adams showed unmistakable signs of thawing, the friendly Clay suggested a confidential conference "upon public affairs." Adams readily agreed, and a few days later—on Sunday evening—the two conferred. Denying any personal interest, Clay declared that he wished to be satisfied with regard to "some principles of great public importance." Adams's diary is cannily silent as to his own side of the conversation, but Clay made it clear that he was ready to support him in the coming House election. The die was cast. Thenceforth the two men were friends.

Yet Adams had other obstacles to overcome. Not all his visitors were as discreet as Clay. Missouri's lone Congressman, with that state's vote in his hands, was concerned about his brother, an Arkansas territorial judge, who had killed a man in a duel. Adams avoided definite promises, but his general attitude assured the Missourian that the brother was safe from removal. Daniel Webster, worried lest Federalists be proscribed, conferred and was satisfied. This involved the vote of Maryland, where a Federalist held the balance of power. One is surprised at the dexterity of Adams in playing the game. Possibly his diplomatic training stood him in good stead, or perhaps his conscience was being subjected to a process of liberal construction. Through his own efforts as well as Clay's, he seemed to be reasonably sure of the votes of the six New England states and of Maryland, Ohio, Kentucky, Illinois, Missouri, and Louisiana. He needed one more to win. Virginia and Delaware were possibilities on later ballots if Crawford were abandoned, but New York seemed to offer better prospects.

Seventeen of the thirty-four House members from New York were ready to vote for Adams; but the wily Van Buren, straining every effort to hold the Crawford lines intact, seemed to have the rest under his control. What his game was, may only be conjectured. Did he plan to transfer his supporters to Adams on the second ballot and claim the honor of electing a President? Crawford's cause seemed hopeless, and Van Buren had as yet no liking for Jackson. His autobiography, written years later, is too disingenuous and is colored by his later relations with Jackson. Whatever his purpose, he seemed to be determined to prevent the election of Adams on the first ballot.

Van Buren's weak point in New York proved to be General Stephen Van Rensselaer, head of an aristocratic family. Elderly, religious, muddleheaded, and much disturbed at the crisis confronting him in the pressure of the Clintonians to support Jackson and of the Van Buren men to vote for Crawford, Van Rensselaer was taken into the Speaker's office by Clay and Webster on the morning of the election and told that the safety of the country depended on the choice of Adams on the first ballot. How an average human being, left alone with Henry Clay and Daniel Webster, could withstand their eloquent persuasiveness is past understanding; yet, according to Van Buren's account, written later, the general held out. Then Providence—or the Adams goddess of luck—intervened. As the vote was about to be taken, Van Rensselaer bowed his head in prayer, seeking divine guidance. It came at once. On the floor in front of him was a ticket someone had dropped with the name of John Quincy Adams written on it. His startled eyes rested on the bit of paper.

A few moments later it was in the ballot box: New York had cast eighteen of its thirty-four votes for Adams, and the New Englander was elected President by thirteen of the twenty-four states.

Crawford had Delaware, Virginia, North Carolina, and Georgia; Jackson, the remaining seven—New Jersey, Pennsylvania, South Carolina, Alabama, Mississippi, Tennessee, and Indiana. In five of the twelve Adams states a change of one vote would have cost him their support. Perhaps a prolonged deadlock would have been disastrous. Yet it is equally possible that much of the Crawford vote would have swung his way. Election on the first ballot without Crawford aid left that group under no compulsion to support the new administration. Van Buren had lost, but he was free to choose his future allies. The prospects for a clever staff officer in the swelling Jackson army soon decided his course.

1828

The circumstances of the House election and Adams's appointment of Clay as his Secretary of State seemed, to Jacksonians, to confirm the charge (which had already incited an angry controversy) that a corrupt bargain had made Adams President. Jackson wrote: "The Judas of the West has closed the contract and will receive the thirty pieces of silver." This and the fact that Jackson had received more popular votes than Adams in the four-candidate race gave the Jacksonians their propaganda weapons for a campaign of vindication and vilification in 1828.

The overconscientious second Adams refused to play politics with the patronage, made only twelve removals, would not punish disloyalty, and kept in office a "neutral" Postmaster General, John McLean, who was placed on the Supreme Court by Jackson in 1829. In his messages to Congress, Adams enunciated broad nationalistic policies, believing that the government should improve the condition of the governed, but his ideas as applied to internal improvements, education, and land policies, affronted southern state-rights beliefs and western individualism.

The heterogeneous opposition was held together only by the prospect of victory with Jackson. There was no unity on tariff and internal improvements; the ruling class in the older planting states did not like rubbing party shoulders with frontier farmers and urban workers; Crawford hated Calhoun but could not swallow Adams's nationalism. In New York, Martin Van Buren and the Albany Regency led the Crawford following into the Jackson camp; but DeWitt Clinton had gotten there first. The factions battled at the polls as in the past, Clinton squeezing in as governor again and Van Buren returning to the Senate; but the embarrassing problem of Jacksonian leadership in the Empire State was solved by Clinton's death early in 1828.

In Congress every administration measure had to face a battery of political criticism. An Adams-Clay proposal to send delegates to a Panama Congress of American republics was finally approved, but only after misrepresentation by critics of its purposes, with charges that the slave trade and recognition of the Negro republic of Haiti would be discussed. With regard to internal improvements and the tariff, the Jacksonians, unable to offer a united front, voted the interests of their states and districts, and their candidate back in Tennessee was discreetly silent. In the case of the tariff, much maneuvering produced the political "Tariff of Abominations" of 1828, constructed by the Jacksonians to divide the Adams supporters sectionally. It was not intended to pass, but did by narrow margins. Its political effects were probably unimportant. The voters are not moved by economics when emotions are aroused.

As the election approached, personal abuse seemed to displace all other considerations. Adams men, angry at the vicious attacks upon the President for misuse of the patronage and the supposed bargain with Clay, retaliated by bringing up various acts of Jackson that showed a violent temper and a quarrelsome nature which unfitted him for the chief office. A Philadelphia editor, John Binns, printed the "Coffin Handbill"—a circular ornamented with coffins, which described purported acts of violence and brutality in Jackson's career. But the Cincinnati *Gazette* and *Truth's Advocate*, a campaign paper—both edited by Charles Hammond, brilliant journalist and friend of Clay—capped the climax by reviving an old story that Jackson's marriage to Mrs. Jackson had occurred before her divorce from her first husband. Legally, the charge was justified; but both parties had been innocent of intentional wrongdoing, and a second ceremony had satisfied both the law and public opinion. Other papers copied the story, and it appeared in pamphlet form. Jackson was aroused to a white heat against Adams and Clay: Why had they not used their influence to suppress the slander? Social relations with the two were thereafter impossible.

Had Jackson followed his natural impulses, the printing of these stories might well have produced further acts of violence. Certainly his enemies hoped for some such result. But the Old Hero realized that he was no longer a private citizen, free to defend his own honor. A committee of friends at Nashville was set up to meet and refute all charges against him and to handle correspondence, while Duff Green, editor of the Washington *Telegraph*, Calhoun's organ, retaliated with counterslanders, even concocting a cruel canard that Adams, while Minister to Russia, had been involved in bringing about the seduction of an American girl by the Czar. A billiard table in the White House, privately purchased for the President's son, was said to have been paid for with public funds. Such a "gaming table," whether sinful or a mark of frivolity, was politically damaging.

The result of the election was foreordained. A new democracy, ignorant, impulsive, irrational, but rooted in the American soil, had its way in 1828. The protagonists of the old order fought not for John Quincy Adams, whom they could not love, but against the new monster, the common man, whom they feared. To a degree, the candidates were symbols of a renewal of the old conflict between popular rule and property rule. This intensified the bitterness and the mud slinging.

When the electoral votes were counted Andrew Jackson had 178; John Quincy Adams, 83. Adams had New England (except for one Maine elector), Delaware, New Jersey, sixteen of New York's thirty-six, and six of Maryland's eleven.

All the rest went to Jackson.[4] Only Delaware and South Carolina chose their electors through the legislature, and so the result was a genuine popular verdict. The total vote for Jackson was 647,376; for Adams, 508,064. Nearly half of Adams's total came from New England and New York. Clay's support brought to the ticket not a single western electoral vote; and only in two states in the West and South, Ohio and Louisiana, was the result even close. Calhoun won the Vice Presidency over Richard Rush of Pennsylvania, but seven of Georgia's nine electors voted for William Smith of South Carolina, in a Crawford gesture of dislike for Calhoun.

[4] In this election Maine, New York, Maryland, and Tennessee used the district system; the other states (except South Carolina and Delaware) used a general ticket. Twenty-four states took part.

CHAPTER III

DEMOCRATS AND WHIGS

1832–1852

1832

JACKSON INTRODUCED the spoils system as a democratic reform, calling it "rotation in office." His removals of septuagenarian clerks with arthritic hands had some justification, but he introduced a new concept of service—that an officeholder's first loyalty was to his party. Thereafter, both major parties practiced the spoils system after each party change. Needy newspapermen fattened at the federal crib, and this helped to provide a loyal administration press.

As to policies, Jackson committed his party to opposition to federal aid for internal improvements, acceptance of a moderate protective tariff, removal to the west of the Indians of Georgia and her neighbors, and hostility toward the United States Bank.

More important than policies in its effects on the next Presidential election was the break between Jackson and Vice President Calhoun. This was a compound of several factors—Jackson's resentment at the snubbing of the bride of his good friend, Secretary of War John Eaton, by Mrs. Calhoun and wives of cabinet members because of rumors of premarital misconduct (the Peggy O'Neale affair); Calhoun's pronouncement in favor of the idea of nullification as a constitutional method of dealing with protective tariff; the belated revelation to Jackson that in 1818 Calhoun, then Secretary of War, had been his critic, not his defender, when

41

he had invaded Spanish Florida; the growing reliance of the President on Secretary of State Van Buren; and the hostility of Jackson's inner circle (the "Kitchen Cabinet") to Calhoun.

To get rid of the Calhounites, Jackson reconstructed his cabinet and sent Van Buren as minister to England. When the Senate rejected the appointment by the casting vote of the Vice President, the break was complete, and Van Buren moved into the role of heir apparent.

Three national conventions provided the candidates in 1832. A third party, the Antimasonic, held the first nominating convention, which met at Baltimore in September, 1831. The Antimasons were the outgrowth of the mysterious disappearance of a certain William Morgan of Batavia, New York, who was preparing a book to reveal the secrets of Masonry. Bitter opposition to the Masonic order developed in western New York when the case remained unsolved. It affected local politics and Antimasons were elected to the state legislature. The movement spread into New England, Pennsylvania, and northeastern Ohio, and national conventions of these opponents of secret orders were held in 1830 and 1831. The second, guided by a coterie of anti-Jackson politicians headed by Thurlow Weed of New York and Thaddeus Stevens of Pennsylvania, nominated William Wirt, former Attorney-General, as its Presidential candidate, after failing to get Justice John McLean to accept. Wirt, a former Mason, virtually repudiated the party's principles in his acceptance statement, but no other candidate was available. He would have withdrawn later if the National Republicans and Antimasons had been able to unite behind a single candidate to oppose Jackson, a Mason.

The old Adams-Clay party, assuming the name National Republican, held a convention at Baltimore in December, 1831, and nominated Clay for President and John Sargent of Pennsylvania for Vice President. The delegates did not adopt a platform, but they favored the policies Clay had long been advocating, particularly protective tariff and internal improvements.

The Democratic Republican (or Democratic) convention

also met at Baltimore, in May, 1832. Jackson had already been nominated by various state legislatures and conventions. The national convention was held to choose a candidate for Vice President. States were allotted their electoral votes regardless of the number of delegates present, and a two-thirds majority was required for a nomination. One ballot made Van Buren the nominee with 208 of the 283 votes. This reflected the will of Jackson, for the Little Magician was none too popular in the South and West.

By far the most stirring and significant event of the campaign was Jackson's veto of a bill to recharter the United States Bank. He had never been friendly toward the Bank, and his attitude should not have surprised anyone. Coming from a section which had had unfortunate experiences with banks and paper money, he hated "ragg, tagg banks" and inclined toward a hard money currency. Ignorant of banking and often the victim of prejudices, he made little distinction between the "wild-cat" banks of the West and the well managed, highly centralized institution at Philadelphia under the efficient Nicholas Biddle. He disliked and feared the Bank, and it was easy for him to say, in bland disregard of John Marshall's decisions, that it was unconstitutional.

Jackson's first two annual messages raised the constitutional issue and questioned whether the Bank had established a uniform and sound currency. He suggested another type of institution "founded upon the credit of the Government and its revenues." Meanwhile, Biddle had established friendly relations with Major Lewis and other politicians, was lending money to Congressmen and editors—including $20,000 to Duff Green—and secured favorable reports from Congressional investigating committees. In the new cabinet Secretary of the Treasury Louis McLane was friendly and only Attorney General Roger B. Taney was openly hostile. The Bank's charter did not expire until 1836, and Biddle was not inclined to ask for a recharter before the election of 1832. Jackson's message of 1831 merely expressed a willingness to leave the matter to the investigation of an enlightened people and their representatives. Henry Clay was not so willing. At first in favor of postponing the recharter question, he felt the need of a popular issue after his nomination—particularly one that would divide the Jacksonians. Biddle was wary, but after sounding out nearly everybody in Washington through a special agent, he accepted Clay's view that the omens were favorable. Congress would pass the bill, and Jackson would hardly dare veto it with the election so near. If he did, he would lose Pennsylvania, home of the Bank, and other eastern states, and Clay would win.

A recharter bill, in charge of a Calhounite in the House and a Jacksonian in the Senate, passed by safe margins, 107 to 85 and 28 to 20. Jackson met this challenge with a ringing veto message that blasted the Bank as monopolistic and unconstitutional. His arguments—or those of Taney, Kendall, and Donelson, who wrote the message—ranged all the way from the clear logic of the strict constructionist to the blatant appeals of the demagogue. Biddle wrote to Clay that the veto had "all the fury of a chained panther, biting the bars of a cage. It is really a manifesto of anarchy." He even circulated it as a campaign document. With the business classes and two-thirds or more of the newspapers aroused against Jackson, the hopes of the Clay men ran high.

But the old Tennessean was wiser in the ways of the common man than Clay, Webster, Biddle, and the whole army of financiers and businessmen who thought the voters would listen to reason and logic. Jackson's instincts told him that, sound or unsound, the Bank was a "Money Monster" and must be crushed, or it would crush democracy. The masses could understand his appeal, and their confidence in his judgment was unshaken. Torchlight processions and hickory-pole raisings showed what they thought. The Bank spent heavily but could not stem the tide. Leading Bank Democrats, seeing the direction of the wind, hastened to make peace with Jackson. Pennsylvania, whose Democratic legislature had urged recharter, remembered only its old loyalty to Jackson. George M. Dallas, who had introduced the Bank bill in the Senate, declared for the Old Hero, "bank or no bank."

In the face of these portents of a Jackson victory, the opposition attempted to unite. Coalition electoral tickets

were arranged in New York, Pennsylvania, and Ohio, with
the understanding that the electors, if successful, should vote
so as to bring about the defeat of Jackson. Whether this
meant Clay or Wirt, no one could tell. Calhoun took no
part in the election, but many of his southern friends supported Clay.

Yet the result was even more overwhelming than in 1828.
Clay won his home state of Kentucky, Massachusetts, Rhode
Island, Connecticut, Delaware, and 5 electors from Maryland, the only state to use the district system—a total of 49
electoral votes. Antimason Wirt had Vermont's 7. South Carolina, through her legislature, chose 11 electors who voted for
John Floyd of Virginia. Jackson had 219; Van Buren, 189, as
Pennsylvania's vote for Vice President went to William
Wilkins.[1] The popular vote is difficult to estimate because
of the fusion electoral tickets in some states, but Jackson's
majority over both his opponents was at least 150,000 in a
total vote well over 1,200,000.

The emergence of the national convention in 1832 was
part and parcel of the democratizing of politics that had
begun long before. Party nominations for local offices had
produced the convention system in the early 1800's, when it
began to supersede the more or less haphazard methods of
self-nomination common in the South, and the mass meeting
or nomination by the candidate's friends used in the North.
The Federalists, generally disdaining party machinery and
democratic innovations, left to their Republican opponents
the establishing of extralegal methods of voicing the will of
the voters.

In the middle states the county convention first came into
general use. In New England the town (township) was the
chief political unit, and the town meeting of the voters
served for most purposes. But in the middle states, where
county officials were elected by the voters and party unity
was necessary for success at the polls, the delegate county
convention was a logical outgrowth of the local mass meet-

---

[1] The popular votes usually cited are: Jackson, 687,502; Clay
and Wirt, 530,189.

ings or primaries. In the early 1800's Delaware and New Jersey Republicans also developed the state convention. Physical obstacles to state-wide meetings were not serious in these small states, and county conventions were already functioning. In Delaware Federalist use of this Republican device may help explain the persistence of Federalism after it ceased to function elsewhere. The use of a party caucus of members of the legislature retarded the development of the convention system for state nominations in other northern states, though occasionally the caucus was modified by the introduction of delegates from counties where the party was unrepresented in the general assembly, making it a "mixed caucus."

With improvements in transportation, and the growing distrust of the masses of new voters for the undemocratic caucus system, the state convention came into its own outside the South in the 1820's. The national convention, for the same reasons, made its appearance in the 1830's to fulfill a need that the old Congressional caucus and the state legislative or state convention nominations of Presidential candidates could not supply. It was representative in character; it divorced nominations from Congressional control and added to the independence of the executive; it permitted an authoritative formulation of a party program; and it concentrated the party's strength behind a single ticket, the product of a compromise of personal rivalries and group or sectional interests. Despite its defects, less evident then than later, it has remained fundamentally unchanged in general structure through well over a century of usage.

Yet, compared with the modern national convention, the early nominating body showed certain irregularities or imperfections. Delegates were chosen in a variety of ways—by state conventions, district conventions, local meetings, informal caucuses—dependent on the organization and strength of the party in each state. A national convention might even recognize as delegates visitors in attendance from a state which sent no delegates. Edward Rucker cast the entire vote of unrepresented Tennessee in the national Democratic gathering of May, 1835, because he happened to be in

Baltimore and was a Van Buren man. At this gathering 181 sons of Maryland appeared as delegates from that state. In the Whig national convention of 1848, the Louisiana delegates cast both their own votes and those of Texas, because a Texas Whig convention had given them its proxies. Distance or lack of interest kept some states from sending delegates to the early Whig and Democratic conventions, while the gatherings of anti-slavery parties were sectional in character and attracted few southerners. From the beginning, however, the major parties limited the voting strength of a state in the national convention to its electoral vote, regardless of oversize delegations or other irregularities.

With the development of a system of committees to accompany this hierarchy of conventions, all unrecognized by the laws, the party organization began its rule of politics, and, indirectly, of government itself, ostensibly as the representative of the voting masses but actually developing into a powerful oligarchy of professionals intent on carrying elections and maintaining the party in power. As a necessary adjunct, the party press flourished as never before. In a state capital the faithful editor of the majority organ expected to receive the public printing of the state government, just as F. P. Blair at Washington benefited from the Jackson administration. In the county seats plums in federal or state civil service or nominations for local elective offices rewarded the editor-printer of the county partisan newspaper, whose struggle for subsistence usually kept him a bare jump ahead of his creditors. In time it came to be almost a tradition in many localities that he should operate the post office for the four years following a national victory.

The Whigs, like the old Federalists, somewhat standoffish toward the masses, soon copied Democratic practices, and the later anti-slavery Republicans took over and improved upon the methods of both. The President found himself the chief dispenser of favors for his party and its national leader, whether he relished the role or not. More than ever the Presidency became a political office, with its control the great aim of each party. Candidates were nominated by conventions of politicians who made availability their prime consideration. More often than not, the nominees were either secondary figures in public life or popular military men. Yet the results were surprisingly good, despite such dubious choices as Pierce, Buchanan, and Frémont.

1836

Jackson's mastery of his party after his triumphant re-election forced dissenters to conform or depart. The opposition gained recruits, especially over two Jacksonian stands: his determination to use force against South Carolina in the nullification struggle of 1832–33 and his renewal of his war on the United States Bank.

Clay, forming an entente with Calhoun in the Senate, was able to end the nullification crisis with his compromise tariff, which both sides accepted. Webster, who had stood with Jackson on nullification, turned against him when he forced the removal of government deposits from the Bank. The Senate's Great Triumvirate secured the passage of a resolution of censure and led a heterogeneous opposition to King Andrew's "executive usurpations."

Under a broad umbrella, National Republicans, Anti-masons, bank Democrats, and state-rights men, mostly southerners, drew together in a conservative alliance against this tribune of the people who was too radical on currency and other economic matters and too high-handed in using the powers of his office. They adopted the name Whig because it had been used in the American Revolution by the opposition to royal tyranny.

The Whigs insisted that they were true Jeffersonians in constitutional theory. They emphasized the supremacy of the legislative branch, and criticized Jackson's free use of the veto power. In effect, they argued for an adulterated parliamentary system with a weak executive and the real power in the hands of Congressional leaders. But too much can be made of constitutional theories. The Whigs, like the wealthier classes on other occasions, raised a hue and cry about destruction of the Constitution by the President because his policies threatened their interests. Executive power was dangerous because Jackson was President.

The election of 1836 was a testing time for the Whigs. It was considered inexpedient to hold a national convention, and this left the leaders in each state free to offer local favorites. In New England Daniel Webster, representing the economic views of the National Republicans, and on friendly terms with the Antimasons, had strong claims. But, as a former Federalist and the paid attorney of the United States Bank, he was too vulnerable to Democratic shafts, and his hopes elsewhere were dashed by the failure of the Pennsylvania Antimasons to indorse him. Their state convention committed itself to General William Henry Harrison of Ohio, a hero of the War of 1812 and a man of considerable political experience, not hitherto regarded as of Presidential caliber. Because of financial reverses, he was then holding the position of clerk of the courts at Cincinnati. Availability was the keynote of his candidacy, for he was popular in the West, had been a Jeffersonian in other days, and had no damning record on national questions. John McLean, kept aloof from party controversies by his position on the Supreme Court, had the support of a number of Whig leaders in Ohio and Pennsylvania; and friends in the Ohio legislature nominated him in 1835 but the movement went no further. The western states were taking up the popular Harrison.

The Democratic legislature of Tennessee furnished a candidate for the Whigs in the South when it nominated Senator Hugh L. White, only recently estranged from Jackson. The Alabama legislature took similar action, and an independent Democratic movement for White was soon under way all through the South, as he was a moderate state-rights man. Van Buren, the "Little Magician," was not popular in this section, and all Jackson's efforts could not bring him a united Democratic support. Except in the border states, where Harrison was favored, the southern Whigs indorsed White electoral tickets.

Meanwhile a Democratic national convention at Baltimore, packed with federal officeholders, had nominated Van

Buren in May, 1835. There was no opposition, but Jackson's choice for Vice President, Colonel Richard M. Johnson of Kentucky, barely received the two-thirds vote required. Johnson, a genial politician and war veteran, reputed slayer of Tecumseh, and long-time foe of imprisonment for debt, provided western balance for the ticket. But he had lived with a mulatto woman, now dead, and had two daughters, whom he educated and presented socially. Such disregard of southern social conventions made him of doubtful value to the head of the ticket, and the Virginia delegation greeted his nomination with hisses.

Whig strategy aimed to defeat Van Buren by running sectional "favorite sons" and throwing the election to the House, where Harrison or White might be chosen. As Biddle put it, "This disease is to be treated as a local disorder— apply local remedies." The scheme failed chiefly because the might of Jackson was behind Van Buren, who received 170 electoral votes to Harrison's 73 (Vermont, New Jersey, Delaware, Maryland, Kentucky, Ohio, Indiana). White's 26 (Tennessee, Georgia), Webster's 14 (Massachusetts).[2] The South Carolina legislature, hostile to White because he had voted for the Force Bill in the nullification crisis, chose eleven electors who voted for Willie P. Mangum of North Carolina. R. M. Johnson had 147 votes for Vice President, one under a majority; the northern Whig states cast 77 votes for Francis Granger of New York, Democratic Virginia gave her 23 votes to William Smith of Alabama, and South Carolina, Georgia, Tennessee, and Maryland cast 47 votes for Whig John Tyler of Virginia. The Senate, for the only time in American history, chose the Vice President, Johnson receiving 33 votes, Granger 16.

The Whigs had cause to feel encouraged. Unlike Clay in

[2] The popular vote was Van Buren 765,483; Whig candidates, 739,795. For the popular votes for the elections 1836–1892, I have used W. Dean Burnham, *Presidential Ballots, 1836–1892* (Baltimore, 1955). Burnham puts minor party votes under the single heading "other." Where there were several minor parties, I have depended on Edward Stanwood, *History of the Presidency* (2 vols., Boston, 1916).

1832, they had polled a large southern vote. They had carried two Jacksonian strongholds, Georgia and Tennessee, and three border slave states, and had given Van Buren a close race elsewhere. Furthermore, Harrison's good showing in the Ohio valley states and in Pennsylvania, which he lost by 4,300 votes, stamped him as a good prospect for 1840. The opposition groups were on the way to becoming a party.

1840

Within two months of Van Buren's inauguration came the collapse of the nation's overexpanded credit system—the Panic of 1837. The Whigs blamed the policies of the Jackson administration for the collapse and demanded that Van Buren take steps to solve the problems of the years of depression that followed.

Van Buren held to a *laissez-faire* position. The government had not caused the panic and things would have to right themselves. He did favor an Independent Treasury system to protect the government from involvements with banks. In the future only gold and silver would be accepted as currency by the federal government. Not until near the end of his term did his proposal become law. Many supporters of state banks went over to the Whigs.

In New York a group of labor-oriented radicals—popularly called Locofocos—who had formed an equal rights party, liked Van Buren's opposition to corporate monopolies and came to his support. The term Locofoco was applied gleefully by the Whigs to all Democrats for many years afterward.

Calhoun, satisfied with Van Buren's narrow conception of federal powers, returned to the Democratic party. Little Van neither looked nor acted the part of a Presidential dictator.

Van Buren's control over his party was unquestioned and he was renominated by the Democratic national convention, meeting at Baltimore in May, 1840. "Tecumseh" Johnson was denied a renomination. Reports from Kentucky indicated that he was continuing to ignore the color line in his social relations. No one was recommended for Vice President. A platform—the first in Democratic history—indorsed the Jackson-Van Buren principles and policies.

The Whigs had already held their national convention at Harrisburg in December, 1839, with three candidates in the running. Clay believed that he deserved the nomination for his services to the party and had a large southern following. But important Whig politicos in New York, Pennsylvania, and Ohio regarded his long record as an inviting target for Democratic arrows. Weed in New York backed General Winfield Scott, but Stevens in Pennsylvania and the Ohio and Indiana delegations liked General Harrison, who had run well in 1836. Clay led on the first ballot, but after a number of ballots and some backstairs maneuvering, the Scott forces shifted to Harrison, and he was nominated. John Tyler of Virginia, a Clay supporter, was named for Vice President. Wisely, the convention made no platform.

The result at first did not seem to augur victory. Clay, disappointed as deeply as a man can be who sees the ambition of years thwarted at the moment of achievement, found liquor and profanity a temporary outlet but not a solace. "It is a diabolical intrigue, I know now, which has betrayed me. I am the most unfortunate man in the history of parties: always run by my friends when sure to be defeated, and now betrayed for a nomination when I, or any one, would be sure of an election." Whether the friend who reported these words quoted him correctly or not, they picture the state of mind of the man who had been most instrumental in creating the party that now rejected him. He had been shabbily treated, but he should not have been surprised. The northern politicians, and behind them the conservative business interests, wanted victory. They could win by an appeal to the democratic masses. Clay was not their man.

The key to victory was furnished by the Democrats. With incredible stupidity a Baltimore newspaper correspondent disparagingly suggested that Harrison be given "a barrel of hard cider and a pension of two thousand a year, and, our word for it, he will sit the remainder of his days in a log cabin by the side of a 'sea coal' fire and study moral philosophy." A Harrisburg Whig sensed the possibilities in the statement, and the sneer became the slogan. Harrison thenceforth was "the log cabin, hard cider" candidate, the simple man of the frontier pitted against the New York aristocrat living in splendor amid the luxuries of the White House. The arguments for Jackson in 1828 could now be used for Harrison, the frontier soldier. Glossed over were his aristocratic Virginia ancestry, his political activities in Ohio, his years of office holding and office seeking. He became the simple soldier-farmer of North Bend who would restore government to the people. His substantial country home was metamorphosed into a pioneer's log cabin.

Conventions and mass meetings, parades and processions with banners and floats, long speeches on the log-cabin theme, log-cabin songbooks and log-cabin newspapers, Harrison pictures, Tippecanoe handkerchiefs and badges, log-cabin headquarters at every crossroads, with the latchstring out and hard cider always on tap—all these devices and more were used to arouse enthusiasm that soon surpassed anything the nation had ever experienced. Crowds of unheard-of proportions turned out for Whig rallies. Ten acres of people (numbers would not suffice) were reported present at a Dayton, Ohio jamboree. The Democrats also held meetings and parades but, with an unaccountable display of moral rectitude, rejected hard cider and posed as the party of virtue. Democratic orators attempted to discuss the issues and—of all things—to belittle Harrison's war record when Van Buren had none. Old Andrew Jackson, on the stump in Tennessee, committed this *faux pas*.

Evading any expression of his bank views except to say that he favored paper money, Harrison talked in crowd-pleasing generalities at a soldiers' rally at Fort Meigs and made briefer speeches confined to Ohio. A Cincinnati committee handled all the correspondence. Whig orators assailed Van Buren's aristocracy with stories of gold spoons in the White House and a gilded coach and the trappings of British royalty. When issues were discussed, the hard times were played up, the Independent Treasury was attacked, and, to alarm state-rights men, a proposal of Secretary of War Poinsett to federalize the state militia was exposed as monarchical centralization and executive usurpation. But always the Whig orators returned to the log-cabin theme. Imposing Daniel Webster, without log-cabin nativity, claimed its virtues by association, through his older brother and sisters.

In the cotton South, Whig tactics were more moderate. Here businessmen and planters, indifferent to log cabins and much concerned about slavery, were assured that Harrison's membership in an antislavery society years before had been a youthful indiscretion, and the candidate himself declared against Congressional interference with their institution. He was pictured as an antique Jeffersonian Republican in contrast with the corruptionists who controlled the Democratic party. Clay recovered from his sulk and did yeoman service in selling Harrison's merits to the South. Even in Georgia, where a State Rights party had operated independently, the Whig candidate was finally accepted.

In the northern cities businessmen used economic pressure for the "Hero of Tippecanoe." Workingmen were warned of the dangers of continued low wages and unemployment if Van Buren should win: prosperity would return if he were defeated. "The subscriber will pay five dollars a hundred for pork if Harrison is elected, and two and a half if Van Buren is." So ran an advertisement in a New York paper. But song and hard cider were better arguments than fear. One of the most popular ditties tells the story:

> What has caused this great commotion, motion,
>   Our country through?
>   It is the ball a-rolling on,
> For Tippecanoe and Tyler too, Tippecanoe and
>   Tyler too.
> And with them we'll beat the little Van, Van, Van;
>   Van is a used-up man.

More expressive was this:

> Old Tip he wears a homespun suit,
> He has no ruffled shirt-wirt-wirt;

But Mat he has the golden plate,
And he's a little squirt-wirt-wirt.

Tobacco chewers spit when they came to the "wirt."

And so Van Buren was sung and drunk out of the White
House and back to Kinderhook. One of the most sincerely
democratic of Presidents was overborne by a wave of popular enthusiasm for a log-cabin myth. Marching in the Whig
ranks with simple artisans and rustic cultivators were bankers,
merchants, landed gentry, mill owners, speculators—for the
log-cabin cult, spreading through the land, had made strange
bedfellows. The rich and the well born had at last learned
that in politics the votes of the humble were not to be de-
spised. "The Goths have taken Rome," wailed Thomas
Ritchie, Virginia editor. But he did not add the bitter explanation that they had borrowed their weapons and their
tactics from the Romans.

The electoral votes indicated a landslide. To Van Buren
went only 60 votes (Virginia, South Carolina, Alabama,
Missouri, Illinois, Arkansas, New Hampshire) out of 294.
The popular vote was less conclusive: 1,274,624 for Harrison, 1,127,781 for Van Buren. Both houses of Congress were
won by the Whigs. Tyler had the same electoral vote as Harrison, but R. M. Johnson had twelve fewer than Van Buren.
South Carolina cast eleven for L. W. Tazewell of Virginia,
while one Virginia elector voted for James K. Polk of Tennessee.

1844

Harrison's death a month from the day of his inauguration
brought John Tyler, reared in the Virginia state-rights
school, into the Presidency. Clay, already at odds with Harrison over patronage matters, assumed the role of Senate
leader and unofficial prime minister when Congress met in
special session. He offered a program of measures covering
the old trinity of banking, tariff, and internal improvements,
which the Whig majorities in both Houses accepted.

Tyler, affronted at both the program, which ran counter
to his constitutional scruples, and Clay's imperious assump-

tion of leadership, vetoed a bill for a third United States Bank. A modified bank measure designed to meet his objections was then passed but it, too, was rejected. The Whig caucus followed Clay's leadership and denounced Tyler as a party traitor, but only a watered down version of Clay's original program was finally enacted. "His Accidency" had turned the Log Cabin victory into ashes, but he had held stanchly to his principles.

But Tyler was ambitious for another term and, as an expansionist, was concerned about British interest in the Republic of Texas, still unrecognized by Mexico. After some secret negotiations he surprised the Senate with a treaty of annexation in late April, 1844. That slavery existed in Texas had been a major obstacle to annexation since the birth of the Lone Star Republic. Now, with a Presidential campaign impending, a critical sectional issue confronted party leaders.

The leading candidates of both parties thought the problem had been solved when each wrote a letter for publication opposing annexation. Clay's letter, written at Raleigh, North Carolina, was more forthright, but Van Buren's wordy explanation of his position was more damaging to his prospects. Annexationists in the Democratic party set out to keep the nomination from him, even though a majority of the delegates were already pledged to him. Led by Robert J. Walker of Mississippi and aided by disloyal Van Buren delegates, they were able to secure the adoption of the two-thirds rule by the national convention when it met at Baltimore on May 27. Van Buren had a majority on the first ballot but his vote declined on later trials and a deadlock resulted. On the ninth ballot a "dark horse," James K. Polk of Tennessee, former Speaker of the House and former governor of his state, was nominated.

For Vice President George M. Dallas of Pennsylvania was the choice after Senator Silas Wright of New York, friend of Van Buren, turned down the nomination. The platform coupled the "re-occupation of Oregon and the re-annexation of Texas." It was a shrewd bid for expansionist support in both North and South.

Meanwhile, the Whigs had nominated Clay and Senator Theodore Frelinghuysen of New Jersey at Baltimore earlier in May. The brief platform was vaguely conservative but did not mention the United States Bank or Texas. Clay's Raleigh letter was clear enough on the Texas issue.

Unexpectedly Van Buren had lost the Democratic nomination, and Clay faced the expansionist Polk on a platform that threatened to make heavy inroads into his southern strength. In general, the Whigs of the South had rallied loyally to Clay, and in the Senate all but one had voted against Tyler's Texas treaty. The large planters and their business allies, except speculators in Texas land, had no stomach for war with Mexico and a stirring up of sectional hatred. "The Union without Texas rather than Texas without the Union," was their slogan. But the powerful appeal of Texas to the land-hungry small farmers and even to some planters, plus the argument of Calhoun that it was necessary to save the institution of slavery, played havoc with Clay's hopes. He began to soften the views of his Raleigh letter and in two letters to Alabama friends made it clear that he had no objection to annexation accomplished without dishonor, without war, with the common consent of the Union, and upon just and fair terms. He would be guided as President "by the state of facts, and the state of public opinion existing at the time I might be called upon to act." The letters encouraged his southern friends, but they damaged him in the North.

Here the abolitionist Liberty party darkened the Whig sky. It had run a candidate, James G. Birney, in 1840 but had been lost sight of in the Log Cabin hullabaloo. Birney had polled some seven thousand votes. But the party had gained recruits and newspaper support since then and was becoming a threat to the major parties in close northern states, where it aimed to swing the balance of power. A national convention at Buffalo in August, 1843, named Birney, now a Michigan resident, and Thomas Morris of Ohio as its ticket. When Texas became a major issue, the Liberty party was in a difficult position. A heavy third party vote might reduce the Whig vote in the doubtful northern states and elect expansionist Polk over Clay, committed against Texas.

The Liberty party leaders, chiefly enthusiasts and fanatics, had little use for Clay under any circumstances; but their opposition would have mattered less had Clay not wavered on annexation. He attempted in September to return to his Raleigh letter position, undoing some of the damage. Whig hopes rose in October when the news spread that Birney had accepted a Democratic nomination for the Michigan legislature—seeming proof of a Liberty-Democratic bargain to defeat Clay. Birney attempted to explain it on the ground of purely local issues, but did openly admit his preference for Polk over Clay for the amazing reason that the latter, far more able, might lead his party to bring about annexation, while Polk was too incompetent to accomplish it. The effect was damaging to the Liberty party and was made more so by a forged letter, appearing in Whig newspapers a day or two before the election, in which Birney promised not to agitate the slavery question in the Michigan legislature. His refutation of it came too late. The Liberty party lost hundreds of votes. But its power in New York still proved decisive.

Yet expansion and slavery were not the sole issues on which the election turned. Oregon and Texas might be Democratic vote getters in South and West, but protectionist Pennsylvania, as important as New York in Democratic strategy, had to be propitiated in other ways. A letter from Polk to John K. Kane of Philadelphia made it clear that he favored a revenue tariff with only incidental protection, but his ardent supporters in the Keystone State used it to prove that he was as good a tariff man as Clay. "Polk, Dallas and the Tariff of '42" was their slogan. "Fifty-four Forty or Fight," long associated with this campaign, appeared after this election.

Organized Native Americanism also appeared locally in New York and Pennsylvania with both parties angling for its support without the curse of its blessing. The Whigs had the advantage here, for the foreign-born were generally Democrats. An antiforeign American Republican party, which had gained some local successes, indorsed Clay and Frelinghuysen. The latter had been active in Protestant evangelical movements, such as the American Bible Society and foreign missions, which weakened Whig appeal to Irish Catholics. The Democrats accused the Whigs of allying with the "church-burning" nativists, and countered by speeding up the naturalization of Irish and German newcomers in the East.

Both candidates were victims of slander and mud slinging. All Clay's chickens came home to roost. He was branded a gambler, a duelist, a profane swearer, a corrupt bargainer. Democratic newspapers printed an alleged letter of a Protestant minister who had traveled on a steamboat with him and bore witness to Clay's free use of strong language and his love of cards. Polk's character was quite exemplary, but Whig journals carried a story that a traveler had observed a gang of slaves being marched to a slave auction in Tennessee, each one branded with the letters "J. K. P." It purported to be an extract from a certain Roorbach's account of a tour of the South and West. Democratic defenders of Polk exposed the story as a Whig fabrication and the name "roorback" passed into the American political vocabulary for a preelection falsehood. One way of belittling the Democratic standard-bearer was to repeat the question many Americans asked just after his nomination: "Who is James K. Polk?" Tom Corwin, popular Whig stump speaker, added, "After that, who is safe?"

The election revealed that the relatively obscure Polk had defeated his more illustrious opponent, 170 electoral votes to 105.[8] Clay had carried only Ohio in the expansion-minded Northwest and only the upper tier of slave states in the South (North Carolina, Tennessee, Kentucky, Maryland, and Delaware). In the East, Massachusetts, Rhode Island, Connecticut, Vermont, and New Jersey gave him their votes. The South and West had voted for Texas and Oregon, but Polk also had Pennsylvania and New York by

[8] The popular vote was as follows: Polk, 1,338,464; Clay, 1,300,097; Birney, 61,998.

narrow margins. Clay needed New York's 36 electors to win. Birney had 15,812 popular votes in that crucial state. One-third of that number added to Clay's total would have meant victory. Had he not wavered on the Texas issue he might have gained these antislavery votes. But there is another side to the picture. His concessions to southern sentiments on Texas possibly tilted the balance to him in Tennessee. His margin there was only 113 votes. Defeat in Tennesseee even with victory in New York would have lost him the election. Tyler, in throwing Texas into the campaign, had confronted Clay with a problem he could not solve, so long as the Liberty party warred on the Whig flanks. It was his misfortune that his Presidential candidacies ran counter to the two most powerful forces in the America of his generation: Jacksonian democracy and territorial expansion. One might add a third, just beginning to build up—European immigration. Millard Fillmore, himself the losing candidate for governor of New York, wrote that the abolitionists and the foreign Catholics had defeated Clay.

While the importance of Texas had tended to give Polk's victory the aspect of a southern triumph, the result in 1844 was more nearly an indorsement of a general expansionist program. The West, as ever, was land-hungry, and the Democrats had pointed the way by linking Oregon and Texas. Locofoco reformism had been diverted into a new channel that was to lead the Democratic party southward, as Benton and Van Buren sensed; but the South was not yet in the even was sometimes called "Young Hickory." Jackson was his mentor, not Calhoun.

1848

Drab, secretive, hard-working James K. Polk was not a popular President, but he left behind him a record of accomplishing every one of his major objectives. He completed the annexation of Texas, approved by joint resolution of Congress after his election. He secured a treaty for the division of the disputed Oregon country with England. His attempts to solve the Texas boundary problem and to pur-

saddle. To the West, Polk was the heir of "Old Hickory" and
chase California failed, and he was largely responsible for
the Mexican War, which followed the breakdown of his
diplomacy. But it resulted in the addition of the vast Cali-
fornia-New Mexico southwest to the United States. On the
domestic front, he was able to secure the restoration of the
Independent Treasury and a lowering of tariff rates.

In the midst of the Mexican War David Wilmot of Pennsylvania introduced in Congress his famous Proviso forbidding
slavery in any territory to be obtained from Mexico. It
passed the House but failed in the Senate. Both parties were
now confronted with a serious sectional division with the
election of 1848 impending.

In the Democratic camp a New York split over patronage
and local issues had produced two warring factions, the
Barnburners and the Hunkers. The more liberal Barnburners came out in favor of the Wilmot Proviso and
appealed for antislavery support. The two factions held
separate state conventions and sent separate sets of delegates
to the national convention, which met at Baltimore on May
22. The convention voted, by a bare majority of two, to seat
both delegations. Both rejected the solution and New York
was unrepresented.

Senator Lewis Cass of Michigan and General William O.
Butler of Kentucky received the party's nominations. Cass
was named on the fourth ballot. A cautious elder statesman
—called a "doughface" because he had opposed the Wilmot
Proviso—he had declared for "squatter sovereignty" in a
territory, which would leave the decision on slavery to the
voters. The platform defended the Mexican War and praised
the work of the Polk administration. Polk had refused to
run for another term.

The Whigs had become critics of the Mexican War and
had taken a position opposing any acquisitions of territory
as productive of sectional discord. But the successful termina-
tion of the war left this program high and dry.

When they held their convention at Philadelphia on June
7, they were presented with the choice of 1840: two generals and a statesman—Zachary Taylor, Winfield Scott, and

Clay, now seventy-one but still ready to battle for the prize that had eluded him so long. But a strong southern contingent and some northern politicians on the lookout for a winner were backing Taylor, and he was nominated on the fourth ballot. Millard Fillmore of New York balanced the ticket as his running mate. No platform was adopted.

Taylor, "Old Rough and Ready," a Louisiana slaveholder who had never voted, had been acclaimed for his early victories in the Mexican War and had been ready to run as an independent when the Whigs took him over. Daniel Webster called him "an illiterate frontier colonel," and a group of antislavery Whigs prepared to bolt the nomination.

The situation seemed to call for a new antislavery party, as both the major parties had ignored the Wilmot Proviso. The Liberty party, which had already nominated John P. Hale of New Hampshire, the bolting Barnburners and their sympathizers, and many "Conscience Whigs" joined to send delegates to a convention held in a big tent at Buffalo in August. They organized the Free Soil party, which was pledged to oppose the extension of slavery and to open the public lands to free homesteaders. Ex-President Van Buren, choice of the Barnburners, defeated Hale for the Presidential nomination. A Conscience Whig, Charles Francis Adams of Massachusetts, son of John Quincy Adams, was named to run with him.

The Free Soilers waged a strenuous campaign to attract antislavery Whigs and Van Buren Democrats. With the former they were less successful. Though the Conscience Whigs in Massachusetts and Giddings and his following in Ohio lent aid, William H. Seward of New York and Tom Corwin of Ohio took the stump to allay antislavery dissatisfaction in Whig ranks. Van Buren's name had no attraction for northern Whigs, and many, doubting his sincerity, were persuaded that Taylor's opposition to the veto power would permit the Wilmot Proviso to become law if Congress passed it. The Free Soil movement played havoc with the New York Democracy but did only slight damage elsewhere. Wilmot, Brinkerhoff, and the Blair family joined the revolt, but Benton, embarrassed by a proslavery backfire at home, remained regular. Former Governor Marcus Morton of Massachusetts favored Van Buren but not the third party. Cass was popular in the Northwest, where he was not regarded as proslavery, and held most of the Democrats in line. He was the first Democratic Presidential candidate from that section, and it proved loyal to him.

Both the major parties fought sectional, rather than national, campaigns. The Whigs of the South argued that southern rights were secure only if a southerner sat in the White House. The Democrats defended Cass as "safe" on slavery and warned that Taylor might die in office, bringing Fillmore, possessor of an antislavery past, into the White House. In view of what actually happened, this has a curious significance. In the North, Democrats praised Cass as faithful to northern interests and asked how antislavery Whigs could stomach Taylor. The Whig answer was to call Cass a doughface and to argue that the North would control a Whig Congress.

The election, the first to be held on the same day everywhere, gave Taylor 163 electoral votes, Cass 127. Taylor carried Massachusetts, Vermont, Connecticut, Rhode Island, New York, Pennsylvania, and New Jersey in the North; the usual Whig states in the upper South, Delaware, Maryland, Tennessee, Kentucky, and North Carolina; and Georgia, Louisiana, and Florida in the lower South. Cass carried Maine, New Hampshire, all of the Northwest (Ohio, Indiana, Illinois, Michigan, Wisconsin, Iowa), and seven slave states (Missouri, Arkansas, Texas, Alabama, Mississippi, Virginia, and South Carolina). Taylor ran well in the usual Whig areas of the South and gained noticeably over Clay's vote of 1844 in the small farmer sections, where his personality seemed to be reminiscent of Andrew Jackson. Pennsylvania, disgruntled over Polk's revenue tariff, and New York, lost through the Barnburner bolt, bitterly disappointed the Democrats. In New York, Taylor received 218,603 votes; Cass, 114,318; Van Buren, 120,510. A united Democracy apparently could have defeated Taylor, though it must not be forgotten that a Liberty party vote was concealed in the Van Buren total and might, as in 1844, have held the balance. Taylor's pluralities were generally larger than those for Cass and his popular vote totaled 1,360,967 to his rival's 1,222,342 and Van Buren's 294,719.

The Free Soilers, though their vote fell below their early expectations, had the satisfaction of holding the balance of power in eleven states and in the national House of Representatives, where they won thirteen seats. The Ohio legislature, controlled by a coalition of Free Soilers and Democrats, sent Salmon P. Chase, Free Soiler, to the United States Senate.

1852

Henry Clay, fearing that the Union was in grave danger, returned to his old Senate seat in December, 1849, and offered his famous Compromise of 1850 to appease sectional grievances. In brief, it included the admission of California as a free state, the creation of two territories out of the New Mexico area with no mention of slavery, the enactment of a stronger fugitive slave law, the abolishment of the slave trade in the District of Columbia, and the settlement of a Texas boundary dispute with New Mexico by a monetary compensation to Texas.

The southern slaveholder President had a plan of his own, more favorable to the North, and opposed Clay's proposals. His sudden death in July, 1850, brought Millard Fillmore, who favored Clay's plan, into the Presidency, and a bipartisan combination put the measures through Congress.

Antislavery radicals attacked the new Fugitive Slave Law but great Union meetings in the larger northern cities better represented public sentiment. Radical southern rights men agitated for disunion, but when a Unionist coalition captured control of a Georgia convention called to consider secession, they lost heart.

The Whig national convention, held at Baltimore on June 16, 1852, adopted a platform which "acquiesced in" the Compromise measures, but sixty-six northern delegates friendly to General Scott opposed it. The struggle for the Presidential nomination went on for fifty-three ballots before Scott triumphed over Fillmore and Webster. William A. Graham, Secretary of the Navy, received second place on the ticket.

The Democratic national convention, opening at Baltimore on June 1, witnessed a marathon battle of three party veterans, Cass, Buchanan, and William L. Marcy, and a brash newcomer, Senator Stephen A. Douglas of Illinois. It took forty-nine ballots to convince the weary delegates that dark horse Franklin Pierce of New Hampshire was the best solution. Veteran Senator William R. King of Alabama was named to run with him.

The platform, mostly a repetition of that of 1848, added a pledge to "abide by, and adhere to" the Compromise measures including the Fugitive Slave Law, and to resist all attempts to renew the slavery agitation. The convention had successfully surmounted all its difficulties, but the query "Who is Franklin Pierce?" was genuine, not a Whig sneer. The nominee had to be explained to the voters, though his availability could not have been higher. Forty-seven years old, handsome, friendly, once a victim of the liquor habit but now a good temperance man, he was a fluent speaker and had no enemies to conciliate and no record to explain away. He had served in both houses of Congress without particular distinction, retiring before sectional issues became acute. He had a Mexican War record as a brave but not brilliant officer. Every element in the party seemed to be pleased with its good-looking New Hampshire nonentity. The Van Burens and the Blairs rejoiced with the southern rights men over the defeat of the leading Compromise candidates, while Compromisers were happy that Pierce and the platform were right on the Compromise.

But the Whigs had no reason to rejoice. Southern party members were disappointed in Scott's letter of acceptance, which merely accepted the nomination "with the resolutions annexed," making no specific mention of the Compromise or the Fugitive Slave Law. To make matters worse, Seward's warm support convinced them of the candidate's unsoundness on slavery. Had not the wily New Yorker drawn poor General Taylor, himself a slaveholder, into his web? Stephens, Toombs, and a few other members of Congress formally repudiated Scott; others were silent, and nowhere in the lower South was there much enthusiasm. Some Georgia bolters, led by Stephens, ran a Webster electoral ticket; elsewhere the dissatisfied either voted Democratic or stayed away from the polls. In the North, Webster's friends were unreconciled to Scott, and those in Massachusetts would have supported a separate electoral ticket but for the great orator's death in October. His bitterness had caused him to hope for Pierce's election. The "higher law" Whigs, as they were dubbed after Seward's Senate speech against the Compromise, were enthusiastic for Scott but not the platform. As Greeley put it, accepting the nominee, they "spit upon the platform."

Yet the Free Soil men had no use for Scott or his platform. In Ohio the Ashtabula *Sentinel*, organ of the redoubtable Giddings, declared, "We do not desire to smuggle antislavery men or measures into the coming or any administration." The third party, under the name Free Democratic, held its national convention at Pittsburgh in August and nominated John P. Hale of New Hampshire for President and George W. Julian of Indiana for Vice President. The platform attacked slavery, condemned the Compromise and the Fugitive Slave Law, and indorsed many proposals including the free homestead policy, cheap postage, river and harbor improvements, and international arbitration. The Barnburners had gone back to the Democrats, leaving behind hardly more than the old Liberty men and some unreconciled antislavery Whigs. Senator Chase of Ohio, after consorting with the Democrats for a year, returned to the fold. Charles Sumner, elected from Massachusetts to the Senate by a coalition of Democrats and Free Soilers in 1851, was the eastern leader.

The campaign was issueless, spiritless, and hopelessly dull. The Whigs made a strong bid for Irish Catholic support, as General Scott's daughters had attended church schools and one, now deceased, had become a nun. He declared in favor of citizenship for foreign-born soldiers after a year of wartime service. The Democrats retaliated with an unwise nativist letter he had written ten years before, and accused him of executing German and Irish soldiers in the Mexican War. The Whigs happily discovered a clause in the New Hampshire constitution disqualifying Catholics from office-holding and blamed Pierce for it. Quotations from English newspapers approving the Democratic low-tariff attitude were reprinted in Whig newspapers to arouse anti-British feeling in Irish breasts. Pamphlets in German were circulated by Whig postmasters. Politicians were aware of the swelling tide of immigration and its political import.

Efforts of both parties to revive the tariff question and to arouse interest in foreign policies accomplished little, and the campaign degenerated further into personalities. Pierce was charged with cowardice in the Mexican War and with habitual drunkenness. Scott, an imposing figure in military regalia, was ridiculed as a pompous ass, and he almost demonstrated this in an ill-disguised electioneering tour of the North; his military career was belittled; and the dangers of electing a soldier despot were held before the voters. On this exalted plane ended one of the dullest campaigns in American history.

The Democrats triumphed by a landslide. Scott salvaged only Massachusetts and Vermont and the border Whig states of Kentucky and Tennessee—42 electoral votes. Pierce had all the rest—a total of 254. The popular vote was: Pierce, 1,601,117; Scott, 1,385,967; and Hale, 155,825.[4] The country was voting to uphold the Compromise. The Democratic stand was clearer, and the candidate safer, on this issue. The decline of the third-party vote is additional proof of the revulsion against agitation. More businessmen and more planters voted Democratic than in any previous election, while large numbers of conservatives gave only perfunctory support to Scott or had refused to vote. The Democratic party, divested of Jacksonian radicalism, was now safe for men of property.

The Whig party was demoralized. Had Webster or Fillmore been nominated, the defeat would have been as bad.

[4] Thirty-one states voted, California having been added in 1850. Webster had 7,425; Troup (Southern Rights), 3,300; Broom (Native American), 4,485.

Thousands of northern Whigs would have repudiated the Compromise nominee, just as the southerners had rejected Scott. With its most available candidate, the party had suffered its worst defeat. Clay's Compromise had saved the Union but had wrecked the party whose foundations he had laid twenty years before. It might have passed away in any case. The growing moral sentiment against slavery, nurtured in Protestant churches, was stirring the middle classes, the backbone of Whiggery. The party was splitting apart in the North. In New England, there were Cotton and Conscience Whigs; in New York, Woolly Heads and Silver Grays; in other places, "higher law" and "lower law" Whigs. The conservatives who sought to repair the breach between the sections were pale reflections of Clay and Webster: Fillmore, Everett of Massachusetts, Bell of Tennessee, Crittenden of Kentucky, all were thin-blooded elder statesmen. The task required dynamic leadership, and this they lacked. Whiggery had gone to seed.

CHAPTER IV

SECTIONAL PARTIES
AND CIVIL WAR POLITICS

1856–1864

1856

IN JANUARY, 1854, Stephen A. Douglas of Illinois introduced in the Senate a Nebraska Bill to organize the Indian
country west of Missouri into a territory. This became, in
its final form, the Kansas-Nebraska Act, which created two
territories out of the area, with the right to decide the
slavery question left to the people of each territory. This
act repealed the provision of the Missouri Compromise of
1820 prohibiting slavery north of the line 36° 30'. Douglas
put in the repeal clause to overcome objections to the bill
from some proslavery men. He was eager to get the territory
organized, possibly because of his interest in having the
projected Pacific Railroad built along a northern route.
Whatever his motives, Douglas and President Pierce, who
yielded to his persuasions, committed one of the costliest
political blunders in American history.

Almost as soon as the Nebraska Bill was introduced, a
group of antislavery members of Congress issued an in-
flammatory appeal to the people denouncing the Douglas
proposal as "part and parcel of an atrocious plot" to ex-
clude free labor from the territory and convert it into "a
dreary region of despotism inhabited by masters and slaves."
Mass meetings all over the North denounced "Pierce, Douglas, and Co.," and presently there was talk of a new party.

The first steps were taken in the Old Northwest. Here

the Whig party was demoralized by defeat and antislavery defections; the Free Soil (or Free Democratic) party had not lost its crusading zeal but was willing to cooperate on a moderate program; and many Democrats felt that the Polk and Pierce administrations had ignored the interests of their section as to policies and patronage, and that the South was responsible for Cass's defeat in 1848. The heavy migrations into the lake regions from New England and New York and the new East-West rail connections were weakening the old economic and social ties with the South.

The first suggestion for the organization of a new anti-slavery party is usually accredited to a meeting at Ripon, Wisconsin, on March 1, 1854, led by Alvan E. Bovay, but other meetings were taking similar steps almost simultaneously. The name "Republican" for a new party was used by Horace Greeley in the New York *Tribune* at Bovay's suggestion, but the old Jeffersonian name was a natural one for such a party. Anti-Nebraska state and Congressional tickets under various names swept the Old Northwest in the fall of 1854. But the East was another story.

The broth of nativism had been simmering for some years in eastern cities, but it boiled over with amazing suddenness in 1854. The great influx of Germans and Irish had been arousing temperance and Protestant America against the poverty-stricken, whiskey drinking, Popish Irish and the less impecunious, beer drinking Germans, many of whom were tabbed as atheistic Red Republicans, "the Forty-eighters." Both groups were Democrats, which made Whigs incline toward nativism.

In the political confusion caused by the Nebraska Bill, Democratic factionalism in New York, and a Maine Law (liquor prohibition) movement, the secret Order of the Star-Spangled Banner burgeoned into a political party. It won some surprising local successes in the East, operating in secret and refusing to reveal its principles. This "Know Nothing" movement soon was spreading southward, largely absorbing the homeless Whigs of that section, who looked upon it largely as a Union-saving force against agitation over slavery. The secret lodges also infiltrated the new Republican party in the Old Northwest and threatened to dilute its antislavery principles with nativism.

But the Republicans had outdistanced the Know Nothings by the end of the year 1855. They made propaganda out of the struggles of antislavery and proslavery men in newly organized Kansas. They elected Salmon P. Chase governor of Ohio and absorbed most of the Know Nothings of that important state. They acquired the New York Whig organization of Seward and Weed, who were antinativist. And the Know Nothings were having difficulties with the slavery issue.

In February, 1856, the Know Nothings, now calling themselves the "American party," held their national council meeting and national nominating convention at the same time. The council adopted a platform which would limit officeholding to the native-born, require twenty-one years residence for naturalization, and deny political station to anyone recognizing allegiance to a "foreign potentate, prince or power." But on slavery it lamely indorsed popular sovereignty for the territories. When the nominating convention assembled and upheld this plank, a secession of antislavery men, loosely called "North Americans," followed. The majority remained and named ex-President Fillmore and Andrew Jackson Donelson as the party candidates.

The Republicans held an organizing convention at Pittsburgh on February 22, which set up a national committee and called a nominating convention to meet at Philadelphia on June 17. The six hundred or more delegates, plus alternates and visitors, made the Philadelphia gathering almost a mass convention, disorderly but as enthusiastic as a religious revival. Astute eastern chieftains passed over Seward and Chase and turned to John C. Frémont, age forty-three, former army officer and famed explorer—called the "Pathfinder"—participant in the California uprising against Mexico, and for a brief period a Senator from that State. Conservatives centering in the Pennsylvania delegation favored elderly Supreme Court Justice John McLean, but the convention nominated the more glamorous Frémont with William L. Dayton, former Whig Senator from New Jersey, as his running mate. The platform declared it the duty of Congress to prohibit in the territories "those twin relics of barbarism, polygamy and slavery." Planks favoring a Pacific railroad to be built with federal aid and advocating national improvements of rivers and harbors were lost sight of in the platform's denunciations of the administration's policies in Kansas.

The seceding "North Americans" accepted both the Republican nominees after offering their own candidate for Vice President.

The Democratic national committee listened to western appeals and chose Cincinnati as the site of its national convention and June 2 as the date. The platform repeated the planks of earlier ones and added resolutions denouncing Know-Nothingism and indorsing the Kansas-Nebraska Act. Pierce wanted a renomination, and Douglas had some support, but James Buchanan of Pennslyvania, who had been minister to England and had escaped involvement in the Nebraska struggle, had friends in both sections and was the most available in all respects. The two-thirds rule delayed his nomination until the seventeenth ballot. John C. Breckinridge of Kentucky was nominated for Vice President.

An old guard of Whigs met at Baltimore in September and indorsed Fillmore and Donelson but not the American party platform.

The course of the campaign was largely determined by the long session of Congress, from December to August, which was marked at every step by sectional and partisan bitterness. It required nine weeks to elect a Speaker, because Republicans, "North" and "South" Americans, Democrats, and Republican-Americans could find no common ground. At last Nathaniel P. Banks of Massachusetts, an American-Republican, was chosen by a plurality. Much time was consumed by the Kansas question. Long debates between "shriekers for freedom" and "subduers of freedom" produced no solution. Democratic Senate and anti-Nebraska House could not agree. Accompanying the excitement in Congress a series of events in Kansas culminated in the "sacking" of Lawrence by a marshal's posse of which former Senator

Atchison was a member—really a proslavery mob. This produced other acts of violence, all luridly misrepresented by reporters for eastern newspapers.

On May 19, while the drunken mob was in possession of Lawrence, Senator Charles Sumner of Massachusetts, eloquent, vain, stuffed with classical learning and master of the dictionary, delivered his carefully prepared and rehearsed masterpiece, "The Crime Against Kansas." Not content with arguments and near-obscene metaphors, he indulged in offensive personalities against Douglas and, for no apparent reason, singled out for special chastisement the elderly South Carolina Senator, Andrew Pickens Butler, who was not present to defend himself. Douglas struck back with caustic comments, but Butler was avenged by his nephew, Congressman Preston Brooks. Two days after the speech, Brooks approached Sumner at his desk in the Senate after adjournment and attacked him with a gutta-percha cane, finally breaking it over his head. Opinion differed then and afterward over the severity of the wounds; but Sumner did not reappear in the Senate for two years, going abroad in search of health. Massachusetts reelected him as a mark of her esteem.

The assault on Sumner was, next to "Bleeding Kansas," the best argument the Republicans had in 1856. A southern bully, fit product of the slavocracy, had brutally assaulted a northern Senator for words used in the supposedly free forum of the Senate. When his district re-elected Brooks after he had resigned as a result of a vote of censure, here was further proof of southern depravity. A leading Democrat predicted that the affair would cost his party 200,000 votes.

The campaign rivaled that of 1840 in excitement and far excelled it in importance. A major party was contesting a national election on frankly sectional grounds. An old Whig, Robert C. Winthrop of Massachusetts, now a Buchanan supporter, caustically described the Republican appeal as one-third Missouri Compromise repeal, for which northerners were largely responsible, one-third Kansas outrages, with no regard for northern provocation, and one-third "disjointed facts and misapplied figures . . . to prove that the South is, upon the whole, the very poorest, meanest, least productive, and most miserable part of creation and therefore ought to be continually teased and taunted and reviled, by everybody who feels himself better off." This anti-southern crusade with its strong moral appeal aroused the Protestant pulpit and gave a religious fervor to the Republican cause. Songs, so effective as campaign weapons in 1840, reappeared as Republican writers exhausted the possibilities of "Freedom, Freemen, and Frémont." And it must not be forgotten that northerners had been exposed to *Uncle Tom's Cabin* in print and on the stage for four years.

The Democrats, with no young hero to exploit and no crusade to conduct, appealed to the fears of conservatives and Union lovers: The elderly, colorless Buchanan typified experienced statesmanship and security for the old American order; Frémont, disunion and possibly civil war. Toombs and Howell Cobb, the Union savers of 1850, publicly announced that the South would not submit to Republican victory. Because Fillmore could not win, Clay Whigs were urged to support Buchanan and northern business did not need to be reminded of southern markets and investments at stake. Democratic leaders in the North forgot their earlier diatribes against the nativists and appealed to Fillmore men to make common cause with them against the specter of sectionalism. In the South, where Fillmore and Buchanan were the only contenders, the battle was sharply fought, with the "Americans" insisting that their candidate was national and at the same time sound on southern rights.

Fillmore's supporters in the North were under the disadvantage of appealing to the same general constituency as the Democrats. Had another Democrat than Buchanan been named, their chances might have been better. Even so, they charged the Democrats with southern leanings, the Republicans with northern fanaticism, and described their own party as the truly national one. To stir up the dying embers of nativism, they concocted a story that Frémont was a Roman Catholic.[1] This invention, taken up by the Democrats, caused

[1] Frémont, an Episcopalian, had been married by a Catholic priest, and an adopted daughter had attended a Catholic school. His enemies went on to insist that he had been reared as a Catho-

the Republicans much embarrassment because they were wooing the German Catholic vote and a public statement by Frémont would be unwise. Friends attempted to refute the charge, but it persisted through the campaign and may have cost some Know Nothing support.

Republican success depended on victories in Illinois, Indiana, and Pennsylvania. In these border free states the antislavery crusade backfired. Too many voters were frightened at Republican radicalism. Attempts to arrange fusion tickets with the Fillmore men were ineffective. In spite of the combined efforts of three of the nation's shrewdest and most unscrupulous political manipulators—local managers Simon Cameron and Thad Stevens helped by Thurlow Weed of New York—the Republicans failed to carry Pennsylvania. After all, it was Buchanan's home state, and it had never had a President. Weed later believed that $50,000 was the margin of Democratic victory.

The electoral college gave Buchanan 174 votes (Pennsylvania, New Jersey, Indiana, Illinois, California, and all the slave states except Maryland); Frémont 114 (the remaining free states); Fillmore 8 (Maryland). Buchanan had 1,832,-955 popular votes; Frémont, 1,339,932; Fillmore, 871,731. The "Americans" were now a conservative third party, their antislavery strength having gone to the Republicans. Nativism had failed utterly as a national issue, but "Bleeding Kansas" had carried the Republicans through their critical period.

1860

The elderly bachelor President proved to be anything but the experienced physician who was to heal the nation's wounds. His administration saw the Democratic party divided and distracted over his support of a bill to admit Kansas as a slave state under the fraudulent Lecompton Constitution, drafted by a proslavery minority. Douglas, upholder of popular sovereignty, won Republican allies in

---

lic, still attended mass, and had shown his Catholicism on various occasions. Witnesses were produced to vouch for the statements.

blocking the measure, but thereby damaged his chances to win southern support for the Presidential nomination.

A further count against Douglas was his refusal to accept the Dred Scott decision of the Supreme Court, which legalized slavery in the territories, as anything but a legal abstraction which would not prevent a territorial legislature from making its own decisions as to the institution. This was called his Freeport Heresy, which he defended in his debates with Lincoln when they were contending for the Illinois senatorship in 1858. Douglas was reelected in spite of the guerrilla opposition of federal "Buchaneers."

The southern Democrats, backed by the Buchanan administration, would accept Douglas as the party's nominee only if he would accept their platform. The Democratic national convention of 1860 met at Charleston, South Carolina, on April 23, and ran on for two hectic weeks. A long and bitter struggle developed over a proposal committing the party to Congressional protection of slavery in the territories, which would put federal power behind the Dred Scott decision. The plank was voted down by the Douglas supporters of popular sovereignty, and a bloc of delegates from the deep South walked out, to the cheers of the crinoline galleries. The balloting for President gave the Little Giant a majority but he could not get two-thirds of the original convention total. The delegates then voted to adjourn and reassemble in the less hostile confines of Baltimore on June 18.

At Baltimore, returning seceders and some new delegates, elected to take their places, contested for seats and the result was a second secession. Finally, the reorganized convention nominated Douglas when he had 181 1/2 of 194 1/2 votes. Senator Benjamin Fitzpatrick of Alabama was put on the ticket with him but later declined, and the national committee substituted Herschel V. Johnson, former governor of Georgia.

Seceders, old and new, met in another hall and nominated Vice President John C. Breckinridge of Kentucky and Senator Joseph Lane of Oregon, an administration supporter, as their candidates. These "Dixiecrats" of 1860 put in their platform the principle of protection of slave property in the territories by the federal government, which, if accepted by Douglas, would have doomed the party in every free state.

Two other parties had made their nominations between the two sessions of the Democratic gathering. A Constitutional Union convention (called "National Union" in the invitation issued by a group of southern "American" Congressmen), meeting in Baltimore, chose veteran Whig John Bell of Tennessee over Sam Houston of Texas, favorite of the "American" contingent, and thrust upon Edward Everett of Massachusetts an unwanted nomination for Vice President. Their platform was a simple pledge to support the Constitution and the Union against all enemies at home and abroad. This was the last effort of graybeards of the faith of Clay and Webster to resist the sectionalism that was engulfing the major parties.

Meanwhile the Republicans had been making political hay out of the Dred Scott decision, Democratic dissensions, and the depression following the Panic of 1857, and their delegates came to Chicago on May 16 with the spirit of victory in the air. This was Chicago's first national convention, made possible by the railroad revolution of the 1850's. A specially constructed "Wigwam" held ten thousand spectators.

The platform attempted to de-sectionalize the party. While it favored Congressional action to preserve freedom in the territories, it upheld the right of a state to determine its own domestic institutions and denounced the lawless invasion of any state (John Brown's raid) as among the gravest of crimes. It bid for Pennsylvania's vote with a vaguely worded indorsement of protective tariff. It satisfied the Germans with a plank opposing any abridgment of the rights of foreign-born and one favoring a homestead act for the public lands. The latter also pleased eastern labor and western pioneer farmers. Planks indorsing river and harbor improvements and federal aid for a Pacific railroad appealed to the Old Northwest and the Pacific Coast.

The need for a candidate who could carry the conservative North—Pennsylvania, Indiana, Illinois, and New Jersey, all Democratic in 1856—produced a "Stop-Seward" movement. The New York Senator was leading the field when the convention opened, but politicos from the doubtful states questioned the wisdom of nominating a man whose record stamped him as an antislavery radical. Chase of Ohio was in a similar position. Edward Bates of Missouri, an old Whig, and Abraham Lincoln of Illinois were more available. In the end, the anti-Seward bloc decided to concentrate on Lincoln and secured his nomination on the third ballot. All manner of pledges, pressures, and deals went into his nominating cauldron.

Nominally four candidates contested for the chief office in 1860. Yet in most states—excluding two or three border slave states and the Pacific coast—it was a two-party fight: Lincoln against Douglas in the North, Bell against Breckinridge in the South. Valiant little minorities of Douglas men put electoral tickets into the field in most of the cotton states, but the great majority of southern Democrats voted for Breckinridge. The Bell-Everett ticket drew the old Whig, "American," and Unionist vote. Both Breckinridge and Bell groups professed loyalty to the South; but the "submissionists" were to be found in the Constitutional Union movement, the "secessionists" in the Democratic camp.

In the North the Bell movement attracted only remnants of "Americans" and old Whigs. The failure of Fillmore in 1856 and the new-found conservatism of the Republicans caused many former Whigs like Thomas Ewing of Ohio and Edward Bates of Missouri to support "Lincoln, the Whig," and the Whig policies in the Republican platform. The Breckinridge following in the North was little more than a corporal's guard of Buchanan officeholders seeking to destroy Douglas, even though it meant Republican success.

The real battle was between Douglas and Lincoln with the cards stacked in favor of the "Rail Splitter." His party was united and seemed to be reasonably sure of New England, New York, Ohio, and the upper Northwest—all carried in 1856. It needed Illinois, Indiana, and Pennsylvania to win. Lincoln's Illinois residence strengthened the Republican cause in his home state and neighboring Indiana. His Whig background attracted conservatives in the Ohio valley, and the homestead plank helped with the foreign-born.

Buchanan vetoed a modified homestead bill in the summer; southern members of Congress had voted almost solidly against it, while both Democratic platforms had ignored it. Using a pamphlet, "Vote Yourself a Farm," and speeches in German by Carl Schurz, Gustav Körner, and other popular German orators under the special direction of a "foreign department" of the national committee, the Republicans made heavy inroads into the German vote in Cincinnati, Chicago, and St. Louis. These were centers of the newer German immigration, more radical and less fixed in party affiliation than the older groups, who still clung to the Democratic party.

In Pennsylvania and southern Ohio the tariff issue was used to win the coal and iron interests and their workingmen. The success of the fusionist "People's" party in Pennsylvania in 1858 prepared the way for 1860 and a similar victory. There was plenty of money, and Simon Cameron, Andrew G. Curtin, Thad Stevens, and other experienced leaders directed the strategy.

There was not the excitement in the North that had prevailed in 1856. The Republican party was neither so novel nor so radical, and its appeal was less emotional. Kansas had long since ceased to bleed; the territories were in little danger of ever becoming slave states; and—a strange vindication for Douglas—some Republicans even accepted popular sovereignty as a safe solution. "The operation of the natural forces of free labor and free emigration is worth a thousand Wilmot Provisos in building up free states," declared the Cincinnati *Commercial*, a powerful western Republican organ. However, most Republican speakers and newspapers were more orthodox in favoring Congressional action against slavery. The southern "intervention" idea—a Congressional slave code for territories—was subjected to bitter attacks; and the South was charged with schemes to reopen the African slave trade. A well organized campaign with numerous speakers and the usual parades and processions aroused moderate enthusiasm but no great excitement. The Wide-Awakes, drilled like military companies, marched in Lincoln-Hamlin parades. Seward overcame his bitter disappointment at his defeat and made what historian James Ford Rhodes has called "the most remarkable stump-speeches ever delivered in this country." He, rather than Lincoln, seemed to be leading the party. The candidate received callers daily at an office in Springfield, was in close touch with campaign strategy, but kept a muzzle on himself.

The opposition parties thundered at the sectionalism of the Republicans and repeated the danger-of-disunion argument of 1856. This was singularly ineffective in the North. "For ten, aye, for twenty, years," taunted Seward, "these threats have been renewed, in the same language and in the same form, about the first day of November every four years . . ." He was certain the Union was in no danger. Republican newspapers were equally sure.

But Douglas, facing certain defeat, was alarmed about the South. Unlike the other candidates, he had made speech after speech, all over the North—a new departure for Presidential candidates and a shattering of old traditions. In August he turned his attention to the South, not to gain votes, for his cause was hopeless there, but to arouse national feelings and bring that section to accept Lincoln's election quietly. There is nothing finer in Douglas's career than his sturdy Union speeches in Virginia and North Carolina, where he declared that no grievance could justify secession, and that he would support the President in enforcing the laws. He returned North to campaign from New York west to Missouri, but after the unfavorable state elections in October he said to his secretary, "We must try to save the Union. I will go South." Taking a steamboat down the Mississippi, he spoke at Memphis, crossed Tennessee to Chattanooga, invaded Georgia, and was in Alabama when the election took place. Threats were made against him, and a few eggs were hurled in Montgomery; but his crusade against secession went on. After the news of Lincoln's election he made his trip up the Mississippi from New Orleans a goodwill tour in an attempt to reconcile the South to a Republican administration.

Desperate efforts to unite the anti-Lincoln forces upon fusion electoral tickets characterized the closing days of the campaign in the North. Complete or partial fusion was effected in Pennsylvania, New York, New Jersey, Connecticut, and Rhode Island. The candidates for electors were apportioned among the Bell, Breckinridge, and Douglas groups with the understanding that, if elected, they would cast their votes so as to bring about Lincoln's defeat in the electoral vote. This would throw the election to the House, where no party had a majority, but where one of the anti-Lincoln candidates might win.[2] A House deadlock beyond March 4 might even make Joseph Lane President, as the Senate was Buchanan-controlled and Breckinridge's running mate, elected Vice President by that body in the event no one had a majority, would assume the Presidency. The Republicans made much of this in criticizing fusion, but the danger was slight. Jefferson Davis wanted all three anti-Republican candidates to withdraw and unite upon Horatio Seymour of New York; but Douglas refused, believing that thousands of his supporters would turn to Lincoln if he abandoned the race. In the South the Bell and Douglas men cooperated in assailing the Breckinridge "disunionists," but only in Texas was there fusion.

The South was the more troubled section in 1860, divided, distracted, fearful—the very antithesis of the antislavery picture of a section held in the grip of a malevolent, aggressive slavocracy. Conservative southern newspapers charged that Breckinridge party leaders such as Yancey and Jefferson Davis were plotting to destroy the Union, and that their demand for Congressional protection of slavery was a subterfuge to divide the national Democratic party. The Breckinridge following held forth on the dangers of disunity in the South and played up stories of abolitionist-slave plots, burning of houses, and poisoning of masters with distant and thinly settled Texas as the favorite locale. This fear campaign may have added votes to the southern rights Democracy, but the large vote polled by Bell in the lower South,

---

[2] Actually Lincoln's chances in the House were excellent. The Republicans had fifteen of the thirty-three states and needed but two more, with Illinois and Oregon offering good prospects, especially if Douglas were eliminated.

especially among the large slaveholders, is proof that the section was far from solid.

The election of Republican governors in doubtful Pennsylvania and Indiana in October indicated the outcome in November; but a vigorous, last-minute fight for the fusion ticket in New York held out faint hopes. Worried about disunion, the city's financial interests poured money into the campaign, but to no avail. Lincoln carried all the free states, except three of New Jersey's seven electors; Bell had Kentucky, Virginia, and Tennessee; Douglas had only Missouri and three electors from New Jersey;[3] Breckinridge won the remaining states, all slave and all from the lower South except Maryland and Delaware. The electoral total gave Lincoln 180, Breckinridge 72, Bell 39, Douglas 12. The popular votes were 1,865,593 for Lincoln, 848,356 for Breckinridge, 592,906 for Bell, and 1,382,713 for Douglas. But in the Senate and the House the Republicans would be in a minority —a strong argument against immediate secession. The "Black Republican" President would have his hands tied.

Sectionalism triumphed in both North and South in 1860. The two moderate candidates, Bell and Douglas, were in a minority. Equally striking was the fact that conservative southerners preferred Bell, a southerner, over Douglas, a northerner, while in the free states the reverse was true. Even conservatives voted for a man from their own section. National parties, so long a unifying force, broke down. The sectionalists had their way.

1864

The Civil War brought about a realignment of parties. Republicans and War Democrats joined in a Union party supporting the war and the Lincoln administration. The more radical Republicans criticized Lincoln for his tardiness in making the war an antislavery crusade, and for his failure

[3] In New Jersey a fusion opposition had a small popular majority; but only three of the seven candidates received united support. Four Lincoln electors won.

to use drastic methods in putting down the rebellion and in reconstructing reconquered states. But they did not carry their opposition to the polls.

The majority of Democrats held aloof from the Union party and criticized the administration for mismanagement and corruption, violating civil liberties, and transforming a war for the Union into an abolitionist war when Lincoln issued his Emancipation Proclamation in September, 1862. A peace group led by Clement L. Vallandigham of Ohio became more aggressive after Democratic gains in the elections of 1862, and demanded an immediate end to the war and a convention to restore the Union on a compromise basis. Vallandigham's campaign for peace ended in May, 1863, when he was arrested and tried before a military court for encouraging resistance to the draft. He was sentenced to prison but Lincoln ordered him sent to the Confederacy. The exile soon made his way to Canada and ran for governor of Ohio *in absentia.* He was defeated overwhelmingly by a War Democrat. Gettysburg and Vicksburg had made his defeat a certainty.

Secretary of the Treasury Chase, consorting with Congressional radicals and other critics of Lincoln, feuded with Secretary of State Seward, then with the influential Blair family represented in the cabinet by Postmaster General Montgomery Blair, a conservative. Chase was put into the Presidential race early in 1864 by a group of friends at Washington, but Ohio and Indiana indorsed Lincoln and he withdrew.

Some four hundred radicals, mostly Germans and abolitionists, met at Cleveland on May 31 and nominated General John C. Frémont for President in the hope of forcing Lincoln to withdraw.

The Union party, with the administration forces in command, opened its national convention in the none too friendly city of Baltimore on June 7 in the cramped quarters of a theater. Lincoln was renominated with only the Missouri delegation opposed. It voted for General Grant. Andrew Johnson, former Senator and war governor of Tennessee, a prewar Democrat, led for second place on the first ballot, and shifts of votes then nominated him. Lincoln was instrumental in his selection. The platform, praising the war President and his policies, called for the complete suppression of the rebellion and a constitutional amendment to prohibit the existence of slavery.

Democratic papers could call the two Union candidates "a rail-splitting buffoon and a boorish tailor, both from the backwoods, both growing up in uncouth ignorance," but these candidates had great popular appeal. Their vote-getting pull was underestimated by many of the party bigwigs, who were not yet ready to accept the work of the convention as final.

For three months Lincoln's reelection seemed to be in the balance. General Grant, on whose military genius the North pinned its hopes, hurled his legions against Lee; but a mounting death toll was the only result. He then settled down for his long siege of Petersburg. General Sherman was making little headway against Atlanta, and a terrible despondency fell upon the North. In July, General Early dashed up the Shenandoah valley, and for a day Washington seemed at his mercy. Greenbacks fell below forty cents on the dollar. The radicals renewed their war on the President by issuing the "Wade-Davis Manifesto," a criticism of his moderate reconstruction policy (which had been applied in Tennessee, Louisiana, and Arkansas) and a reply to his pocket veto of a radical measure of Senator Ben Wade of Ohio and Representative Henry Winter Davis of Maryland. The two vented their spleen in the manifesto with a large bloc of Republican Senators and Representatives in sympathy with them. They called the veto a "studied outrage on the legislative authority," charged that Lincoln held the electoral votes of the reconstructed rebel states at his dictation, and warned him to confine himself to his executive duties—"to obey and execute, not make the laws."

Chase had offered to resign late in June when miffed over a trivial patronage difficulty, and the President had surprised him by accepting his resignation. Now his hopes rose as defeatism threatened to engulf the North. If a new pilot was needed, he was ready. Radical leaders were not prepared to commit themselves to a particular candidacy, but in August an undercover movement centered in New York set about securing the withdrawal of both Lincoln and Frémont and the immediate calling of another national convention. Vindictive spirits like Wade and Davis, the erratic Greeley, the critical Sumner, the moderate John Sherman of Ohio, Governor Andrew of Massachusetts, the friends of Chase, and many practical politicians agreed that Lincoln must go. Even those good friends of the administration Thurlow Weed and Henry Raymond, chairman of the national committee, whose *New York Times* was the only avowed administration organ in that city, began to despair.

In the midst of this season of intrigue and gloom, the Democrats held their national convention at Chicago on August 29, with high hopes of victory and a popular candidate at hand. On the first ballot, with but slight opposition, General George B. McClellan was nominated. Military authorities credit "Little Mac" with organizing ability and a certain cautious type of generalship; but his insufferable egotism, his contemptuous attitude toward the President and the War Department, and his inability to act when action was required had caused his removal late in 1862. He had two assets, his popularity with soldiers of the Army of the Potomac and his grievances against the administration, upon which he placed the full responsibility for his military failures. Democratic politicians, eager for a soldier candidate, found him a ready tool, and he became the party nominee on a platform that pronounced the war a failure and declared in favor of immediate efforts "for a cessation of hostilities with a view to an ultimate convention of the States, or other peaceable means" to restore the Union. Attacks upon the subversion of civil liberties, the exercise of unconstitutional powers by the administration, and military interference with elections in the border states were included in the brief platform, along with a resolution praising the soldiers and sailors and promising to protect and care for them.

The peace plank reflected the influence of the indomitable Vallandigham who had quietly returned from Canada and become a delegate to the convention from his home district.

George H. Pendleton, an Ohio Congressman, was nominated to run with McClellan. The combination of a war hero and a peace platform seemed to be well contrived to attract united Democratic support for the ticket in the face of a quarreling, disunited Union party.

But on September 1 an event revolutionized the whole political situation. General Sherman captured Atlanta, key to the lower South, and broke the military backbone of the Confederacy. The Gulf States were cut off from Richmond, and Lee's fate was sealed. The tight-lipped Sherman, who had no use for politics and politicians, had inadvertently proved to be a master politician. As northern crowds cheered and rejoiced, Lincoln's star rose again, and the radicals hastened to make their peace.

All talk of a second convention was dropped. The *New York Tribune* pronounced for Lincoln on September 6. Chase, by mid-September, was ready to go on the stump. Wade and Davis, seeking a way to cover their retreat, were induced by their radical colleague, Senator Chandler of Michigan, to accept the removal of Blair from the cabinet as a peace offering. Lincoln, with the game in his hands, might have rejected Chandler's proposal, but the Postmaster General, unpopular even with many good Lincoln men, had become a liability to the administration. The President requested his resignation, and he promptly and graciously acceded, showing his loyalty to his chief by speaking soon afterward before a great Lincoln meeting in New York City. Wade and Davis, appeased, went on the stump, but it was reported that Davis would not mention Lincoln's name.

Frémont's withdrawal was almost simultaneous with Blair's resignation, and Chandler believed it was due to his own indefatigable efforts. But Frémont had already made his decision, regardless of the status of Blair. His candidacy had become hopeless, and he was seeking a way out. Efforts to sound out McClellan and possibly make a deal with him had been ignored. Sullenly acquiescing in the inevitable, this overrated man withdrew in the interest of Union success but in a final bitter fling declared that the Lincoln administration was "politically, militarily, and financially a failure," and "that its necessary continuance is a cause of regret to the country." Thus ungraciously the once popular Pathfinder passed into political oblivion.

Fate dealt Lincoln a final trump, no longer needed, in his game with the radicals: Chief Justice Taney died on October 12. Chase, eagerly desirous of Taney's office, next in importance to the Presidency itself, must have felt keenly humiliated at seeking it from the man he had so often criticized and belittled. His friends, however, ate humble pie for him and pressed his candidacy. Lincoln, amused at the situation, waited until after the election. Then he duly appointed Salmon P. Chase to the highest judicial position, and on the 4th of the following March received the oath from the solemn-visaged Jovian Chief Justice whose pettiness of spirit had so gravely marred his public career.

General McClellan, facing a united and harmonious Union party, saw his own candidacy threatened with shipwreck between the militant peace faction and the less militant war supporters. Vallandigham, still antiwar and fierce for peace, importuned the candidate not "to insinuate even a little war" into his letter of acceptance as it would cost him two hundred thousand votes in the West. He stated on September 6 at a public meeting in Dayton, Ohio, that the convention "meant peace, and it said it." But eastern Democrats, conscious of the war prosperity their section was enjoying and seeing the political appeal to the soldiers of a war stand, pressed the general to insist on restoration of the Union as a condition of peace. August Belmont, New York financier and chairman of the Democratic national committee, warned McClellan that he must emphasize this point. Bedeviled by such conflicting opinions, Little Mac wrote his letter of acceptance several times, at first with a decided swing toward the viewpoint of an armistice without conditions, then back to an unconditional Union stand. The final draft gave cold comfort to the peace men. "I could not look in the faces of my gallant comrades of the army and navy who have survived so many bloody battles," he wrote, "and tell them that their labors and the sacrifices of so many of our slain and wounded brethren had been in vain—that we had abandoned the Union for which we have so often periled our lives." The candidate had repudiated the platform, and the War Democrats were satisfied.

But the peace element, deeply disappointed, gave a grudging support or remained away from the polls. Vallandigham reluctantly stumped for the ticket, but a group of western peace Democrats attempted to put another candidate into the field. A meeting at Columbus, Ohio, chose Alexander Long, a Cincinnati member of Congress, but he refused to run.

The inconsistencies of the Democrats made their campaign a two-faced affair. A *McClellan Campaign Songster* contained both war and peace songs. To the tune of "Dixie" crowds were expected to sing:

> For rebel traitors we've a halter,
> They falsely swore at freedom's altar
> Cheer away, cheer away,
> Cheer away, cheer away.
> We've tried all means to keep 'em quiet,
> Shot and shell their only diet,
> Cheer away, cheer away,
> Cheer away, cheer away.

And on another page, to the air of "The Battle Cry of Freedom," they could chant,

> We'll extend the hand of peace,
> That this wicked war may cease,
> Shouting McClellan, boys, and freedom.

Politicians have been notoriously adept at riding two horses, but a bloody civil war compelled men to take sides. The strain on party loyalties was a heavy one. The Democratic effort to play both sides became untenable when the Union party harmonized its differences and military success cleared the air.

Democratic prospects, so bright in August, faded with the first frosts of autumn. Following the fall of Atlanta came the successes of Sheridan in the Shenandoah valley while Grant's tentacles slowly and relentlessly extended around Petersburg without relaxing their grip. Cheered on by a season of victory in the field, radicals and conservatives alike worked for Lincoln and the Union party, and officeholders and government contractors filled Chairman Henry J. Raymond's campaign chest. On Election Day Lincoln carried all the loyal states except Kentucky, Delaware, and New Jersey. He had 212 electoral votes to McClellan's 21. The popular majority of the Union party was four hundred thousand[4]—an amazing refutation of the dire predictions of radicals and Democrats but a few weeks before.

Before counting the electoral vote, February 8, Congress adopted the Twenty-second Joint Rule whereby no electoral votes objected to in joint session should be counted except by concurrent votes of both houses. This was to insure the rejection of the electoral votes of Louisiana and Tennessee, newly reconstructed under the President's plan. Elections had not been held in the other seceded states.

[4] Lincoln had 2,206,938 popular votes; McClellan, 1,803,787.

CHAPTER V

GRANT AND HAYES

1868–1876

1868

LINCOLN'S ASSASSINATION occurred when he seemed to have gained the whip hand over the radical element in his party. The involved story of the struggle between his successor and the radical leadership in Congress boils down to Johnson's stubborn insistence on a moderate policy toward the defeated South and the determination of a Congressional oligarchy to keep ex-Confederates out of power and create Republican bastions in the former Confederate states. In the end, military rule and a process of readmission including compulsory Negro suffrage became the Congressional solution. The Stevens-Sumner leadership tried to remove Johnson as a dangerous obstacle to the success of their program, but the impeachment proceedings against him failed of conviction by a margin of one vote.

Radical reconstruction was certain to be a major issue in the campaign of 1868, but "greenback-ism" was becoming its rival in both parties. The greenbacks, issued without gold backing because of the stresses of war financing, were being called in, but pressure from western farmers stopped the progress of this deflation in 1868. Instead, there was a growing demand for the payment of war bonds with new issues of paper money instead of gold as the treasury had promised. The problem was embarrassing to both parties, for it tended toward an east-west division.

The "National Union Republican" party solved the problems of Negro suffrage and the greenbacks at its national convention at Chicago, May 20–21, by some skilfully evasive planks. The platform declared that Negro suffrage in the reconstructed states was necessary to protect the loyal men of the South, but in the North it properly belonged to the people of the states. The currency plank favored the payment of the national debt according to the letter and spirit of the laws without defining either. The platform defended the reconstruction policy of Congress and catalogued the misdeeds of Andrew Johnson.

General Ulysses S. Grant was the unanimous choice to head the ticket, but it took five ballots to give Speaker Schuyler Colfax the Vice Presidential nomination.

Having been deprived of Grant, a prewar Democrat, by the Republican convention, the Democrats were confronted with a concerted movement by eastern leaders to nominate a radical Republican, Chief Justice Salmon P. Chase. His ambitious daughter, Kate Chase Sprague, was his manager. But more orthodox Democrats were in the race and a wide-open battle got under way when the national convention opened its sessions in newly built Tammany Hall in New York on July 4. The platform assailed radical reconstruction and approved a greenback plank, a concession to western demands. But the western favorite, George H. Pendleton of Ohio, who led on the early ballots, was blocked by eastern opposition and a long deadlock developed. Just when it seemed that Chase might be offered as the solution, a stampede was started to nominate the chairman of the convention, Horatio Seymour, former governor of New York. Seymour protested but on the twenty-second ballot he became the nominee. Francis P. Blair, Jr., of Missouri was named to run with him. He had recently written a strongly worded letter suggesting the use of force to disperse carpetbag governments in the South, a political blunder, as it was used against him in the campaign.

The campaign of the Democrats bogged down almost from the start. Seymour and the eastern leaders did not repudiate the greenback plank, but their evasions indicated their feelings. The candidate aroused no enthusiasm in the inflationist West and the plank did not help. Although Seymour's letter of acceptance virtually repudiated Blair's Broadhead letter, it did not prevent the Republicans from playing up the issue and declaring that Blair would rule the administration if Seymour won. They even charged that the Democrats would try to pay the Confederate debt. Instead of campaigning aggressively on the reconstruction issues, the Democrats were thrown on the defensive and were unable to make headway.

Money and propaganda generally were with the Republicans, although wealthy Democrats such as August Belmont, Cyrus H. McCormick, and Samuel J. Tilden did their best. Tariff benefits, land grants to railroads, and the Republican currency position induced the Astors, the Vanderbilts, Jay Cooke, and other men of wealth to give freely to the campaign chest. The metropolitan newspapers and the leading weeklies—*Harper's*, the *Nation*, the *Independent* and *Leslie's*—were mostly Republican and conservative in their economic views, though radical enough toward the South.

Old Union party conservatives and Johnson men had to make a hard choice between the radical-sponsored Grant and the orthodox Democrat, Seymour, whose party bore the stigma of Copperheadism. President Johnson himself tardily indorsed Seymour, though he made no speeches, and his cabinet was badly divided. Chief Justice Chase was friendly toward Seymour but hostile to Blair, and held aloof from expressions of opinion. The conservative Republican Senators who had voted for Johnson in the impeachment proceedings remained Republican despite the torrent of denunciation from party organs. Had they been forced to choose between Seymour and an out-and-out radical, many conservatives might well have preferred the Democrat; but Grant's reputation as the strong, silent soldier—he refused to make speeches—the moderation of his past views and actions, and his "Let us have peace" statement induced most of them to take him on faith.

The general trend of the October state elections toward the Republicans produced a movement, started under cover earlier, to have both Seymour and Blair withdraw. The national committee would then select a new ticket, with Chase presumably to head it. Alexander Long and some other Chase men were involved, while the New York *World* called for Blair's resignation and, by inference, Seymour's as well. But the national committee did not countenance the move, the eastern leaders were hostile, and the party newspapers disapproved almost unanimously.

One effect of the October reverses was the appearance of Seymour on the stump, actually against his wishes. He was an excellent speaker, and it was felt that he might stir the admittedly lagging spirits of the Democrats. He covered the Middle West as far as Chicago, returning through Pennsylvania. He criticized the Republicans as violators of the Constitution and emphasized the moderate, peaceful character of his own party's views. It was a fine but futile attempt to undo the damage done by Republican misconstruction of Blair's position.

The November results verified the October forecasts. Grant and Colfax had 214 electoral votes; Seymour and Blair, 80, with the popular vote running 3,013,421 to 2,706,829.[1] Seymour had New York, New Jersey, and Oregon from the North, Delaware, Maryland, and Kentucky from the border, Georgia and Louisiana from the South.

Grant's victory rested on two pillars that Democratic campaigning could not overturn: the widespread popular confidence in the man, and the operation of radical reconstruction. The former gave him the North; the latter, the South. The effect of Negro suffrage is evident. Without the colored vote Grant would have had a smaller popular vote than Seymour, though possibly an electoral majority because of his strength in the white-voting North.

To Republican leaders the value of the Negro vote was clear. But it was needed in the North as well as in the South, and this required a constitutional amendment. The retiring Congress, disregarding the statement of the Republican plat-

[1] Florida chose electors through the legislature; Virginia, Mississippi, and Texas, still under military rule, did not vote. Thirty-four states took part in the election.

form that control of the suffrage in the North could be safely left to the states, passed the Fifteenth Amendment providing that the right to vote should not be denied or abridged on account of race, color, or previous condition of servitude. With Republican legislatures already chosen in the great majority of states and subject to party control, ratification was possible without giving the voters a chance to express themselves at the polls. Twelve state legislatures ratified the amendment within a month. Within a year three-fourths of the states had ratified,[2] and Negro suffrage was made compulsory everywhere with the Republican party the beneficiary.

1872

Widespread dissatisfaction with Grant's harsh southern policy, together with his failure to bring about tariff reductions and civil service reform, caused a Liberal Republican movement to get under way to defeat him at the polls in 1872. Reformers of all stripes and some dissatisfied politicians met at Cincinnati on May 1, 1872, to name candidates and draw up a platform. Its variegated composition caused some difficulties, but a platform was adopted which indorsed the three war constitutional amendments, universal amnesty and local self-government for the South, civil service reform, and a speedy return to specie payments for greenbacks.

The practical politicians, however, succeeded in manipulating the convention, burdened with too many candidates, to bring about the nomination of Horace Greeley, long-time editor of the New York *Tribune*, over Charles Francis Adams, minister to England during the Civil War, and the choice of eastern reformers and intellectuals. B. Gratz Brown, governor of Missouri, where the Liberal movement had started, was made the Vice Presidential choice. He had had a hand in Greeley's nomination.

The Democratic convention swallowed the bitter dose

[2] Texas, Virginia, and Mississippi were required to accept it as a condition of reconstruction. They were not readmitted until 1870.

when it met at Baltimore on July 9. Greeley and Brown became their candidates on the Cincinnati platform, although the New York editor had been flaying Democrats all his journalistic life. A group of bitter-enders revolted and nominated Charles O'Conor of New York at a Louisville meeting in September. He rejected the nomination but electoral tickets were run under his name in twenty-three states.

The regular Republican party leaders and eastern business and finance were satisfield with Grant and wanted the Hero of Appomattox renominated. The Republican convention at Philadelphia on June 5 complied without a dissenting voice. Senator Henry Wilson of Massachusetts replaced Vice President Colfax as Grant's running mate. The platform pointed with pride to the party's past and paid lip service to civil service reform.

Appalled at Greeley's nomination, many of the Liberals found Grant more acceptable. But Carl Schurz, Senator from Missouri, who had inaugurated the Liberal movement in that state and had presided at the Cincinnati convention, and Lyman Trumbull, one of the candidates for the nomination, urged support for Greeley as the only practical course.

The campaign was a strange one. Never in American history have two more unfit men been offered to the country for the highest office. The simple soldier, inexperienced in statecraft, impervious to sound advice, and oblivious to his own blundering, was pitted against the vain, erratic, reforming editor whose goodness of heart could not make up for his sad lack of judgment. The man of no ideas was running against the man of too many. Intelligent voters, in perplexity, might well have preferred Grant and the evils that went with him to Greeley and evils they knew not of. But many a good American saw no problem involved in the choice. The indomitable Grant of Civil War days was resurrected by press and politicians to save the blundering, ineffectual Grant of the White House.

The legend prevailed, but not against the real Greeley. His foibles and eccentricities were exaggerated and cruelly ridiculed so that the country saw him in grotesque caricature.

Thomas Nast's cruel pencil in *Harper's Weekly* held him up to ridicule in cartoons so merciless that George William Curtis, the editor, even protested. Yet it was so easy to laugh at Greeley. His appearance was anything but imposing or dignified. He was usually in a long linen duster that covered wrinkled clothes; a white hat concealed his frontal baldness but not the long silver locks at the back; metal-rimmed spectacles were hooked over his ears; and a fringe of whiskers framed his smooth round face like a miniature fur piece. A friendly observer might have detected a resemblance to Franklin, but the savage Nast cartoons made him more like a nearsighted German professor with the heavy body of a peasant, the mind of a fool, and the vanity of a child. Partisan editors dragged forth choice morsels from old files of the *Tribune* to reveal his inconsistencies and eccentricities. The courageous humanitarian editor was forgotten, and a scarecrow Greeley appeared in his place. Democratic and Liberal papers savagely attacked Grant, shouting Caesarism and corruption, but the silent soldier quietly enjoying the summer at Long Branch played the role his managers had marked out for him, without speeches. How could a caricature contend against him?

Yet even Grant could not have won in the face of a great depression. This would have torn the legend to shreds. Fortune smiled on the Republicans, however, and prosperity continued another year. Business, pleased with Grant and his party, contributed liberally to the campaign coffers. A disciplined party organization, with the patronage of the federal government and most of the states at its disposal, did the rest. The Liberals, poorly organized and embarrassed for funds, could hardly have won against such odds, even with a stronger candidate.

Greeley's strong points proved to be of slight value. His long record of friendliness to the workingman did not draw a heavy labor vote, for labor was not well organized and was politically impotent. His antislavery record and equal-rights principles failed to attract the colored vote, though Sumner gave his blessing. Gratitude toward the Republican party and fear of the Democrats outweighed the appeals of these two veteran defenders of the black man. Greeley's efforts to bridge the "bloody chasm" were treated by exponents of the "bloody shirt" as treason to the North, and the old prejudices against the Copperhead Democracy were stirred up. Yet many Copperhead Democrats could not make themselves vote for Greeley.

The North Carolina state election in August indicated the probable defeat of the Liberals, but it remained for Pennsylvania, Ohio, and Indiana, vitally important "October states," to settle the question. Greeley went on the stump for several weeks in a remarkable oratorical campaign before large crowds. To the surprise of most people he spoke with dignity, breadth of vision, and restraint, exhibiting none of the eccentricities for which he had been lampooned. But the results were not evident on election day. Pennsylvania and Ohio went Republican, and, while Indiana elected the popular Hendricks governor, the majority of the legislature and most of the Congressmen were Republican. The Liberals lost hope, and thousands of their Democratic allies failed to vote in November.

Grant carried every northern state and most of the carpetbag South; Greeley had three border states (Missouri, Kentucky, and Maryland), Tennessee, Texas, and Georgia. Louisiana, according to the official returning board, was apparently carried by the Liberal-Democratic coalition; but a Grant returning board reported different results, and Congress rejected both sets of electors.[8] It also threw out three Georgia electoral votes for Greeley because the electors had voted for a dead man. Arkansas, carried by Grant, was

[8] Greeley died before the electoral college met, and so the Liberal-Democratic electors voted for other choices. The official vote, accepted by Congress, was as follows: Grant, 286; Hendricks of Indiana, 42; B. Gratz Brown of Missouri, 18; Charles J. Jenkins of Georgia, 2; David Davis of Illinois, 1. Henry Wilson had the same vote as Grant, but the Liberal-Democratic electors scattered their votes for Vice President, Brown receiving 42, seven others dividing the remainder. The popular vote, including Arkansas and the more official of the Louisiana returns, gave Grant 3,596,745, and Greeley 2,843,446. O'Conor, straight-out Democrat, received 29,489; James Black, Prohibitionist, 5,608.

thrown out on a technicality. The coalition had made a poorer showing than Seymour in 1868. Grant's popularity seemed to be greater than ever.

For Greeley the result was fatal. His wife died October 30; he was crushingly defeated on November 5; reports came to him soon afterward of a movement to deprive him of the *Tribune*; and on November 29 he was dead. "The poor white hat!" said Harriet Beecher Stowe. "If, alas, it covered many weaknesses, it covered also much strength, much real kindness and benevolence, and much that the world will be better for."

The Liberal Republican movement disappeared with Greeley's defeat. Loosely organized and dependent upon the Democrats for most of their votes, the Liberals collapsed under the shock of a disastrous defeat. Represented in Congress by a mere handful, with no patronage to sustain them, they could not preserve their separate identity.

Despite seeming failure, the Liberal Republican movement did not live wholly in vain. It was an honest attempt to end the vexatious southern question, whose very existence imperiled any reform movement. Not until federal interference in the South ceased and local self-government was restored could the attention of the voters, northern and southern alike, be directed to the new America that had come into existence. In Grant's second term the country realized this truth, and the policy of Hayes in 1877 vindicated the Liberal position. The amnesty act of 1872 was due to Liberal pressure, and the alignment of southern conservatives in a united front was aided by the national Democratic-Liberal coalition. The Liberal movement also infused a reform leaven into the old Copperhead Democracy and committed it to acceptance of the finality of the war amendments, thus closing the books on the past. It loosened party ties in the West and made that section more receptive to the appeal of agrarian reformers. Perhaps the most significant accomplishment of the Liberal movement was the creation of a group of independents who, held together by a common interest in civil service reform and honesty in government, would play a notable part in the battles of the next twenty years. The Liberals had failed as party organizers, but the spirit of reform did not die with Greeley.

1876

The years of Republican rule seemed about to end as the time for choosing Grant's successor drew near. The Panic of 1873 and the six years of hard times that followed destroyed the Republican prosperity argument, while appalling revelations of corruption in the national government seemed to demand the overthrow of the party in power. Impervious to criticism, Grant was willing to run again but was clearly not wanted.

When the delegates to the Republican convention came to Cincinnati on June 14, 1876, a reform candidate seemed to be the party's only hope. Nevertheless, Senators Oliver P. Morton of Indiana and Roscoe Conkling of New York, party stalwarts, and popular Speaker James G. Blaine, recently tarred by a "Mulligan Letters" scandal, had strong delegate support. Reform hopes rested with Secretary of the Treasury Benjamin Bristow. To prevent a Blaine nomination (Conkling was a bitter enemy), spoilsmen and reformers joined in support of innocuous Rutherford B. Hayes, governor of Ohio, whose reputation was unblemished and whose war record was excellent. He was nominated on the seventh ballot. The platform was vaguely reformist and said little about Grant's policies. Representative William A. Wheeler of New York was the Vice Presidential choice.

The optimistic Democrats assembled in convention at St. Louis on June 27 with a reformer candidate far in the lead, Governor Samuel J. Tilden of New York. He received the necessary two-thirds of the votes on the second ballot. His chief rival, Thomas J. Hendricks of Indiana, was named to run with him. The platform was a stirring indictment of Republican misdeeds but sidestepped the greenback issue, which the depression was bringing to the front.

Samuel J. Tilden was a veteran in New York politics, from

the days of Martin Van Buren and Silas Wright; but his earlier interests were in party management rather than officeholding. Acclaimed for his part in exposing and prosecuting the Tweed Ring, he was elected governor in 1874 and showed a high order of ability as a reform administrator. That he could carry New York, essential to Democratic success, was a powerful argument for him, although Bayard, Thurman, and Hendricks were better known. Yet he was a strange choice. Sixty-two years old, unmarried, in rather poor health, this coldly intellectual, secretive corporation lawyer was far removed from the popular conception of a crusading knight of reform. Worst of all, he was a multimillionaire, having amassed his fortune in part through skill in reorganizing insolvent railroads. Such a man might give a clean, efficient administration to the country and relieve the South of carpetbag misrule, but his political and economic tenets were thoroughly conservative. The temple of business would suffer no profanation from a Tilden in the White House. He and Hayes, if not two peas from the same pod, at least gave indications of coming from the same parent vine.

The problem of the greenback Democrats, it was hoped, had been solved through the nomination of the friendly Hendricks for second place and through Hayes's outspoken stand against inflation. But, with both parties unfriendly, the extreme inflationists launched the Independent, or "Greenback," party, a threat to Democratic unity in the West. Tilden's letter of acceptance, intended to harmonize differences, hurt him in the East, where concern was also expressed over the possibility that Hendricks, an avowed greenbacker, might become President if the none too robust head of the ticket did not live out his term.

Hayes, in accepting the Republican nomination, went beyond the party platform. He definitely favored resumption of specie payments, a policy of noninterference with the South, "thorough, radical and complete" reform of the civil service, and a single term for President. Republican politicians were taken aback, and Grant was annoyed at the implied criticisms of his policies; but reformers were enthusiastic. Schurz took the stump and frequently wrote letters of advice to Hayes; the former Liberal Republican organs, Bowles's *Springfield Republican*, Halstead's *Cincinnati Commercial*, and White-law Reid's New York *Tribune*, extolled the virtues of the candidate in contrast with the delinquencies of Grant; and most of the eastern reformers also expressed faith in the nominee. Joseph Pulitzer in the New York *World*, angry at reformer support of Hayes, could find but one reason: "Hayes has never stolen. Good God, has it come to this?"

The Conkling-Morton-Chandler group, saddled with a re-former candidate, made the best of the situation by working for party victory and ignoring Hayes, whom they did not even consult about the national chairmanship. With a better ap-preciation of the realities of politics, they saw that the reform issue was an admission of Republican guilt and was playing directly into Tilden's hands. A political newcomer, Colonel Robert G. Ingersoll, acclaimed for his nominating speech for Blaine, was put on the stump and drew huge crowds all the way from Maine to the Mississippi River, waving the bloody shirt as it had never been waved before and assailing the Democratic party as the party of treason and rebellion. A South Carolina riot in July in which several Negroes were slain served to point the moral of southern depravity and to show the dire consequences to be expected if the southern-controlled Democratic party came into power.

This stirring of old hatreds reached such a stage that late in the campaign the Democratic national chairman, Abram S. Hewitt, forced from the excessively cautious Tilden a public declaration against any payment of Confederate debts, any compensation for loss of slaves, or any recognition of damage claims of disloyal persons, a touchy point.

Republican orators assailed Tilden's private character, charging that he was a railroad wrecker, a grasping penny pincher, an income-tax evader, a sham reformer, and—Ingersoll added—a dried-up, old bachelor, as bad as Bu-chanan. Zach Chandler, Republican chairman, managing the Hayes campaign with no illusions about reform, collected large sums from federal officeholders and concentrated on New York and Indiana, to the neglect of other states. "A

bloody shirt campaign, with money, and Indiana is safe,"
wrote one party leader in a letter which got into the newspapers; "a financial campaign and no money, and we are
beaten." Hayes, aware of the straits of the party in these
two states and even in Ohio, came down from his pedestal
and urged Blaine to play up in his speeches the dread of a
solid South and rebel rule to distract people's thoughts from
hard times. Nor was he averse to stirring up anti-Catholic
prejudices against Tilden whose record was combed to provide some evidence. The secret anti-Catholic, antiforeign
"Order of the American Alliance" indorsed Hayes.

Tilden's "barrel," as depicted by the cartoonist Nast, was
supposed to finance the Democratic campaign; but this was
far from the case. The candidate kept a tight hold on his
purse strings, offended Chairman Hewitt and the organization managers by his indifferent attitude toward their arduous
work, and failed to supply funds which might have made
safe the three doubtful southern states. As it was, the national headquarters centered its efforts and funds on New
York and Indiana, and did a good job. The South was left
to shift for itself—a fatal error.

In the October state elections Indiana was Democratic by
a small margin, Ohio Republican by a slightly larger plurality.
The Democrats were encouraged. Indiana, New York, and
a solid South would mean victory. Betting odds favored
Tilden, while Hayes calmly prepared himself for an unfavorable verdict, though worried over the possibility of a
disputed outcome.

Early returns indicated before midnight of November 7
that Tilden had been elected. New York, Indiana, Connecticut, and New Jersey had gone Democratic, and while there
was some uncertainty about the "solidity" of the South, Tilden could spare two southern states and still win.[4] Republi-

[4] The popular vote is difficult to determine accurately because of
disputed returns. Stanwood gives as the Republican count, Tilden
4,285,992 and Hayes 4,033,768; the Democratic count gave Tilden
4,300,590 and Hayes 4,036,298. Peter Cooper, Greenbacker, had
81,737; Green Clay Smith, Prohibitionist, 9,522. The more recent
compilations of Burnham accredits Tilden with 4,284,020 and
Hayes with 4,036,572.

can headquarters in New York closed up, and Chairman Chandler, discouraged at reports from Louisiana and Florida, went to bed. Hayes admitted his defeat in his diary, and nearly all the Republican papers gave up hope.

In the early hours of the morning of November 8, while the editors of the *New York Times*, stanchest of Republican organs, debated whether to concede Tilden's election, a message came from Democratic state headquarters asking for the *Times* estimate of the electoral vote. This indication of Democratic uncertainty encouraged the editorial staff to hold out a little longer. The *Times*, without basis, thereupon claimed Louisiana and South Carolina for Hayes, but left Oregon, New Jersey, and Florida in doubt. John C. Reid, managing editor, then hastened to the Fifth Avenue Hotel headquarters of Chairman Zach Chandler, picking up an ally on the way, William E. Chandler of New Hampshire, national committeeman and lobbyist. The two aroused the exhausted, uncomprehending national chairman and secured his permission to send telegrams alerting party leaders in South Carolina, Florida, and Louisiana to the fact that the national outcome depended on holding these states. Without this prod, they might have accepted as final the reported returns. Agents well supplied with money were soon heading southward, and National Chairman Chandler, belatedly aware of the situation, announced that Hayes had 185 electoral votes; Tilden, 184.

Everything seemed to depend on the official count in the three doubtful states, and both sides sent "visiting statesmen" south to watch the count.

The situation in the three states was similar. The Republicans, controlling the state governments and the election machinery, had relied upon the Negro masses for votes, and had practiced frauds as in the past. The Democrats used threats, intimidation, and even violence when necessary, to keep Negroes from the polls; and where they were in a position to do so they resorted to fraud also. The firm determination of the whites to overthrow corrupt carpetbag rule contributed to make a full and fair vote impossible; carpetbag hold on the state governments made a fair count impossible. Radical reconstruction was reaping its final harvest.

In Florida a small Tilden majority was wiped out by a Republican-controlled election board, and the Hayes electors received the official certificates. In South Carolina Hayes had a small margin of the popular vote, though the Democrats elected Wade Hampton governor and carried the legislature. In both states the Democratic electoral candidates claimed the election and cast their votes for Tilden, though officially the Republicans had the better case.

In Louisiana a Republican election board, by throwing out the votes of whole parishes where there was any evidence that violence or intimidation had affected the result, changed a Tilden majority into a Hayes margin of some 3500 votes and awarded the governorship and legislature to the Republicans. Three members of the board later received federal offices from Hayes. In Oregon, carried by the Republicans, the Democrats contested an electoral vote on a technicality.

A Democratic House and a Republican Senate had to decide which of the double sets of electoral votes from the disputed states should be counted. Twenty votes were involved.

The Constitution states that the President of the Senate shall, in the presence of the two Houses, "open all the certificates, and the votes shall then be counted." Did this confer any power on the presiding officer to decide which votes should be counted or rejected when double sets of returns came from a state? Most authorities were inclined to answer in the negative, and this was in accord with all the precedents, though Hayes personally held to the other viewpoint. Senator Ferry of Michigan, a Republican, presided over the Senate (Vice President Wilson was dead) and would doubtless act in the interests of his party. But, granted the right of the two Houses to decide such matters, how could a Republican Senate and a Democratic House of Representatives be expected to agree?

A joint committee of the two houses, after long discussion, evolved a plan for an Electoral Commission to consist of five Senators, five Representatives, and five Supreme Court Justices. The two houses were to elect their representatives (in each case, three from the majority and two from the minority); four Justices (two from each party) were designated in the bill, and they were to choose a fifth, presumably David Davis, of uncertain political affiliations. This Electoral Commission was to have final authority in the cases of double sets of electoral votes, unless both houses agreed to overrule it. The plan was accepted by large majorities, most of the opposition coming from die-hard Republicans. The Democrats felt certain that such a commission could not be so partisan as to award all the disputed votes to Hayes—and Tilden needed only one to win. Without arbitration, the cards were stacked in favor of the Republicans, who controlled the executive (and the army), the Supreme Court, and the Senate.

Democratic hopes were suddenly dashed to the ground on the very day the bill passed the Lower House. News of a startling character arrived from Springfield, Illinois. The preceding day, a coalition of Democrats and independents in the Illinois legislature had elected Justice Davis to the United States Senate, rendering him unacceptable for service on the Electoral Commission. Fortune seemed to reserve her smiles for the Republicans through these years; but in this case asinine blundering by Illinois Democrats would seem to be a more logical explanation. National Chairman Hewitt and the Congressional leaders, intent on getting the Electoral Commission bill passed, realized too late the dangers in the Illinois situation.

There was still the possibility that the judicial members of the commission would show the fair-mindedness of true judges and not the spirit of partisans. At least the fifth Justice, on whom the burden of the final decision must rest, would surely realize the gravity of his position and put aside partisan considerations. That unfortunate individual, chosen by the four Justices already on the Commission after Davis became disqualified, was Justice Joseph P. Bradley. Bradley had the approval of Democratic leaders as he appeared to be the most independent of the remaining members of the Court, all of them Republican.

The electoral count began before the two Houses on February 1, with a great crowd present in the hall of the House of Representatives. When Florida was reached, objections were raised against the certificates of both Republican and Democratic electors, and the problem went to the Electoral Commission. The first and most important matter for it to settle was whether it should go behind the returns. After long arguments by eminent counsel, it was voted, 8 to 7, that the Commission was not competent to receive evidence which was not submitted to the two Houses in joint session. In other words, the regularity of the certificates would be considered, but not the proceedings and measures in Florida responsible for them. After such a decision, arguments were futile. Regularity was with the Republicans, and the Commission, 8 to 7, awarded the Florida votes to Hayes, with Bradley casting the deciding vote.

The Democratic House rejected the Commision's decision in the Florida case; but the Republican Senate upheld it, and so it was final according to the law. Similar verdicts in the Louisiana, Oregon, and South Carolina cases gave Hayes their disputed electoral votes. House and Senate separated to vote on each disputed state.

While the South Carolina case was under consideration, an alarming possibility developed. Democratic die-hards in the House were ready to inaugurate a filibuster that would prevent resumption of joint sessions and completion of the count before March 4. What would then happen, no one could say. Civil war might begin. But the danger was more apparent than real.

Actually, negotiations had been under way for many weeks to take care of such a situation. William Henry Smith, general agent of the Western Associated Press, acting for the Hayes inner circle, had established contacts with important southern conservatives, chiefly former Whigs, and reached a tentative agreement with them that would insure their support for the peaceful acceptance of Hayes as President. As finally worked out, the terms of the bargain included assurances that Hayes would live up to his letter of acceptance and bring to an end federal support of carpetbag rule;

that at least one cabinet post, and other patronage favors, would go to southern conservatives; that Hayes would favor federal aid for education and internal improvements in the South, including a government subsidy for the Texas & Pacific Railway. The lower Mississippi valley was eager for a rail connection with the Far West, but the panic had stalled the project. Thomas A. Scott, president of the Pennsylvania Railroad, was interested in the Texas & Pacific and played a part in the consummation of the bargain.

Hayes made these commitments cautiously, through intermediaries. In return, he received promises of equal rights and fair treatment for southern Negroes and assurances that the electoral count would proceed unobstructed. He also believed that a coalition to elect James A. Garfield Speaker of the new House might be arranged. Southern Democrats, especially those of Whig background, saw more loaves and fishes for their neglected section in a deal with the Hayes men than in a resolute stand beside their intransigent northern colleagues. Hayes had once been a Whig.

The well-known conference in late February at Wormley's Hotel in Washington, long supposed to have produced the solution to the filibuster threat, actually was only a last-minute meeting to reassure worried southerners that the terms already agreed upon would be respected. A number of persons participated in the negotiations at various stages, including the indefatigable William Henry Smith, General Henry Van Ness Boynton, a Washington correspondent, Andrew J. Kellar of the Memphis *Avalanche*, Major E. A. Burk of Louisiana, Tom Scott's Pennsylvana Railroad lobby, several conservative southern members of Congress, and a group of Ohio friends of Hayes. Although not involved in the deal, Speaker Randall and National Chairman Hewitt also worked to prevent delays in completing the count of the electoral votes. In the early hours of March 2 the two Houses finished their tabulation: Hayes had 185 electoral votes; Tilden, 184.

Hayes arrived at the Capital that day and took the oath of office privately the next evening at the White House, because March 4 was a Sunday. On Monday, with due ceremony, he was formally inaugurated.

CHAPTER VI

REFORM AND TARIFF ELECTIONS

1880–1892

1880

HAYES DETERMINED THE political course of his party by two actions. He removed the federal troops from Louisiana and South Carolina, after which the Democrats evicted the carpetbag governments from those states, angering Republican Stalwarts who termed Hayes supporters "Half-Breeds." He attempted to reform the civil service system by Presidential edict, and clashed with Senator Conkling of New York when he removed Chester A. Arthur and Alonzo B. Cornell from the top federal posts at the port of New York. Both were important cogs in the Conkling machine, and the angry boss tried to get their successors rejected by the Senate. He lost out after a long battle.

The New York Colossus, determined to recapture the White House for the true-blue Republicans, decided that Grant, recently returned from a leisurely trip around the world, should run again. Grant was willing. Conkling controlled New York, J. Donald Cameron accounted for Pennsylvania, and John A. Logan for Illinois. Those against a third term supported Blaine, John Sherman of Ohio, and some favorite sons.

When the convention opened at Chicago on June 2, a dramatic clash ensued between Conkling and James A. Garfield, Sherman's manager and leader of the anti-Grant forces. Conkling was defeated in an attempt to secure the adoption of the unit rule, which would have suppressed anti-Grant minorities in the three large Grant states. When the balloting began, Grant led with 304 votes, but this was far from the 378 votes needed for the nomination. After thirty-five ballots the Blaine and Sherman forces combined and made Garfield the nominee on the thirty-sixth. Over Conkling's objections, Chester A. Arthur, the recently removed collector of the port of New York, accepted the offer of the Garfield forces to run for Vice President. Except for a condemnation of Chinese immigration, the platform merely rephrased the planks of 1876.

The Democratic convention met at Cincinnati on June 22 with Tilden out of the picture, presumably because of impaired health. The brief platform indorsed "tariff for revenue only"—a blunder—opposed Chinese immigration, and deplored the "great fraud of 1876–77." On the first ballot for President, nineteen persons received votes with General Winfield S. Hancock of Pennsylvania in the lead. He had less than one-fourth of the total, but received the nomination on the second ballot, almost by default. There was little enthusiasm for any of his rivals, and his soldier record was a major asset. Former Congressman William H. English, a banker with a "barrel," completed the ticket. His residence in doubtful Indiana helped his cause.

The campaign of 1880 was barren of issues and devoid of drama. Labor troubles and farmer unrest had subsided, though the Greenback party, headed by General James B. Weaver, tried to keep the embers alive. Neither major party had a program, and only on the tariff question was there any divergence. The Republicans waved the bloody shirt rather feebly and talked of southern disfranchisement of Negroes and the power the white South would exercise in a Democratic administration. The Democrats did not overlook the "fraud" of 1876–1877 and repeated the old charges of Republican corruption, though the honest administration of Hayes gave these small weight.

The reformers, or Independents, again seemed to be in a position to decide the election. Both platforms had indorsed civil service reform, but more to the point were the records of the candidates. Here Garfield's garments were slightly spotted. As the recipient of a share of stock in the Crédit Mobilier, which had been exposed in Grant's administration, he had collected $329 in dividends. His explanations of this and of a large attorney's fee in a Washington paving contract scandal satisfied even the impeccable *Nation* and G. W. Curtis's *Harper's Weekly*. Schurz added his praises as well. But Garfield's letter of acceptance was not the positive statement on civil service reform the reformers expected, and during the campaign he seemed to cater to the machine leaders. In spite of this, the Independents turned down Hancock, with an unblemished record, apparently because of his lack of experience in government. Sneers at his imposing physique—"a good man weighing two hundred and forty pounds"—and Nast's cartoons portraying his naïve ignorance were the extent of Republican assaults on the man.

Conkling was the chief Republican problem. Arthur, Cameron, and Logan did their part but "Lord" Roscoe sulked in his tent. Garfield visited the East in August to appeal for financial support and secured Jay Gould's help. Thomas C. Platt and other New York Stalwarts conferred with the candidate and apparently received some general assurances about patronage. Conkling did not appear, but his lieutenants were satisfied and went to work. In September he went on the stump in New York for the Republican cause, if not for Garfield.

Maine startled Republican leaders by electing a Democratic-Greenback governor in September, and fears were felt for Indiana and Ohio. Conkling then went West to speak; Grant joined him, making a seven-minute speech at Warren, Ohio, and the two, with a number of retainers, were maneuvered into a brief call on Garfield in his home, at Mentor. Out of this call later grew Platt's story that the grateful candidate rushed out in the rain to embrace Conkling and pledge him control of New York appointments. Historians have given little credence to the "treaty of Mentor." Garfield was not given to making rash pledges, particularly to the domineering New Yorker.

Conkling also spoke in Indiana, where the situation was

serious. Money as well as oratory flowed like water in the Hoosier State, where S. W. Dorsey, secretary of the national committee, had things in his hands. The fears of business and industrial leaders were played upon with a belated use of the Democratic "tariff for revenue only" plank. Hancock denied that the Democrats would not protect the manufacturer and declared with much truth that the tariff was "a local question." Republicans seized upon this as an example of the General's ignorance, and ridiculed his views. The Greenback character of the Maine outcome was a further argument used by Republicans to draw money from reluctant financiers, for Garfield's record was consistently anti-inflationist. At the candidate's own suggestion John D. Rockefeller was importuned to bring his Standard Oil agents into line for the Republican ticket in Indiana. In the end Republican money and organization carried the October state elections in Indiana and Ohio, foreshadowing success in November.

At this juncture appeared the forged Morey letter, a desperate attempt to turn the Pacific coast against Garfield. The letter, addressed to "H. L. Morey of the Employers' Union, Lynn, Massachusetts," and apparently signed by the Republican candidate, approved of Chinese immigration "until our great manufacturing and corporate interests are conserved in the matter of labor." Garfield learned of its existence on October 20, and at once declared it a forgery; but *Truth*, the New York paper publishing the letter, insisted on its genuineness. Doubtless it injured him in the Far West where the Chinese question was a vital issue, though every effort was made to show that the letter was simply a campaign roorback.

Democratic hopes were dashed on Election Day when the Republicans carried the entire North and West except New Jersey, Nevada, and five of California's six electors. Garfield had 214 electoral votes; Hancock, 155. However, the victor's popular plurality was small.[1] The Democrats took what little consolation they could from the "solidity" of the South: every former slave state had voted for Hancock.

[1] Garfield, 4,453,295; Hancock, 4,414,082; James B. Weaver, Greenback, 308,578; Neal Dow, Prohibitionist, 10,305.

The leading factors in the Republican victory were prosperity, the support of the business and financial interests, and the improvement in reputation of the party during the Hayes administration. That it was a party victory rather than a personal one was shown by the Republican majority in the Lower House, the first in six years. In the Senate two Independents held the balance of power and divided between the two parties, creating a tie on organization questions and giving Vice President Arthur the deciding vote. In effect, party government was restored in 1880 after a six-year deadlock.

1884

Garfield appointed Conkling's Half-Breed enemy, James G. Blaine, Secretary of State and did not satisfy Conkling with some other appointments. But open war began when he made a Blaine henchman collector of the port of New York. Conkling fought the nomination with characteristic verbal violence and abuse, but when the appointment was about to receive Senate confirmation, he and his colleague, "Me, Too" Tom Platt, resigned and went to Albany to ask the legislature to vindicate their stand by returning them to Washington. They were turned down, but Garfield did not live to enjoy his triumph. His assassination by a mentally unbalanced Stalwart made Arthur, a Conkling liegeman, President and Blaine resigned as Secretary of State.

Arthur was a pleasant surprise as President. He displayed independence and good judgment, and made a record that seemed to warrant his nomination in 1884. The Pendleton Act to reform the civil service was passed in 1883, certain vetoes were generally praised, and in his appointments, he did not give special preference to Stalwarts. But the Half-Breeds wanted Blaine, and even among the Stalwarts, with Conkling out of power, there was the feeling that Blaine's turn had come. The reform group preferred Senator Edmunds of Vermont to Arthur, and John Sherman of Ohio and John A. Logan of Illinois had their friends.

The Republican convention met again at Chicago, on

June 3. To the customary platform generalities was added a stronger protective tariff plank. In spite of delegate and gallery enthusiasm for Blaine, it took four ballots to nominate him. John A. Logan, Illinois Stalwart, received second place on the ticket.

The Democrats, confronted with Blaine and Logan, needed a reform candidate to draw the independent vote. One appeared in 1882 when Grover Cleveland was elected governor of New York. His record at Albany won the reformers but antagonized the Tammany machine headed by John Kelly. Kelly controlled part of the New York delegation but was muzzled by the unit rule.

A generally harmonious convention assembled at Chicago on July 8. "Cockeyed" Ben Butler turned up with two third-party nominations, but his past party shiftings and southern remembrance of his wartime rule of New Orleans eliminated him from serious consideration. His attempts to amend the platform were voted down. That document was long, platitudinous, and on the tariff question, verbosely ambiguous. But reform was too important an issue to be sidetracked by tariff, currency, or any other controversial question, and the platform's indictment of Republican misdeeds was well stated.

Ill-timed attacks on Cleveland by Tammany henchmen were greeted with hisses, and the galleries roared their approval of Bragg of Wisconsin when he said that Cleveland's friends "love him most for the enemies he has made." The New York governor was far in the lead on the first ballot and received the necessary two-thirds on the second. Hendricks of Indiana, Tilden's running mate, a soft-money westerner, balanced the ticket. He was not a reformer.

The campaign for Cleveland was a double-headed affair in which the forces of darkness and of light joined hands. On the side of darkness were Daniel Manning, Democratic boss of the Empire State, William C. Whitney, a wealthy young lawyer of tremendous energy and proper Wall Street connections, and Senator Arthur P. Gorman of Maryland, an astute, hard-headed politician who headed the national executive committee (a figurehead, ex-Senator Barnum of Connecticut, was chairman of the national committee). These unregenerate partisans collected a larger campaign fund than usual from a segment of business and from Democratic state and municipal officeholders, made terms with recalcitrant or sulking local bosses, and used methods on occasion that might not have commended themselves to the candidate, had he been fully informed. Their problem was to get every real or half-hearted Democrat to the polls. On the offensive they joined hands with the Independents in vicious attacks on Blaine.

Schurz, heading a separate organization with a small, poorly manned office in New York City, led the Independents, popularly called "Mugwumps," and the Republican bolters into battle. Among them were many eminent American intellectual leaders: President Charles W. Eliot and almost the whole Harvard faculty, Henry Ward Beecher, James Freeman Clarke, Thomas Wentworth Higginson, and the veteran civil service reformers Godkin and Curtis. The important periodicals *Harper's Weekly*, the *Nation*, and *Puck*, and independent or Republican papers including the *Herald, Times, Evening Post* and *Telegram* in New York, the *Transcript, Herald*, and *Advertiser* in Boston, the *Springfield Republican*, the *Brooklyn Union*, the *Times* and the *Record* of Philadelphia, and the *Times* and *News* of Chicago, were anti-Blaine.

Yet many Republicans who had opposed Blaine before the Chicago convention now became mute or openly conformed. The whip of party regularity brought those looking to the future into line. Congressman Henry Cabot Lodge, young Massachusetts aristocrat, refused to sacrifice his seat to principle and stated that bolting would "destroy all the influence and power for good I possess." His fellow Harvardian Theodore Roosevelt, after weeks of uncertainty, returned from a Dakota ranch to speak for Blaine; earlier, as a New York State assemblyman, he had found much about Cleveland to commend. Senator Edmunds of Vermont was harder to move. Toward the close of the campaign he made one speech for his party but refused to mention Blaine's name. But Blaine's old enemy, Roscoe Conkling, in a reputed reply to requests for his support, was devastating: "I do not engage in criminal practice." His home county, usually Republican, was carried by Cleveland.

The Mugwump fire was centered on the Republican candidate's record, particularly the Mulligan letters. In 1869, Blaine, Speaker of the House, after helping secure renewal of a land grant for an Arkansas railroad, worked with a Boston broker, Warren Fisher, to sell its bonds. When they declined in value Blaine refunded the money to investors by secretly selling the nearly worthless bonds to the Union Pacific at a high price. Letters supplied by Fisher's bookkeeper, James Mulligan, to a House committee in 1876 were secured by Blaine on a pretext and not returned. Instead, he read extracts to the House and made a brilliant, if disingenuous, defense. There the matter rested until Blaine's nomination in 1884 revived the old charges. Worse even was a new batch of letters uncovered during the campaign, including a draft of a letter exonerating him which he himself had written and sent to Fisher to copy and mail back. On it in his own hand was the significant request "Burn this letter." The request had not been carried out, and the draft letter had not been sent. Both now appeared in print to humiliate the candidate.

Bernhard Gillam, the cartoonist of *Puck*, who outdid Nast of *Harper's Weekly* in vindictiveness, stamped the Republican candidate unforgettably in the public mind as the "tattooed man," marked on his body with "Bribery," "Mulligan Letters," "Little Rock," and other unpleasant reminders of his record.

The unrestrained abuse of Blaine drew a savage retaliation from Republican sources that might well have been deadly, had it been better timed. In July the Buffalo *Evening Telegraph* gave the world the sordid story of Mrs. Maria Halpin. This prepossessing widow, employed in a Buffalo store in the early seventies, had been on intimate terms with several men. When a son was born to her in 1874 she named Cleveland as the father. He accepted the responsibility, perhaps to shield the others involved, and made some financial arrangements for the child. Eventually, because of the mother's misconduct, he had the boy placed in an orphanage, from which he was adopted by a good family. Few people knew of the matter until it appeared in print in 1884.

Jubilant Republican papers printed all the details, and many partisan Protestant ministers preached sermons against moral laxity and the danger of placing men of debauched character in high office. Cleveland astonished friends and enemies alike by admitting his sin and offering no excuses. His confession threw the Democratic-reformer camp into confusion. But the witty comment of a clever anonymous Chicagoan at a New York conference of Mugwumps let sunlight through the dark clouds. Let Blaine, he argued, whose private life was blameless, be remanded to private life, and let Cleveland, whose public life was a model of integrity, be kept in public life. Two famous Protestant ministers, James Freeman Clarke and Henry Ward Beecher, championed Cleveland; and Republican charges of gross immorality began to lose their weight. By Election Day the Halpin affair had become no more effective than any stale gossip after the truth has been clearly revealed. Cleveland's frankness was refreshing after Blaine's dissembling evasions of the Mulligan letters.

As the contest drew to a close, Republican strategists, alarmed at the situation in the Middle West, violated Republican precedents and put Blaine himself on the stump. His tour stirred the Republican masses as he preached on the benefits of protective tariff, and dilated on his favorite theme, the dangers of rebel rule. In less spectacular fashion, Colonel W. W. Dudley, Commissioner of Pensions, and a hundred special examiners appeared in Ohio and Indiana to pressure the soldier vote.

If the Middle West, except Indiana, seemed to be safe by mid-October, New York was not, and the pleadings of Blaine's managers—or, perhaps, some inexorable fate—called him back to his destruction. The New York situation was complicated. John P. St. John, former Republican and governor of Kansas, was campaigning in New York as Prohibition candidate for President; and Frances E. Willard and the Woman's Christian Temperance Union, angry at contemptuous treatment accorded to a temperance petition at the Republican national convention, were supporting him. Temperance advocates, usually Republican in the past, might be drawn to St. John to punish Blaine just as the abolitionists had punished Clay in 1844. To offset this danger, the Republican national committee was secretly financing Ben Butler, the Antimonopoly-Greenback candidate, in an attempt to draw Democratic votes from Cleveland. John Kelly of Tammany was suspected of secret friendliness to Butler.

Tied up with the Tammany and Butler problems was the Irish vote. Blaine was of Irish descent. His mother was a Roman Catholic, a cousin was the mother-superior of a convent, and he himself had long exhibited a tendency to twist the British Lion's tail, to the edification of all good Irishmen. The *Irish Nation* and the *Irish World* of New York indorsed him, and a great meeting of Blaine Irish-Americans was held on July 28. Cleveland, son of a Presbyterian minister, had no particular appeal to the sons of Erin except as traditional Democrats. The Republicans, calling the Mugwumps and Democrats free traders, dubbed him the "British candidate," whose success would imperil American industries. The *Irish World*, speaking for the more vociferous "professional" Irish-Americans, charged that all the great British dailies were opposed to Blaine.

To New York City came Blaine with the scales so evenly weighted that a straw might unbalance them. On the morning of October 29 he spoke to a group of Protestant ministers at the Fifth Avenue Hotel. In welcoming the candidate, Samuel D. Burchard, a Presbyterian minister, carved his niche in history with one asinine sentence: "We are Republicans, and don't propose to leave our party and identify ourselves with the party whose antecedents have been rum, Romanism and rebellion." Blaine did not catch the remark, and made no mention of it in his reply. A shorthand reporter took it down, turned it in to Chairman Gorman at Democratic headquarters, and within a few hours "Rum, Romanism and Rebellion" was doing its work. Newspapers and handbills carried the story of Burchard's insult to Roman

Catholics and Blaine's apparent acquiescence. No explanation could undo the damage. Enough Irish votes were probably lost to change the result in New York.

As if this were not enough for one day, Blaine was again victimized in the evening by supposed friends. Unwisely, and against Chairman Elkins's advice, he attended a dinner at Delmonico's given by the wealthiest men in the city. Present were John Jacob Astor, Jay Gould, Cyrus W. Field, Russell Sage, Levi P. Morton, and many other millionaires. The solitary reporter present (from Jay Gould's Associated Press) heard Blaine extol the tremendous increase in the country's wealth under Republican rule. Then all went into a private room (with the reporter excluded) and discussed campaign funds. Next day a New York *World* cartoon pictured "Belshazzar Blaine and the Money Kings" dining in splendor on "Monopoly Soup," "Lobby Pudding," "Navy Contract" and "Gould Pie," while a starving workingman and his wife appealed in vain for food. In a year of hard times the reaction of labor to the incident was bound to be unfavorable.

Cleveland made two formal speeches—at Newark, New Jersey, and at Bridgeport, Connecticut—and attended a great celebration at Buffalo. On the Saturday before the election he reviewed a parade of forty thousand in New York City, listening to the tramping thousands chanting "Blaine, Blaine, James G. Blaine, the Monumental Liar from the State of Maine," and "Burn this letter, burn this letter, kind regards to Mrs. Fisher," while the marchers held lighted matches to sheets of paper. Twice in this same week Blaine had had his innings when the Republican hosts paraded past him roaring "Blaine, Blaine, James G. Blaine, O-O-O-hi-O, No-No-No Free Trade," though some were not above chorusing "Ma! Ma! Where's my pa? Gone to the White House, Ha! Ha! Ha!" Not since 1840 had Americans worked so hard at politics.

As the returns came in on the night of November 4, it was evident that New York would decide the outcome. Cleveland had the Solid South, Indiana, Connecticut, and New Jersey, a total of 183 electoral votes; Blaine had the rest, except New York, 182 in all; New York's 36 were in doubt. The weather had taken a hand at the last minute and a driving rain in upstate New York, "good weather for Democrats," made it hard for the farmers to get to the polls. Blaine was the loser thereby, for more Democrats lived in the cities.

Cleveland's plurality in New York was 1,149 in a total vote of 1,167,169.[2] The scales had indeed been tipped against Blaine by a straw. But what was the straw? Was it the much publicized Burchard remark, or the banquet of the millionaires, or Conkling's ill will, or the unexpected strength of St. John, who polled 25,000 votes, or Butler's poor showing, or the rain of November 4, or some other fortuitous circumstance? Blaine believed that the suppression of the southern Republican vote had forced the party to depend on New York, and that the Independents, the Prohibitionists, and the Burchard remark accounted for that state. Better known is his message to Murat Halstead: "As the Lord sent upon us an ass in the shape of a preacher and a rainstorm to lessen our vote in New York, I am disposed to feel resigned to the dispensation of defeat which flowed directly from these agencies."

More fundamental were two factors that accounted for heavy Democratic inroads into Republican strength everywhere in the North. One was the failure of Republican economic appeal in a year of much unemployment and business stagnation. The other was the Independent, or Mugwump, uprising. The reform groups held the balance of power in the four northern states carried by Cleveland and reduced the Republican vote in other states. But for their activity in New York, Blaine would have won by such a margin that preacher, Prohibitionist, and rainstorm combined could not have changed the result.

The parties had not come to grips over economic issues. Both sides had ignored or touched lightly such matters as

[2] The popular vote was as follows: Cleveland, 4,918,507; Blaine, 4,850,293; Butler, 175,370; St. John, 150,369. In New York the vote was: Cleveland, 563,154; Blaine, 562,005; Butler, 16,994; St. John, 25,016. The electoral vote was 219 for Cleveland, 182 for Blaine.

labor unrest, farmer problems, public-land policies, railway regulation, the growth of monopolies, and even tariff reform. The evasion was deliberate but not at all strange. Why should party leaders, whose function was to carry elections, attempt to formulate programs upon which few people were agreed? Third parties had tried and failed dismally. Reform in government thousands of honest Americans regarded as necessary before other reforms could come. For years corruption and a vicious spoils system had been undermining confidence in democratic government. The election was a contest to see whether a sentimental loyalty to a party in power which had long promised reform but had performed slowly and half-heartedly for its own Presidents, and whose candidate was now suspect, should triumph over a party whose chief pledge was a candidate of unquestioned integrity with a record to match. The majority of the voters decided that the party that had saved the Union should no longer misgovern it.

1888

Cleveland, a neophyte in national politics who was confronted with a Republican Senate, learned as he went along. Neither party spoilsmen nor reformers were satisfied with his handling of appointments, but civil service reform did make some progress. He antagonized the Grand Army of the Republic by vetoing several hundred private pension bills and by an order, later rescinded, to return to their states captured Confederate battle flags.

Cleveland's ideas of economy and the application of business principles to government were affronted by the growing surplus in the federal treasury, chiefly from tariff revenues. Protectionist Democrats helped Republicans in blocking bills to revise the tariff, but Cleveland devoted his entire message to the problem in 1887 and committed his party to a policy of rate revision to reduce the surplus.

The task of the Democratic national convention, assembled at St. Louis on June 5, was the easiest that had confronted the party since 1840. The platform contained a long statement on the tariff, which, in spite of its ambiguities, was taken to mean an indorsement of a downward revision policy. A separate resolution approved the moderate Mills bill, pending in the House of Representatives. Cleveland's record was the real platform. He was renominated by acclamation; former Senator Allen G. Thurman of Ohio became his running mate.

The Republicans came to Chicago on June 19, jubilant over Cleveland's commitment of his party to a lower tariff. Blaine would have been renominated but for a formal declination sent from Italy to the chairman of the national committee. A flock of favorite sons got into the race and fourteen persons received votes on the first ballot. John Sherman of Ohio, making his third effort, had 229 votes. Judge Walter Q. Gresham of Indiana, hope of the unbossed, was second with 111. But bosses Matthew S. Quay of Pennsylvania, Tom Platt of New York, and some lesser lights seemed to determine the nomination after the deadlock forced an adjournment over the weekend. In any case, on the eighth ballot on Monday, ex-Senator Benjamin Harrison of Indiana was chosen. He was Ohio-born, had been a Civil War brigadier, was the grandson of a President, had no scandals to cover up, and was a faithful Presbyterian. Levi P. Morton, New York banker and businessman, represented the East on the ticket.

The platform contained an uncompromising protective tariff plank and promised to dispose of the surplus revenue with increased appropriations for defense, pensions, and public works.

The Republican campaign manager was Matthew S. Quay, who had succeeded the Cameron dynasty in the boss-controlled state of Pennsylvania, and whose organization methods were thorough and unscrupulous. Colonel W. W. Dudley, former head of the pensions bureau, was campaign treasurer. Money was presently raised on an unprecedented scale. John Wanamaker, Philadelphia merchant, acted as liaison officer to tap the vast resources of American business. Heading an advisory committee of businessmen, he was soon engaged in what came to be called cynically "frying out the fat."

Mark Hanna, businessman-politician, raised over $100,000 in northern Ohio. A key figure was James M. Swank of Pennsylvania, head of the American Iron and Steel Association, which, with kindred organizations, sent hundreds of thousands of pamphlets to propagandize the partially industrialized Middle West on the merits of protection. No longer were officeholders expected to carry the chief burden of financing a national campaign. If businessmen felt that the security of their investments depended on Republican control, they must expect to pay a good, stiff price for it.

Harrison, a small man, aristocratic in bearing, aloof and difficult in personal contacts, called "Kid Glove" Harrison in Indiana, made surprisingly effective public addresses from his Indianapolis front porch. His good Civil War record was contrasted with Cleveland's hiring a substitute, and helped to make the G.A.R., already angry over the pension vetoes, into a Republican auxiliary. It remained for Blaine, however, to quicken Republican heartbeats with his compelling eloquence, to give to a dry tariff argument a dramatic touch, to expose the British Lion and the Confederate Brigadier hiding behind the Democratic free-trade ramparts. It was a memorable 10th of August when Blaine rode up New York harbor on a tender amid a din of whistles, horns, band music, and frantic cheers to throw his spellbinding energy into the rather apathetic campaign. Tens of thousands greeted him, and other tens of thousands fought to hear him at Indianapolis and elsewhere in the Middle West in October. Finishing in doubtful Connecticut and New York, he had done more for Harrison than he could have done for himself.

Meanwhile, what of Cleveland? With Congress on his hands all summer and far into October, he had little time for campaign matters. His one public appearance was to read his letter of acceptance. The campaign was left to his managers, William H. Barnum of Connecticut, chairman of the national committee as in 1884, and Calvin S. Brice, chairman of the executive committee, a wealthy railroad financier and Wall Street speculator with a home in Ohio. Neither had any interest in tariff reform—Barnum being a member of the Iron and Steel Association—and neither had the President's interests closely at heart. The American Free Trade League headed by David A. Wells circulated pamphlets by the thousands; the American Tariff Reform League operated after a fashion in the Middle West; Godkin, Curtis, William Graham Sumner, Henry George, and others engaged in a campaign of education; but the heavy weight of the money bags unbalanced the scales against them. Most of the old Mugwump papers remained loyal to Cleveland, but civil service reform attracted little attention. The scandal of 1884 was not revived. Cleveland had married in 1886, but stories did circulate that he beat his young wife and was drunk on the Presidential yacht.

As in 1884, New York and Indiana were the key states. In the Empire State, Governor David B. Hill, candidate for re-election and no friend of Cleveland or reform, had the strong backing of Tammany and the urban liquor interests. He was indifferent to Cleveland's fate, and Republican Boss Platt was willing to sacrifice his own party's candidate for governor, Warner Miller. A deal was apparently cooked up between three local machine leaders in the metropolis and the Republican organization. Harrison and Hill benefited at the expense of Cleveland and Miller. The *New York Times* and loyal Cleveland men charged that Hill himself was a party to the deal. The bolting of German Republicans, opposed to Miller's antiliquor position, may have been a factor. At least Harrison carried the state, and Hill won the governorship.

In New York corruption may have affected the result; in Indiana it was the deciding factor. That state no longer held its state elections in October, but a Republican poll sixty days before the November election showed the Democrats ahead. National headquarters then came to the relief of the state organization. "Divide the floaters into blocks of five," wrote Treasurer W. W. Dudley to Indiana lieutenants, "put a trusted man with the necessary funds in charge of these five and make him responsible that none get away and that all vote our ticket." This letter, put into Democratic hands by a railway mail clerk, created a sensation. Chairman Quay denounced it as a forgery and Dudley brought libel suits—later dropped—against newspapers printing it. But stories of floaters, locked up the day before the election, then marched to the polls with Republican ballots in their hands and as much as fifteen dollars each in their pockets, have been well authenticated. Never had that considerable number of poor Hoosiers who were accustomed to turning a dishonest dollar at the polling places been so well rewarded. Afterwards, an investigation was launched into Dudley's activities; but he threatened to "explode a lot of dynamite" if he were made the scapegoat, and a federal judge saw fit to dismiss the case. At all events, Indiana voted for Harrison by the scant margin of 2,348.

More widely used than direct bribery was the fear appeal. Industrialists warned employees of wage cuts and unemployment if Cleveland should win. Although he did not advocate free trade, it became the bogy of Republican orators; and such a good friend of labor as Henry George played into their hands by preaching its benefits while speaking for the Democrats.

Anti-British sentiment was stirred up by the publication of a letter from Sir Lionel Sackville-West, the British Minister, to "Charles F. Murchison" of California, favoring Cleveland over Harrison. "Murchison," a Republican, posed as a former British subject writing for advice. The stupid Minister was at once dismissed, but the episode may have cost Cleveland some Irish votes.

The election was close, but the outcome was clear by midnight. Harrison had the 36 electoral votes of New York by a margin of about 13,000. Cleveland lost Indiana but carried Connecticut and New Jersey. The rest of the North and West went Republican as in 1884, though in most cases Cleveland ran better than before and had a popular plurality of 90,728.[3] The unrepresentative electoral system gave him only 168 electoral votes to Harrison's 233.

[3] Cleveland had 5,537,857 popular votes; Harrison, 5,447,129; Clinton B. Fisk (Prohibitionist), 249,506; Alson J. Streeter (Union Labor), 146,935. A United Labor candidate polled 2,818 votes in New York and Illinois, and an "American" candidate had 1,591

Cleveland's courageous if inexpedient tariff stand made him the leader of his party and, in defeat, its most popular figure. He had ended its halting expediency and had given it an issue. More important, his four years in office had finally given the lie to the old cry that rebels would rule if the Democrats won. The party of the Copperheads had at last attained respectability.

1892

Party rule returned with Harrison. The Presidency and both Houses of Congress were Republican. Blaine became Secretary of State and Thomas B. ("Czar") Reed Speaker of the House. The promises of the platform of 1888 were carried out by the passage of the highly protective McKinley Tariff Act and liberal appropriations for defense and pensions. This policy disposed of the treasury surplus but was not popular, and coupled with a farmer uprising, product of droughts and falling farm prices, produced a disastrous Republican defeat in the mid-term elections.

Party bosses Quay, Platt, and J. S. Clarkson of Iowa were dissatisfied with Harrison for personal and patronage reasons and attempted to prevent his renomination at the Republican convention, which met at Minneapolis in the discontented farm belt, on June 7, 1892. Secretary of State Blaine resigned suddenly three days before the convention met without giving any reasons. The anti-Harrison alliance offered him as their candidate, but Harrison was renominated with 535 1/6 votes out of 905 cast. Blaine had 182 5/6, and William McKinley, without being a candidate, received 182 votes. Whitelaw Reid of the New York *Tribune*, a longtime foe of Platt, was nominated for Vice President. The platform reaffirmed the tariff position of 1888 and defended the measures of the Republican Congress.

Eastern business interests, alarmed at the farmer revolt, looked to the Democrats to nominate Cleveland, who could

---

in California. Socialist and scattering votes totaled 7,006. Other totals vary slightly from these.

be trusted to stand stanchly against free silver and agrarian radicalism. The New York Democratic machine backed Senator David B. Hill, who avoided commitments on issues by saying, "I am a Democrat," but Hill had slight support outside his home state. William C. Whitney managed Cleveland's pre-convention campaign skilfully, and the former President was nominated on the first ballot at the national convention, which opened at Chicago on June 21. Adlai E. Stevenson, a silver Democrat and former First Assistant Postmaster General, was named for the Vice Presidency, a peace offering to the free silver advocates.

The platform committee's moderate tariff plank was revised on the convention floor to commit the party to a tariff for revenue only. The currency plank denounced the Sherman Silver Purchase Act of the Republicans as a cowardly makeshift but otherwise was as evasive as the Republican plank.

A formidable third party, product of a swelling farmer discontent in West and South, was launched at Omaha on July 2. Delegates from various farmer, labor and other liberal organizations adopted with wild enthusiasm a platform that condemned the major parties for engaging in sham battles, and demanded a national paper currency along with the free coinage of silver, a graduated income tax, government ownership of railroad, telegraph, and telephone systems, and other reform proposals of a radical character. The convention nominated for President James B. Weaver of Iowa, who had been the Greenback candidate in 1880, and for Vice President James G. Field of Virginia, a coupling of Union and Confederate generals. The new party called itself the People's party but was better known by the term Populist.

Except where agrarian discontent fed the fires of Populism, the campaign was the dullest in many years. Honest bearded Benjamin Harrison confronting honest mustached Grover Cleveland in a tariff debate was a repeat performance that did not inspire parades with torches or the chanting of campaign ditties. Neither candidate appeared on the stump, Harrison because of Mrs. Harrison's illness and death and Cleveland out of respect for his rival's sad affliction. The Democrats, out of power, could assail Republican tariff policy without clarifying their own position. Cleveland's acceptance letter made it clear that he was no theoretical free trader—a necessary precaution, as the extreme tariff plank declaring that protection was unconstitutional was a boon to Republicans picturing the dangers of Democratic radicalism. The Republicans also had to defend their spending policy against charges of waste and extravagance while the Sherman Silver Purchase Act suited neither silver men nor gold advocates.

The argument that labor benefited from protection received a stunning blow when a great strike occurred in the Carnegie steelworks at Homestead, Pennsylvania. Wage reductions were the ostensible cause, but the company's desire to break the power of the steel workers' union soon became evident. After much violence and bloodshed, the strike ended in failure; but its lesson was clear. A prohibitive tariff wall might confer huge profits on monopolistic industries, but labor would get little enough. Cleveland's letter of acceptance hammered this point home. Labor troubles in other places added to Harrison's woes.

The "fat-frying" tactics of 1888 worked poorly in 1892. Industrialists contributed to the Republican campaign, but the amounts apparently were smaller. The McKinley Tariff rates were so high that the moderate reductions to be expected from the Democrats were not alarming. Spending for corrupt purposes, however, was not much in evidence.[4] The secret Australian ballot, already adopted by thirty-three states in 1892, made vote buying more difficult. Voters might still be bribed, but it was harder to check on their fidelity.

Another aspect of this dull campaign was the lethargy of the professional politicians. Quay, Platt, and Clarkson, the active leaders of 1888, were still sulking, and did little. Hanna of Ohio worked chiefly to advertise the virtues of William McKinley by having him speak for Harrison and

---

[4] Tabulations of campaign expenditures since 1860 list those of 1892 as the largest in any campaign to that time. However, the estimates are largely guesswork.

the tariff all the way from Iowa to Maine. Blaine, stricken by disease and the shock of the sudden death of his son Emmons, was in no condition to play his customary part. He visited Whitelaw Reid at his country estate in New York and read a ten-minute address to a crowd of citizens from the neighboring towns, his only speech of the campaign. He came to Washington shortly before the election, was cordially received by Harrison, and walked home from church with him. Within three months he was in his grave.

In the Democratic camp the indefatigable Whitney handled the campaign efficiently, without blunders. The central organization was small, and finances for a time troubled him; but his Wall Street contacts helped bring in the necessary funds. The biggest problem was Grover Cleveland. Promises of jobs and favors were foreign to his nature, and he could not forgive his enemies. In the midst of the campaign he broke with Henry Watterson, the powerful Kentucky editor; and the two were never reconciled. When Whitney undertook to gain the good will of the Hill machine, Cleveland would make no pledges as to patronage. Sensing a national victory, Hill and his cohorts fell in line and worked for the party, if not the candidate.

Whitney also advised Cleveland to take a more sympathetic attitude toward silver, as the newly organized Populists were charging him with subservience to the eastern money power. A vague sentence in his letter of acceptance about remedying "the wants of our people arising from the deficiency or imperfect distribution of money circulation" was the limit of his concession. However, Democratic state organizations in half a dozen western states where the Republicans had the upper hand joined forces with the Populists and gave twenty-two electoral votes to Weaver, the third-party leader.

While late indications pointed to a Democratic victory, the margin was surprising. It was a near landslide. Cleveland had the South, the doubtful northern group—New York, New Jersey, Connecticut, and Indiana—and normally Republican Illinois, Wisconsin, and California (except one elector). He also had 5 of Michigan's 14 (a Democratic legislature had districted the state for electors) and one from Ohio where a Democratic elector, oddly enough, led the ticket followed by 22 Republicans. Fusion in North Dakota produced one Cleveland elector also. The totals were: Cleveland, 277; Harrison, 145; Weaver, 22. The popular vote gave the victor a substantial margin.[5] Fusion arrangements with the Populists in some states gave Weaver many Democratic votes. In New York, Cleveland had a plurality of over 45,000; but the Empire State for once did not decide the result. The Democrats would have won without it.

The verdict was too decisive to be explained by anything except a widespread revulsion against Republican policies and an abiding confidence by voters of all classes in the integrity of Grover Cleveland. Had the four years which followed brought prosperity and domestic peace, he might have retired in 1897 with the popularity of a Coolidge. But panic, business collapse, unemployment and labor troubles, farmer discontent, and the strife of classes and sections brought out in a cruel light his fundamental conservatism, the negative character of his virtues, and the inflexibility of his mind. He saw only the necessity of resisting discontent; he did not know how to allay it. In the end his party was torn apart, and his leadership repudiated.

[5] The popular vote was as follows: Cleveland, 5,555,426; Harrison, 5,182,690; Weaver, 1,029,846; John Bidwell, Prohibitionist, 255,841; Simon Wing, Socialist Labor, 21,532. Forty-four states participated in the election, six having been admitted since 1888. Kansas, Idaho, Colorado, and Nevada chose Populist electors. North Dakota, carried by a Democratic-Populist coalition, gave Weaver and Cleveland each an electoral vote, while one Republican elector was successful. One Weaver elector was chosen in Oregon. A joint electoral ticket was defeated in Wyoming.

CHAPTER VII

McKINLEY AND BRYAN

1896–1900

1896

THE COUNTRY SEETHED with discontent during the depression following the Panic of 1893. Cleveland insisted on upholding the gold standard at all costs, to the anger of the inflationist silver-coinage forces. Labor was aroused over the federal government's drastic actions in the Pullman Strike at Chicago. The Supreme Court was sharply criticized for its five-to-four decision that the income tax (in the Wilson-Gorman Tariff of 1894) was unconstitutional.

The People's party, advocating free coinage of silver among its list of reforms, was threatening to swallow the Democratic party in the farmer-silver West and was challenging its control of the South. Democratic silver advocates such as veteran Congressman Richard P. Bland of Missouri and young William Jennings Bryan of Nebraska set to work to convert their party to free silver and make it a farmer-labor vehicle which might absorb Populism and unite South and West against the conservative East. The Republican party gained ground in the mid-term elections of 1894, but was also divided into "gold bugs" and "silver bugs."

The Republicans faced the currency problem first. Their national convention opened at St. Louis on June 16, 1896, with a new operator displacing the old state bosses at the controls.

Marcus A. Hanna, wealthy Cleveland business leader, was

better known as a fund raiser than a political manager when he formed an alliance with William McKinley, northeastern Ohio Congressman, author of the tariff law of 1890, war veteran, and experienced campaigner for public office. Hanna worked and spent to elect McKinley governor of Ohio for two terms, and then planned a pre-convention strategy to get him the Presidential nomination. He operated so skilfully that "he had the South practically solid before some of us waked up,"—Boss Platt's version. The old bosses encouraged favorite son candidacies but Hanna's lieutenants, such as Charles G. Dawes in Illinois, won delegates for McKinley over local favorites.

Hanna handled the currency problem skilfully. McKinley had been a "straddle bug" on the issue but reluctantly agreed to a gold plank. When the eastern leaders arrived, Hanna created the impression that he was not committed to the gold standard and seemed to capitulate to their demands as the convention opened. Actually his close associates had already drafted the gold plank that went into the platform. As adopted, it opposed the free coinage of silver except by international agreement which "we pledge ourselves to promote and until such agreement can be obtained the existing gold standard must be preserved."

A free silver substitute offered on the floor of the convention by Senator Henry M. Teller of Colorado was tabled, 818 1/2 to 105 1/2. Then followed a secession of twenty-four delegates and some alternates, nearly all from the silver-producing mountain states.

The platform blamed Democratic policies for the panic and depression and promised protective tariff to right things. It foreshadowed the imperialism of the next few years by its statements on foreign policy, but these were overlooked in the tumult over silver.

The balloting for President gave McKinley 661 1/2 votes; Speaker Thomas B. Reed, 84 1/2; Quay, 61 1/2; Levi P. Morton of New York, 58; William B. Allison of Iowa, 35 1/2; and Donald Cameron of Pennsylvania, 1. Garret A. Hobart of New Jersey, a loyal member of the McKinley organization, was nominated for Vice President.

The Democratic national convention opened at Chicago on July 7. The silver men were in control, but the credentials committee strengthened their hold by seating the Bryan delegation from Nebraska and awarding four Michigan seats to silver men. The resolutions committee presented a silver majority report and a gold minority report to the convention. David B. Hill of New York led the gold debaters. It was Bryan's good fortune to be the closing speaker on the silver side. His famous effort appeared to be extemporaneous, but he had tried out parts of the speech on smaller audiences in his pre-convention campaigning for silver, and only the arrangement was improvised. His magnificent voice reached every part of the great hall, and the audience responded "like a trained choir," he wrote afterward. He concluded with the sentence that has given the speech its name. "You shall not press down upon the brow of labor this crown of thorns, you shall not crucify mankind upon a cross of gold."

The majority report was upheld and an indorsement of Cleveland's administration voted down. The platform declared for the free and unlimited coinage of silver at the ratio of sixteen to one without waiting for the aid or consent of any other nation. It criticized the Supreme Court sharply for declaring the income tax unconstitutional, opposed the importation of foreign labor, favored arbitration of labor disputes, and denounced the use of injunctions by federal courts and federal interference in local affairs—a reference to the recent Pullman Strike. Other resolutions demanded enlargement of the powers of the Interstate Commerce Commission and condemned President Cleveland's bond sales to banking syndicates. Such a platform seemed anarchistic to conservative easterners, and 178 delegates refused to vote on the balloting for President.

Richard P. Bland of Missouri, veteran silver leader, and Senator Henry M. Teller of Colorado, bolting silver Republican, had been regarded as the favorites in the large field of candidates, but Bryan's electrifying speech had altered the situation. It took five ballots to dispose of instructions and pledges. On the fifth ballot Bryan had 652 of the 930 votes in the convention. He had celebrated his thirty-sixth birthday on the preceding 19th of March.

For the Vice Presidency Arthur Sewall of Maine, a shipbuilder, railroad director, and bank president—and yet a silver advocate—was named on the fifth ballot over John R. McLean of Ohio.

With their silver thunder stolen by the Democrats, the People's party, meeting at St. Louis on July 22, had a hard choice between independent action and expediency. The latter won. Bryan was indorsed but a separate candidate, Thomas E. Watson of Georgia, was named for Vice President. The platform was much more radical than the Democratic, but Bryan did not have to accept it. Thus the Populists became "Popocrats."

The bolting Silver Republicans and a National Silver party also joined the coalition by indorsing Bryan.

The Gold Democrats held a convention at Indianapolis on September 2 and nominated General John M. Palmer for President and General Simon B. Buckner of Kentucky for Vice President. By this strategy Cleveland, Carlisle, and other conservatives avoided voting Republican. But David B. Hill, who did not bolt, was quoted as saying, "I am still a Democrat, very still."

The action of the Democratic convention had upset the Republican plan of campaign. Expecting to throw the responsibility for the depression and the blunders of Cleveland's administration on the Democratic party and to advocate a return to a higher tariff as the way of economic salvation, the party of McKinley and Hanna had counted on an easy victory over a disorganized foe. But the Democrats had repudiated the Cleveland administration, had set up a standard to which all the forces of discontent were invited to repair, and were threatening to sweep the upper Mississippi valley from its Republican moorings with a far more plausible method of curing the hard times than Republican tariff policy. It was now poor strategy for the Republicans to center their guns on Cleveland as it would only antagonize the Gold Democrats whose support was worth attracting.

Instead, McKinley was forced to defend the existing gold standard, for which he had little heart, and place less emphasis on protection, in which he thoroughly believed. To make concessions to silver now would only play into Bryan's hands.

McKinley determined his own role in the canvass. A fluent public speaker, he could talk generalities more impressively than any man then in public life. His formal friendliness had none of Harrison's chill, and his solid figure and careful dress—with wing collar, starched shirt, long double-breasted coat, white vest, and red carnation—convinced audiences that they were looking at a statesman before he uttered a word. As a candidate for lesser offices, he had pleaded his own cause. But a Presidential candidate, he felt, must remain in dignified waiting until the voters made their decision. He then devised a curious compromise. He might not go to the people but the people might come to him. The idea of delegations and committees calling upon the candidate was familiar enough, but the excursions to Canton in 1896 amounted to mass pilgrimages. People came by the thousands in special trains—farmers, merchants, G.A.R. posts, railroad workers, religious and racial groups, and many others, often with their expenses paid—to see McKinley and listen to a few well chosen remarks, or, in the case of large delegations, a formal address of some length. Nothing was left to chance. McKinley would have no "Rum, Romanism and Rebellion" upset his careful planning. He invited the chairman of every visiting group to Canton ahead of time and asked him to submit his remarks in writing. These were carefully edited, unfortunate or embarrassing expressions deleted, and sometimes whole sections rewritten. Then, on the appointed day, the chairman would take his delegation to McKinley's home, recite his prepared speech to the appreciative candidate, and listen to a most felicitous response on the significant issues of the campaign, particularly attuned to the interests of the group of listeners. The speeches in this "front porch" campaign of course appeared in the newspapers and added to McKinley's stature as a candidate.

Hanna's management problem was not easy. No longer was

it one of raising sufficient funds to buy floaters in Indiana and deal with venal Tammany politicians in New York. The East seemed to be safely Republican, but every state west of Pennsylvania was listening to the silver siren. To win on such an extended front would require organization and propaganda on a large scale. Money must be provided by the wealthy East, if business and financial leaders wanted to save their system from the deluded "anarchists" of the midlands. The sums Hanna demanded seemed to be excessive in a period of business distress; but the wave of enthusiasm for Bryan immediately following his nomination, and the united front established by the silver groups, frightened bankers and businessmen and made Hanna's task easier. James J. Hill, railroad magnate, introduced him to Wall Street, and the money began to pour in. Ability to pay, not generosity, determined the contributions. For banks the assessment was fixed at one-quarter of 1 per cent of their capital. Life insurance companies contributed liberally, as did nearly all the great corporations. The Standard Oil Company gave $250,000 to Hanna's war chest. The audited accounts of the national committee revealed collections of about $3,500,000. Charles G. Dawes, who handled all funds at the Chicago headquarters, recorded in his diary a total of $1,962,325.59 spent at Chicago. He estimated the New York total at $1,600,000.00. The wild guesses of $10,000,-000 to $12,000,000 by unfriendly writers seem to be impossibly large.

Very little of this disappeared into the capacious pockets of grafting politicians. Hanna demanded results, and from the national headquarters in New York City and the well-organized regional headquarters at Chicago he directed his army of workers with admirable efficiency. A group of veteran political strategists managed the New York headquarters, but he entrusted the more important Chicago center to aggressive younger men including Henry C. Payne of Wisconsin, Charles G. Dawes of Chicago, W. T. Durbin of Indiana, and Cyrus Leland, Jr., of Kansas.

Pamphlets and leaflets by the millions were sent out from Chicago, some of them in seven or eight foreign languages, to catch the interest of voters of all classes, creeds, and nationalities. Everything from boiler-plate matter for small-town newspapers to McKinley buttons for schoolboys poured out of Hanna's mill, while billboards along country roads carried the likeness of "The Advance Agent of Prosperity." Some fourteen hundred speakers were available to preach the Republican gospel in the doubtful areas.

But as the campaign grew in heat and bitterness ugly aspects appeared for which Hanna had no direct responsibility. Men of wealth, alarmed at the enthusiasm aroused by Bryan and taking at face value the extreme utterances of Populist orators, fought back with powerful economic weapons in an attempt to coerce, where persuasion might fail. Labor, the uncertain partner in Bryan's poorly constructed farmer-labor coalition, was threatened with loss of employment in case Bryan won. Buyers gave orders for materials subject to cancellation if McKinley lost. In some cases workers were told not to report Wednesday morning after election unless McKinley won. Such methods, coupled with the steady pounding away at the workingman with the prosperity argument, made of little account the efforts of those champions of the downtrodden, Governor Altgeld of Illinois, Eugene V. Debs, and Henry George.

In farming areas pressure of a different sort was attempted. Reports went around that agents of the great insurance companies, large holders of farm mortgages, were promising extensions at lower rates of interest if McKinley were elected. This was used to offset the boon of easier credit supposed to come when free silver went into effect.

Bryan's campaign was almost a one-man show. The "Boy Orator of the Platte" was a novelty in American politics. The "Cross of Gold" speech had made him a popular hero, and Americans clamored to see and hear him. A front-porch campaign was out of the question. The only sensible strategy was to send him around the country to carry his message to the largest possible number. There followed the most famous stumping tour in American history.

His first trip East was made early in August to receive formal notification of his nomination at New York City.

The thousands that jammed Madison Square Garden wanted a fiery, fighting speech, a challenge to battle against the powers of mammon. Instead, the candidate read a carefully phrased but tiresome treatise on the economics of the currency question, while they squirmed and perspired, and some even departed. Opposition newspapers—nearly the whole metropolitan press—ridiculed the performance as a false alarm, and even the friendly *New York Journal* admitted that the audience was disappointed. Bryan had used a manuscript because he was in "the enemy country" and felt that he must make no slips in this keynote speech. This was a mistake. He had missed a great opportunity to arouse the eastern masses. Men of wealth slept more soundly after this.

The return trip provided opportunities for numerous speeches in upstate New York, Pennsylvania, and the Middle West as far north as Milwaukee. Bryan then made the most extensive trip of the campaign, a speaking tour all the way from Nebraska to Maine, and from the upper South to the Canadian border. The Middle West, the great battleground, received most attention. The trip ended at Lincoln, Nebraska, his home town, the Sunday before the election. He devoted Monday, November 2 to his home state, addressing twenty-seven audiences on that day. All together, by his own estimates, he covered 18,009 miles and made some six hundred speeches to possibly five million persons. Fears that his magnificent voice would not hold out led to all manner of throat treatments—compresses, gargles, cough drops; but finally he discarded them all and found his vocal chords in fine condition at the end of his oratorical marathon.

Democratic difficulties centered around money and the fusion of the silver forces. The paltry $650,000 with which they tried to match Hanna's millions was the smallest fund since Hancock's campaign of 1880. But for the contributions of a group of wealthy silver-mine owners, the campaign chest would have been insignificant. On the other hand, donations from the Republican national committee solved in part the financial problem of those Democrats who had bolted and nominated Palmer and Buckner.

Securing the cooperation of all the silver forces was an

awkward problem. Three organized parties—Democratic, Populist, and National Silver, each with its national committee—and a group of Silver Republicans were supporting Bryan and attempting to preserve their separate identities at the same time. The Populists even had their own Vice Presidential candidate, Tom Watson, and a platform which Bryan did not accept. This duality was solved by the nomination of joint electoral tickets of "Popocrats" with part of the electors apportioned to Bryan and Sewall and part to Bryan and Watson. In twenty-six states where division was agreed upon, Sewall had 198 possible electoral votes to Watson's 78. Watson naturally resented this arrangement as it rendered his defeat certain. Even if Bryan won, he would finish third and the Senate would choose from the two highest, Hobart and Sewall. Yet no other course was possible. Except in Louisiana, Arkansas, and North Carolina, the Democrats of the South rejected fusion, forcing the Populists to accept their tickets. In a few states separate electoral tickets for Bryan and Watson were nominated; but they had no effect on the election.

Fusion on state and Congressional tickets was far more complicated and was not always achieved. In the South the Populists tended to work with the Republicans; in the West, with the Democrats, though the independent Silver Republicans followed their own course and fusion became confusion in the mountain states.

The Bryan campaign headquarters, despite limited funds, sent out a considerable amount of literature. The best-known piece used by either side was *Coin's Financial School*. A primer of the silver question first published in 1894 by William H. Harvey, a lawyer then living in Chicago, it recited in simple dialogue the merits of free coinage of silver, leaving the gold advocates in its pages utterly confounded. The cracker-box philosophy of the little book, like the panacea of the later Townsend Plan, struck home in a period of hard times and gave it a circulation of several millions.

One of Bryan's greatest handicaps was lack of newspaper support in the larger cities. The Republican press, the independent journals, the influential weeklies such as *Harper's*

Weekly, the *Nation,* and the *Independent,* and most of the larger Democratic papers in the metropolitan centers were against him. In New York City only William Randolph Hearst's *Journal* was loyal; even Pulitzer's *World* joined the bolters. Not again until 1936 was there such a journalistic phalanx on one side of a great political contest.

Near-hysteria seemed to grip the conservative East by autumn, and a campaign of fear and hate broke loose that outdid in vituperation the most rabid utterances of the Populists. Bryan was derided as a boy orator and a political faker; but more effective was the cartoon representation of him in *Harper's Weekly* as a huge silver dollar with Governor Altgeld of Illinois, the "anarchist," hiding behind him. Altgeld had outraged conservatives by pardoning the anarchists imprisoned for the Haymarket bombing of 1886, in Chicago. Bryan was now linked with Altgeld and Debs, the Pullman strike leader, in a trinity of subversive infamy. Theodore Roosevelt compared them in a campaign speech to "the leaders of the Terror of France in mental and moral attitude"; and he declared in an unguarded moment in a private conversation later made public that he expected to meet Altgeld and his followers "sword to sword on the field of battle." The metropolitan Protestant pulpit entered the campaign, and many eminent reverend figures, including T. DeWitt Talmage and Charles H. Parkhurst, upheld the cross of gold.

Against the tide of abuse and denunciation Hearst's *New York Journal* retaliated in kind. Its cartoonist, Homer Davenport, pictured Hanna invariably as a bloated plutocrat stamped with dollar signs, and McKinley as his puppet. Alfred Henry Lewis wrote articles so offensive that Hanna, unaccustomed to this political in-fighting, considered court action; but he decided that this might be just what Hearst wanted.

As Election Day approached, close observers could see that the result was no longer in doubt. After weeks and weeks of careful work the great Hanna organization had everything in hand. The Middle West, the battleground, was safe. Historians have usually given some credit to a fortuitous circumstance. The wheat crop of 1896 was a bumper one, yet a heavy foreign demand in the fall brought a sharp rise in price. This came without free silver and may have helped the Republican argument for gold; but the higher wheat prices seem to have benefited speculators rather than farmers, and prices of other products continued to slump.

Before midnight November 3, Bryan knew that he was beaten. The Middle West as far as Minnesota, North Dakota, and Iowa had gone Republican, as had the East, the southern border states of Delaware, Maryland, West Virginia, and Kentucky, and California and Oregon on the Pacific coast. McKinley had 271 electoral votes to Bryan's 176. Bryan had the South and the newer western farming and mining states, admitted after 1860, except North Dakota, and also one elector each from California and Kentucky.

McKinley had 7,098,474 popular votes; Bryan, 6,379,830 including fusion electoral tickets.[1] Both Houses of Congress were Republican by safe margins.

Bryan had failed to corral the industrial workers. The cities outside the South and the silver-mining West were nearly all Republican. Hanna had sold the prospects of prosperity and good wages to labor, though pressure and intimidation played a part. Bryan's farm vote fell short of his expectations. The debt-burdened and impoverished followed him; the better off, as so often in the past, voted Republican. The rural South and the silver-mining states did as expected, but his margin of victory in the distressed Populist belt was small, for cities and towns voted against him. In the older

[1] John M. Palmer, Gold Democrat, had 131,529; Joshua Levering, Prohibitionist, 141,676; Charles E. Bentley, National Party (Prohibition seceders), 13,969; Charles H. Matchett, Socialist Labor, 36,454. Bryan's total is often given as 6,467,946, or even higher, by adding in the votes cast for him on independent electoral tickets running against regular Democratic candidates. In Texas a separate Populist ticket polled 77,985 votes. For the elections from 1896 through 1916 I have supplemented the popular vote of the major parties given in E. E. Robinson, *The Presidential Vote, 1896–1932* (Stanford University Press, 1934), with the vote given by the *World Almanac* for minor parties. For the elections 1920–1964, I have used *America at the Polls* (Pittsburgh, 1965), compiled and edited by Richard Scammon.

Middle West he shared the farm vote with McKinley, but in the rural parts of the East he failed badly. He lost every county in New England and carried but one in New York. He ran proportionately better in the seaboard cities than in the neighboring country districts. His effort to unite South and West was too late by at least two decades. Industrialism and urbanization, spreading westward, even had outposts beyond the Mississippi, while the older farm states were almost as conservative as the East.

The People's party had been swallowed by the Democratic party; but it had liberalized the older organization in the process, and while its reform program was forgotten in the din raised over silver, the best features were to be revived and accepted later by the major parties. Even free silver was vindicated in a way, for unexpectedly large increases in the world's gold supply provided the currency expansion Bryan and the "Popocrats" were demanding.

1900

The violent shift of American political issues from domestic problems to foreign relations made McKinley's term of office very different from what he had expected. The Spanish-American War, the acquisition of Puerto Rico and the Philippines, the annexation of Hawaii, and the demand for an interoceanic canal tell the story of the breakdown of isolation and the emergence of America as a world power. The angry voices of the Leases, the Donnellys, and the other prophets of Populism fell on deaf ears as prosperity returned and imperialism took over the political stage. The Gold Standard Act of 1900 seemed to settle the currency problem, and Republicans gave the new Dingley Tariff much of the credit for the good times.

The Republicans held their convention at Philadelphia on June 19, 1900, with everything but the Vice Presidential nomination planned in advance by the President and Mark Hanna. The gold standard, the Dingley Tariff, the Spanish-American War, and the fruits of the new adventure in glory were extolled in the long platform. McKinley refused to express a preference for a running mate, and after his own nomination by acclamation, the delegates took matters out of Hanna's hands by nominating Theodore Roosevelt, governor of New York, and Rough Rider hero of the Spanish-American War. Behind the scenes Boss Platt of New York, who wanted to keep Roosevelt from another term as governor, and Boss Quay of Pennsylvania, who had some scores to pay with Hanna, helped manipulate the stampede. Roosevelt had been reluctant to run, but, to Hanna's annoyance, decided to accept the nomination.

The Democrats again turned to Bryan, still the popular hero to the masses of Democratic voters. The chief problem faced by the national convention at Kansas City on July 4 was indorsement of free coinage of silver. Bryan insisted on it over the opposition of eastern delegates and some of his own friends and had his way. The platform attacked Republican imperialism and the administration's policies toward Cuba, Puerto Rico, and the Philippines, and demanded more stringent anti-trust laws. Bryan was renominated with much enthusiasm and former Vice President Adlai Stevenson was named as his running mate.

The Populists were divided. A fusion group and some Silver Republicans indorsed Bryan, but a middle-of-the-road group ran independent candidates. A newly formed Socialist party nominated Eugene V. Debs.

Although insistent that free silver go into the platform, Bryan did not plead for it in his campaign but made imperialism the paramount issue, with the trust question second in importance. He attempted as in 1896 to make it a struggle between democracy and plutocracy, but the class and sectional appeal was less evident in 1900. He appeared rather as the defender of American liberal traditions in opposing an imperialism that would exploit weaker peoples, "civilize with dynamite and proselyte with the sword." He promised in his notification speech at Indianapolis before fifty thousand people to set up a stable form of government in the Philippines, and then to give the people independence under American protection. The strong religious strain in Bryan came to the surface repeatedly in his assaults upon the immorality of holding weaker peoples in subjection. "The command 'Go ye into all the world and preach the Gospel to every creature' has no Gatling gun attachment," he shouted. Imperialism had no warrant in the Bible, he insisted, and he flung scriptural citations at the Republicans with the fervor of a traveling evangelist.

However, the Democratic candidate began to shift his emphasis as the campaign went on. The dangers of imperialism were not arousing the voters. The woes of the little brown brothers whom unsympathetic American soldiers were "civilizing with a Krag" were not like the woes of the debt-burdened agrarians four years earlier. Then Bryan had voiced magnificently the demands of impoverished Americans for a more abundant life, and his words had struck home. In 1900 he was preaching sermons to well-fed audiences on the right of self-determination for far-away Filipinos. His appeal was not much more exciting than that of a returned foreign missionary seeking funds for Christianizing the heathen. "It sounded like music, and it read like the prophets of old," was one listener's comment on a Bryan speech. But it was not stirring the masses. Bryan sensed this, and he began to play up the trust question and the need to curb special privilege. This was a note more in keeping with the Bryan of 1896 and, under more propitious circumstances, might have been powerfully effective. But Americans, relaxing from the stresses and strains of the depression years, were content for a season to enjoy the fruits of prosperity without examining too closely the warped and misshapen tree that produced them. Bryan was on the right track but he had chosen the wrong moment.

His plan of campaign, like that of 1896, involved a long speaking tour, and large crowds turned out. In the East he was particularly well received. Richard Croker, head of Tammany, had become a Bryan convert—from reading the candidate's book, *The First Battle*, so he said—and the Tammany braves made the welkin ring when the Nebraskan descended on Madison Square Garden. "Great is Tammany," said Bryan, "and Croker is his prophet." But the Gold Democrats were still hostile. Had Bryan abandoned free silver, most of them would have supported him, for nearly all were anti-imperialists. Instead many voted for McKinley, as in 1896.

Cleveland apparently did not vote. He refused to say a word that could be construed as an indorsement of either candidate, despite all manner of requests that he commit himself. While bitter towards "Bryanism," he could not swallow "McKinleyism." Richard Olney, Judson Harmon, William L. Wilson, and J. Sterling Morton—all former members of his cabinet—and the veteran editor, Henry Watterson, chose Bryan as the lesser evil. "I am going to shut my eyes, hold my nose, vote, go home and disinfect myself," wrote Morton to his old chief.

Among Republican anti-imperialists the problem was equally difficult. Andrew Carnegie, Senators Hoar and Hale, and many other old-fashioned Republicans found Bryan's silver views and his reputation for instability sufficient justification for a vote for McKinley. Thomas B. Reed, eased out of the Speakership and now retired from politics, took refuge in a stony and embittered silence. Carl Schurz, despite his lifelong advocacy of sound money, accepted Bryan, though with a wry face. George S. Boutwell, Secretary of the Treasury under Grant and now heading the Anti-Imperialist League, and Erving Winslow, the League's secretary, gave loyal support to the Nebraskan, but Republican bolters were not very numerous. It is doubtful whether the omission of the silver plank would have drawn many of these Republican anti-imperialist conservatives to Bryan. He repelled them in too many other ways. In the end, the difficulty of uniting Gold Democrats, Bryan Democrats, Populists, Silver Republicans, and anti-imperialists on one ticket was too great to be overcome.

Hanna's management of McKinley's campaign involved fewer problems than in 1896. His organization functioned efficiently, and collected approximately $2,500,000 principally from big business interests pleased with McKinley's policies and fearful of Bryan's antitrust program. The party machine under Hanna had become a systematic, well organized business that could be trusted to conduct a campaign honestly and efficiently. No special favors were granted, as a Wall Street group discovered when its ten-thousand-dollar contribution was returned because it had strings attached to it.

McKinley was now more than ever averse to descending from his pedestal, and so the defense of the administration was turned over to the hero of San Juan Hill—known to the average man as "Teddy," though Roosevelt thoroughly disliked the nickname. His tours were a grand success. In part, he followed Bryan's trail; and the duel of these two rabble rousers gave color to a campaign that was otherwise apathetic. Bryan preached—Roosevelt shouted. The Nebraskan quoted Scripture—the Rough Rider waved the flag. The great Democratic leader was an artist with words—his Republican rival was a better tub thumper. Roosevelt's voice, often cracking into a high falsetto, began to give way toward the end; but he waved his arms and pounded his fists and at least impressed his audiences with his tremendous vigor and his certainty as to what was right. References to "my opponent" made it almost seem as if Roosevelt himself were running for the Presidency.[2] No Vice Presidential candidate had ever before stolen the show from the head of the ticket.

Hanna had become a successful stump speaker since 1896, and the organization functioned so efficiently that he could devote some time to campaigning. People wanted to see the bloated, dollar-decorated ogre of the hostile cartoons, and there were many requests for him. Invariably he captured his audiences. A genial, unaffected soul, he spoke to a thousand in the same informal manner that he talked to three or four. He would talk on whatever came into his head at the moment, and his listeners liked it. In 1900 he confined most of his attention to South Dakota and Nebraska, home states of his particular enemy Senator R. F. Pettigrew, bolt-

---

[2] Mrs. Bryan, in the joint memoirs of her husband and herself, inadvertently refers to his defeat "by Mr. Roosevelt" in 1900.

ing Silver Republican, and of Bryan. His invasion of South
Dakota partook of the nature of a private vendetta, for Pettigrew had attacked the validity of his election to the Senate. McKinley, dubious about the undertaking, sent an
resigning as chairman, but his old loyalty soon reasserted itself. However, he went ahead with his tour.
emissary to dissuade the national chairman. Hanna, discovering who had sent his caller, answered angrily, "Return to
Washington, and tell the President that God hates a coward."
Sensitive over this reflection on his judgment, he considered

Accompanied by Victor Dolliver of Iowa and Senator Frye
of Maine, Hanna stumped the Populist belt by special train.
Large crowds gathered at every stop, and occasionally he
was heckled. At one place a sign read: *"Populist Farmers,
Beware ! ! Chain Your Children to Yourselves or Put Them
Under the Bed. Mark Hanna Is in Town."* But his good humor, his sallies of rough wit, and his blunt, straightforward
style of speaking won admirers everywhere and helped dispel the bogy-man belief where it was most strongly held.
It was disarming to the crowds of farmers at little railroad
stations to hear the generalissimo of plutocracy in his own
defense. In a tour lasting one week he made seventy-two
speeches.

In declaring that there was but one issue in the campaign,
"Let well enough alone," Hanna touched upon the strongest
argument of the Republicans. Economic conditions were so
much improved that "the full dinner pail" became the slogan
of party orators and newspapers. Only in a limited sense
was the election a referendum on imperialism.

The defeat of the Democrats was greater than in 1896.
McKinley had 292 electoral votes to Bryan's 155, compared
with the earlier 271 to 176. He added Kansas, Nebraska,
South Dakota, Utah, Wyoming, and Washington to his total,
more than making up for the loss of Kentucky. The silver
states, Colorado, Idaho, Montana, and Nevada, remained
loyal to the Democrats, but the entire agricultural West was
again Republican. Bryan had the South as before, though
West Virginia, Maryland, and Delaware on the border were
still Republican. The popular vote was: McKinley, 7,218,491;

Bryan, 6,356,734.[8] The former had exceeded his total of 1896, while Bryan had declined proportionately. Hanna was delighted. Even Nebraska was Republican and Pettigrew lost his Senate seat from South Dakota.

[8] The other candidates had these totals: Woolley, Prohibition, 209,157; Debs, Social Democratic, 94,864; Malloney, Socialist Labor, 33,432; Barker, Populist ("Middle-of-the-Road"), 50,599; Ellis, Union Reform, 5,698; Leonard, United Christian, 1,059.

CHAPTER VIII

PROGRESSIVISM AND WAR

1904–1916

1904

McKINLEY'S ASSASSINATION brought "that damned cowboy" into the Presidency and shifted party leadership from Hanna and the standpatters to the energetic, pugnacious, reforming "T. R." The latter responded to a growing progressive sentiment for ending the capitalist-politician partnership in the temple of government by instituting anti-trust suits and asking for legislation for more effective regulation of railroads and large-scale business enterprises. Hanna avoided a clash with the President, but his death in 1904 removed the only possible obstacle in Roosevelt's path to the nomination for another term.

The Republican national convention at Chicago, June 21–23, was a tame affair. The platform pointed with pride and promised a continuance of the McKinley-Roosevelt policies, but left it to the candidate to clarify its generalities. The 994 delegates nominated Roosevelt by acclamation and put Senator Charles Warren Fairbanks of Indiana, a staid conservative, on the ticket with him.

The conservative Democrats, with Bryanism twice turned down, wanted a safe-and-sane easterner on a conservative platform to draw business support and turn the tables on the Republicans, afflicted with a problem child as unpredictable as he was uncontrollable. A dearth of northern governors and Senators forced them to turn to the bench. Judge

Alton B. Parker of the New York court of appeals seemed to be the best solution. Journalist William Randolph Hearst offered himself with a reform program but did not fit the situation. Parker was nominated on the first ballot over Hearst and some favorite sons. Bryan conducted a battle for a liberal platform and secured a strong anti-trust plank and some other liberal commitments.

The platform's silence on the gold standard evoked a telegram from Parker pledging himself to uphold it and offering to decline the nomination if this was unsatisfactory to the majority. Bryan and his following were incensed, but the convention voted that the gold standard had been omitted because it was not an issue and that Parker's views did not preclude him from accepting the nomination.

The convention nominated wealthy eighty-year-old Henry Gassaway Davis of West Virginia for Vice President. From Republican sources came this gibe at the Democratic ticket —"an enigma from New York and a ruin from West Virginia."

The convention had not actually healed the breach in the party. The Bryanites were angry and, without bolting, gave only a perfunctory support to Parker. Bryan took the stump, but his purpose was to retain his hold on the masses of Democrats and to recover control of the party after the election. He was shrewdly demonstrating his regularity to teach the bolters of 1896 a lesson in loyalty. Ten days before the election he announced in the *Commoner*, for many years his personal organ, his intention of reorganizing the party "along radical lines."

The general management of the Democratic campaign was in the hands of Thomas Taggart, chairman of the national committee and Indiana's shrewdest politician, with William F. Sheehan of New York at the head of the executive committee. But the hoped-for support of the business interests did not materialize. August Belmont, Thomas F. Ryan, Daniel S. Lamont, and a few other loyal Democrats helped, but Republican businessmen were not to be weaned away from the party that had protected their interests. E. H. Harriman, J. P. Morgan, George J. Gould, James Stillman, H. C. Frick, the Standard Oil interests, and a number of other wealthy corporations and individuals contributed liberally to the Roosevelt cause. The Republican candidate knew big business was supporting him; but Cornelius N. Bliss, treasurer of the national committee, kept his own books on the more than two millions he raised, and Roosevelt showed no unseemly curiosity.[1] His attitude toward the trusts had not changed, but he maintained a discreet and dignified silence during the campaign, sticking to the Presidential tradition of abstaining from speech-making. His excessively long letter of acceptance reviewed the measures and policies of his administration and invited the opposition to make them the issues.

That even a huge campaign chest could have elected Parker is highly improbable. Regardless of the fact that the Democratic platform was more liberal, the voters tended to regard Roosevelt as the dynamic progressive and Parker as the cautious conservative. Even if Parker had attempted a vigorous offensive, it would have spoiled the picture of the well balanced, dignified judge who was to save the nation from the erratic, spectacular "T. R." The Democratic candidate belonged in the Republican camp, conducting a front-porch campaign, while Roosevelt, given the leadership of the opposition, would have been freed from his inhibitions and could have assailed Wall Street, the trusts, and the corruptions of boss rule with sledge-hammer blows. The labels were mixed in 1904.

The achievements of Roosevelt were so generally popular that Democratic guns had to be leveled at methods rather than measures. Even the much criticized "rape of Panama" was an asset to Roosevelt. To the average man it meant merely that the canal, talked about for a quarter of a century, would be built at once instead of encountering further delays. Old issues were devoid of interest, while Roosevelt's trust prosecutions deprived the Democrats of ammunition in that area. Of necessity they assailed the man and his meth-

[1] Not until the investigations of the Clapp Committee of the Senate in 1912 was the extent of corporation contributions revealed, although much had been surmised before this.

ods. Bryan attacked him for sword waving and militarism, and Henry Watterson called him "as sweet a gentleman as ever scuttled a ship or cut a throat." More staidly the Parker Constitutional Club of eminent New York lawyers pointed to Roosevelt's "arbitrary usurping of legislative functions" and his "massing enormous power in his own hands," and called for a man of "safe tendencies."

The dull campaign furnished only one lively incident, near the close. Joseph Pulitzer of the New York *World*, with his keen perception of realities, pointed to Republican Chairman Cortelyou's former headship of the Department of Commerce and Labor, containing the Bureau of Corporations, which had been strangely inactive since its creation. Did the corporations, pouring money into the campaign, assume that they were buying protection? Pulitzer called on Roosevelt to make public the contributions of big business. The Republican candidate was silent, but when Parker, rather belatedly, repeated the insinuations about Cortelyou and the Bureau of Corporations he angrily termed the charge a wicked falsehood. The campaign closed on this triumphantly righteous note.

Roosevelt did not deny the fact of corporation contributions, though not informed by Cortelyou and Bliss of their extent. In one case at least he was personally responsible. Alarmed at the prospect of defeat for the Republican state ticket (and possibly the national ticket) in New York because of local issues, he invited Edward H. Harriman, the railroad magnate, to the White House and asked him to raise funds to save the day. Harriman returned to New York and raised $250,000, which he turned over to Treasurer Bliss. Over a year later he wrote to a friend explaining his relations with Roosevelt. In April, 1907, the letter, sold by a discharged employee, appeared in the New York *World*. Roosevelt, angry over Harriman's hostility toward railroad legislation and cynical remarks about his ability to buy legislatures and courts, flamed at this revelation of their former relations. "I never requested Mr. Harriman to raise a dollar for the Presidential campaign of 1904," he stormed, insisting that the story was utterly false. The money was for the *state ticket.* Roosevelt seemed to be arguing that $250,000 spent on behalf of the state ticket would have no influence on the outcome of the national election in the Empire State.

But no revelations of corporation connection with the Republican campaign could have saved the Democrats. Roosevelt had captured the popular imagination, and nothing short of a complete economic collapse could have prevented his election. Even in that contingency he might have escaped by blaming Wall Street. Not since Jackson had there been such a popular hero. The king could do no wrong. And so Judge Parker went down to defeat on November 8 by a record-breaking margin in the popular vote. Roosevelt had 7,628,461; Parker, 5,084,223.[2] Only the South remained loyal to the Democrats—Missouri, West Virginia, and Maryland (popular vote) were lost. Roosevelt had 336 electoral votes to 140 for Parker, the largest majority since the Grant-Greeley election of 1872, when the South was under carpet-bag rule. Both Houses of Congress were Republican by large majorities. The Democratic conservatives' bid for power had been a disastrous failure.

Roosevelt celebrated his astounding triumph with an amazing blunder. On election night he issued this statement: "The wise custom which limits the President to two terms regards the substance and not the form, and under no circumstances will I be a candidate for or accept another nomination." This most energetic of Presidents, barely forty-six years of age, was relegating himself permanently to the painful estate of an ex-President at the expiration of his term. In effect, he was notifying the party leaders in Congress that his power to reward and punish was of limited duration. For so astute a politician the statement was inexcusable. Exuberance over his great victory had betrayed

[2] Maryland gave Roosevelt one electoral vote, Parker the rest. Delaware was consistently Republican from 1896 to 1936, except for 1912. The vote of the minor parties was as follows: Swallow, Prohibition, 259,257; Debs, Socialist, 402,460; Watson, People's, 114,753; Corregan, Socialist Labor, 33,724. Debs's vote had risen from 94,768 in 1900 to 402,460—a surprising increase, indicating a growing protest against the conservatism of the major parties.

his judgment. The club of a possible third term (in his case actually a second elective term) would have served him well in dealing with a recalcitrant Congress in the years to follow. And in 1912 he was made painfully aware of this entirely unnecessary pledge when he chose to run again.

1908

Roosevelt's second term did not produce the results he had expected. The Hepburn Act—extending the powers of the Interstate Commerce Commission over railroad rates—a Meat Inspection Act, and a Pure Food and Drugs Act, were major achievements, but the Senate led by Nelson W. Aldrich of Rhode Island and the House under Speaker Joseph Cannon blocked further Roosevelt reform measures, especially after the Wall Street panic of 1907.

To stop rumors that he wanted a third term and to provide a successor after his own heart, Roosevelt decided to back Secretary of War William Howard Taft of Ohio, who had been a federal judge and the first civil governor of the Philippines. The southern delegates, usually chosen by federal officeholders, were easily drawn into the Taft-Roosevelt fold, and in the northern states only a group of favorite sons, called the "Allies," offered opposition.

Chicago was again the scene of the national convention, which opened on June 16, 1908. The problem of 223 contested seats, mostly from the South, was solved in Taft's favor in most cases. A proposal to reduce southern representation—the party's rotten borough system—was defeated by a narrow margin. The platform, far too long for what it contained, declared for revision of the tariff, strengthening of the anti-trust law, conservation of natural resources, and a more elastic currency.

A last-minute attempt to stampede the convention for Roosevelt had gallery support for forty-six minutes, but Chairman Henry Cabot Lodge stopped it with the roll call. Taft had 702 votes and the opposition 277. Veteran Congressman James S. Sherman, an arch-conservative member of Speaker Cannon's inner circle, was New York's choice for

Vice President; he was nominated with 816 of 979 votes cast.

Having tried Parker and conservatism, the Democrats were ready for Bryan again, when the delegates assembled at hospitable Denver on July 7. A progressive platform, largely the Commoner's own handiwork, included downward revision of the tariff, more teeth in the anti-trust laws, an income tax, direct election of United States Senators, and restrictions on the use of injunctions in labor disputes. A seventy-minute demonstration greeted the presentation of Bryan's name. The one ballot gave him 888 1/2 votes to 59 1/2 for Governor John A. Johnson of Minnesota and 46 for Judge George Gray of Delaware. John Worth Kern, an Indiana Bryanite, was nominated for Vice President.

The usual array of minor parties presented candidates, and a new one appeared. The Socialists again offered Eugene V. Debs with high hopes of another large gain in voting strength. The Socialist Labor party named August Gillhaus and the Prohibitionists Eugene W. Chafin. The feeble remnant of Populists made their last stand, led by the veteran agrarian Tom Watson. The new party was the Independence party, a Hearst-financed, one-ring circus with Thomas L. Hisgen as candidate and Hearst as ringmaster. Its platform, occupying ground between the Democrats and Socialists, was decidely progressive. Hearst had not yet tossed overboard the liberalism of his early years, though his recent dealings with Tammany had made progressives view him with suspicion.

The Republican campaign got under way slowly. Taft, burdened with his judicial temperament, would have preferred a front-porch affair but was persuaded that stumping was necessary to counteract the appeal of Bryan. Frank H. Hitchcock, his manager, withheld the Republican fire for the closing weeks, and as late as September Bryan and Taft seemed to be running neck and neck. Then Taft went on the stump, Hearst attempted to expose men prominent in both parties, Roosevelt started a debate by letter with Bryan, and the tepid campaign warmed up a little.

Hearst had secured letters from the files of the Standard Oil Company revealing that Ohio Republican Senator Foraker and Governor C. N. Haskell of Oklahoma, treasurer of the Democratic national committee, had had intimate connections with the great oil trust. Foraker defended himself by showing that his dealings with Standard Oil were on a purely business basis; but the fact that a United States Senator, in a period of bitter public feeling toward trusts, had sought favors from the most hated of the species was enough to damn him. Roosevelt, with the Hepburn bill and the Brownsville affair[3] fresh in his memory, was eager to destroy Foraker and urged Taft not to appear with him at a public meeting. Foraker solved the problem for Taft by staying away, but Roosevelt was not satisfied. "He ought to throw Foraker over with a bump," he wrote to his son-in-law. "I have decided to put a little vim into the campaign by making a publication of my own."

His "publication" was an interview attacking Bryan for retaining Haskell as campaign treasurer and showing that Taft, by contrast, had refused to have dealings with Foraker long before. Then followed a lively public controversy between Bryan and Roosevelt. Bryan went back to 1904 to show that the President's skirts were not clean of corporation assistance. He charged that the trust magnates were supporting Taft, and demanded publicity for all contributions. Charges and countercharges followed, Haskell resigning as treasurer in the midst of the controversy.

The question of publicity of campaign contributions, raised by Bryan, was an awkward one. He had announced earlier that a $10,000 limit would be placed on individual contributions, and that the names of donors of more than $100 would be made public. The Republicans were embarrassed, but Taft declared that the law of New York State,

---

[3] Brownsville, Texas, had been mysteriously shot up on the night of August 13, 1906, presumably by colored soldiers of a United States infantry regiment stationed there. One man was killed and another wounded. The evidence of guilt was not very clear, but the President dismissed three companies from the service on the ground that the men not guilty had refused to expose the culprits. Foraker defended the soldiers in the Senate and criticized Roosevelt. The two men clashed bitterly at a banquet of the Gridiron Club, famed Washington press club.

which required a statement of receipts and expenditures after the election, would be observed. This was less frank than the Democratic position but was in advance of earlier methods. Roosevelt privately protested to the Republican campaign treasurer, George R. Sheldon, against reported requests for funds from John D. Archbold of Standard Oil and Edward H. Harriman. Sheldon responded with the disagreeable information that Standard Oil money had been accepted in 1904, contrary to Roosevelt's wishes. Neither party was particularly well financed in 1908, though as usual the Republicans fared better than their rivals.

Apart from the interest injected by Roosevelt, the campaign dragged. Trusts, tariff, and currency developed no sharp differences. Taft declared that the ambiguous Republican tariff plank meant revision downward, which seemed to place the parties rather close together on this question. Samuel Gompers, head of the American Federation of Labor, indorsed Bryan because of the anti-injunction plank in his platform, but there was little evidence of any pronounced swing of labor to the Democrats.

Bryan found that Roosevelt's liberalism had cut the ground from under his feet in the West while the East, as in his earlier campaigns, saw no reason to change its Republican allegiance. He was no longer the glamorous "Boy Orator of the Platte," but a middle-aged political preacher whose ideas, fed to Chautauqua audiences year after year, had become a familiar story. Roosevelt had altered his opinion of the Nebraskan for the better since 1896 and now spoke of him as "a kindly man and well meaning in a weak way; always provided that to mean well must not be translated by him into doing well if it would interfere with his personal prospects. But he is the cheapest fakir we have ever had proposed for President." Yet a conservative Republican of the McKinley stamp would have found this "fakir" a formidable opponent. The country was turning liberal, but Roosevelt had postponed the day of reckoning for his party by giving it the habiliments of reform.

November 3 wrote finis to Bryan's efforts to be elected

President. He had 6,412,294 votes to Taft's 7,675,320.[4] His total was larger, but his percentage was slightly smaller, than in 1896 or 1900. His popular vote was far above Parker's in 1904, but his electoral defeat was almost as bad, for he had only 162 to Taft's 321. He had the usual southern bloc plus six of Maryland's eight electoral votes, Kentucky, newly admitted Oklahoma, Colorado, Nevada, and his home state, Nebraska. The rest of the North and West and Missouri, West Virginia, and Delaware went Republican as in 1904. Judged by the total vote, the Democratic party was no better off than it had been when Bryan ran before. It had merely recovered the ground lost by Parker.

But there were bright spots in the Democratic picture. Bryan's vote was less sectional and better distributed than before. In five states carried by Taft, Democratic governors were chosen. In several other states Republican state candidates ran far behind the head of the ticket. The progressive movement was spreading eastward. Unless the dominant Republicans recognized reform demands, a reviving Democracy under new leadership might serve the purpose of the progressives.

1912

Beginning with the Payne-Aldrich Tariff, Taft antagonized the progressive Republicans by his measures and actions, and by the aid and comfort he gave to the standpat elements in the party. Roosevelt, returning from an African hunting trip, was soon campaigning for progressive Republicans and drawing away from Taft. His speeches and editorial comments in the *Outlook* clashed with Taft's basically conservative views and policies and brought on the break in 1912.

Progressive Republicans, fearing that Senator LaFollette of Wisconsin, their original choice, could not defeat Taft, put pressure on Roosevelt to run after LaFollette had suf-

---

[4] The minor parties had these totals: Debs, Socialist, 420,820; Chafin, Prohibition, 252,683; Hisgen, Independence, 83,563; Watson, People's, 28,131; Gillhaus, Socialist Labor, 13,825.

fered a temporary breakdown. Roosevelt was easy to persuade and the battle of 1912 was on. The President and the ex-President, now bitter rivals, stumped the important states having primaries, and soon name-calling prevailed over discussions of principles. The net result of a dozen primaries gave Roosevelt 278 delegates; Taft, 48; LaFollette, 36. In the convention states, the organizations gave Taft most of the delegates. The Roosevelt forces, charging fraud and trickery, especially in the southern states, sent contesting delegates for 254 of the 1,078 seats.

The Taft forces, controlling the national committee, gave the seats to their claimants in most cases. This was the situation when the national convention opened its sessions in the Coliseum at Chicago on June 18. The test vote, taken on electing a temporary chairman, was 558 to 501 for the Taft choice, Elihu Root, who also became permanent chairman. Defeated in the credentials committee and on the floor of the convention, the Roosevelt forces refused to participate further in the proceedings.

Taft was renominated with 501 votes. Roosevelt received 107; LaFollette, 41; Cummins, 17; Hughes, 2; not voting 349. Vice President Sherman was also renominated. A rather liberal platform had been adopted and forgotten.

The convention was one of the most disorderly on record. The pro-Roosevelt galleries added to the tumult with boos and whistle imitations of steam rollers. Roosevelt came to Chicago to direct the strategy and told reporters he felt like a bull moose. This animal of the north woods became the symbol of his cause.

The bolting Rooseveltians called for a new party, and on August 5 more than two thousand delegates came to Chicago to nominate Roosevelt and Governor Hiram Johnson of California as their candidates. The platform included almost every reform the progressive movement had spawned or inherited. The convention could have been mistaken for a religious revival as delegates and galleries sang "Onward Christian Soldiers" and the stirring "Battle Hymn of the Republic." Roosevelt gave his Confession of Faith. He was standing at Armageddon and battling for the Lord (his earlier description of his cause).

The party took the name Progressive but Bull Moose was the more popular term.

The delegates of the jubilant, yet worried, Democrats came to Baltimore to make their nominations on June 25. The progressive-conservative division was present but less serious for a party long out of power and now in sight of the promised land.

Bryan created a turmoil at the opening session by opposing the national committee's choice of Alton B. Parker for temporary chairman. He lost by 579 votes to 508, but he had stirred up outside sentiment for the progressive cause. Bryan served on the resolutions committee and helped write a progressive platform. After the preliminary work of the convention was out of the way, he offered a resolution that the convention declare itself "opposed to the nomination of any candidate for President who is the representative of or under obligation to J. Pierpont Morgan, Thomas F. Ryan, August Belmont, or any other member of the privilege-hunting and favor-seeking class." After great uproar and confusion the resolution was adopted by a large majority. Belmont and Ryan were delegates.

In the pre-convention struggle Speaker Champ Clark of Missouri had bagged the most delegates. His House record and his strong western support seemed to vouch for his liberalism, but state machines tended to line up for him and Hearst's newspapers sang his praises.

Governor Woodrow Wilson of New Jersey, former president of Princeton, had made a fine record as governor after dumping the bosses and ranked next to Clark in delegate strength. He had ditched his early conservative sponsor, Colonel George Harvey of *Harper's Weekly*, and stood out as the leading progressive contender. Governor Judson Harmon of Ohio, who had been Attorney General under President Cleveland, and Oscar Underwood of Alabama, floor leader of the House of Representatives, were respected conservatives, but did not fit the situation or suit Bryan. Of the favorite sons, only Governors Thomas Marshall of Indiana and Simeon Baldwin of Connecticut were placed in nomination at the convention.

On the first ballot Clark had 440 1/2; Wilson, 324; Harmon, 148; Underwood, 117 1/2; Marshall, 31; Baldwin, 22; William Sulzer, of New York, 2; Bryan, 1; not voting, 2. On the tenth ballot New York shifted from Harmon to Clark, giving the latter a majority. A Clark victory parade lasting an hour proved to be premature. A Wilson-Underwood agreement to hold out kept Clark well short of the required two-thirds. On the fourteenth ballot Bryan surprised the convention by announcing his intention to change his vote from Clark to Wilson because Clark might be under obligation to the interests represented by the New York delegation then voting for him.

The convention adjourned over the weekend after twenty-six ballots with the deadlock unbroken. Thousands of telegrams poured into Baltimore on Sunday demanding the nomination of Wilson. The battle continued into Tuesday when the July heat, the strain on delegate pocketbooks, and the shift of Roger Sullivan, boss of Illinois, to Wilson brought it to an end. On the forty-sixth ballot the New Jersey governor received the nomination. Underwood would not accept second place, and it went to Governor Marshall of Indiana on the second ballot. He was the choice of the Wilson managers.

The platform, adopted after the nominations, was moderately progressive, favoring tariff reduction, more effective anti-trust measures, banking reform, and the passage of constitutional amendments for an income tax and direct election of United States Senators.

The campaign of 1912 really ended with the three conventions. Woodrow Wilson's liberal views and aggressive campaigning soon made it clear that he would poll the normal party vote; and it would be sufficient to elect him, regardless of any other consideration. Had the Democrats nominated a conservative, a Progressive tidal wave might have carried Roosevelt to victory. Fortunately they had named their strongest man. Wilson, an easterner and once a conservative, had won the liberals by his courageous course as New Jersey's governor and had received the blessing of Bryan. Yet he steered clear of extremes and conducted a campaign that kept him safely between the conservatism of Taft and the radicalism of Roosevelt.

To nullify the fiery aggressiveness of Roosevelt, Wilson was put on the stump. Curiosity drew many to see what a professor-politician was like, and they were pleasantly surprised. The tall, homely, long-jawed candidate was no owlish, dry, remote scholar but a skillful phrase maker, occasionally witty, always clear and convincing, who knew what he wanted to say and said it well. In dealing with issues he dwelt on tariff and trusts; but he was more concerned with the regeneration of politics through a spiritual awakening. This sometimes worried his friends. Like the evangelist's appeal to "get right with God" and thus solve all mundane problems, it hardly seemed to come to grips with the hard facts of life. Roosevelt battled with devils and had a weapon to slay each one. Wilson's faultless sentences pleaded for a "new freedom," but his listeners too often were more inspired and uplifted than enlightened. Rather naïvely, he proposed to destroy private monopoly and restore competition, thus making business free and giving to every man the just rewards of his talents. Roosevelt termed such ideas "rural toryism." The Progressives' program of government regulation was more realistic. Yet, as President, Wilson came far nearer the Progressive position than his speeches forecast.

Samuel Gompers supported Wilson. The anti-injunction plank in the Democratic platform pleased him, and he also developed a great admiration for the candidate. The appeal of the Progressives' program of social justice failed to overcome union labor's doubts of Roosevelt himself and the segment of big business in his camp.

The party campaigns were managed much as in the past. William F. McCombs, manager of Wilson's pre-convention campaign, became Democratic national chairman. Suffering from ill health, he had to leave much of the work to William G. McAdoo, with whom he often disagreed. Henry Morgenthau handled Democratic finances efficiently, ending the campaign with a cash balance. Nearly ninety thousand persons contributed $1,159,446.33. Wilson warned the party treasurer not to accept contributions from certain dubious sources, and one gift was returned to avoid embarrassment to the candidate.

The Progressive chest was better filled than a third party had any right to expect.[5] Supporting Roosevelt were a few men of wealth such as Frank Munsey, magazine publisher, and George W. Perkins, once a partner of J. P. Morgan and an important figure in the International Harvester Company and other large corporations. Without their financial backing Roosevelt might have refused to run. Perkins, chairman of the executive committee, managed the campaign. Senator Joseph M. Dixon of Montana, although chairman of the national committee, was relegated almost to a figurehead role. The Democrats accused Roosevelt of favoring the International Harvester Company and the United States Steel Corporation during his Presidency by not prosecuting them under the Sherman Act, and much was made of his intimacy with Perkins.

Charles D. Hilles, Taft's private secretary, was chairman of the Republican national committee, and George R. Sheldon, a New York banker, was treasurer. Business, angry at Taft's trust prosecutions, gave niggardly.[6] Taft made few speeches, as his cause was recognized as hopeless. In his acceptance speech he made an able defense of his administration but revealed his essential conservatism by picturing the dangers of socialism and the destruction of American institutions if either of his opponents triumphed.

The usual third parties appeared: the Socialists with Debs again as candidate; the Socialist Labor group with Arthur E. Reimer; and the Prohibitionists with Eugene W. Chafin. The Socialists, despite dissension at their national convention

[5] The national committee reported receipts of $676,672.73, disbursements of $665,500.00, and liabilities of $5,714.31.
[6] Receipts were reported at $1,076,391.51; disbursements, $1,076,548.57. These and the figures reported for the other parties were filed with the clerk of the House of Representatives in accordance with the act of 1910.

between conservatives and direct actionists, conducted an aggressive campaign. The unrest that had produced the progressive movement in the old parties helped their cause, and a number of victories in local elections encouraged them to believe that 1912 would bring a great increase in their vote, even though the new third party would attract many radicals.[7]

The campaign drew to its close without the excitement that the convention struggles had seemed to foreshadow. The most dramatic incident occurred on October 14 in Milwaukee when an insane man attempted to assassinate Roosevelt. The bullet entered the right side of his chest and lodged in a rib. Showing his usual fortitude, Roosevelt delivered his scheduled speech without medical treatment. Although the wound proved to be not too serious, it ended his speaking tour. Both Taft and Wilson telegraphed their regrets and suspended campaign activities until he recovered. On October 30 he addressed a great New York gathering at Madison Square Garden, where the faithful showed their loyalty in the shadow of defeat.

On November 5 the Democrats were successful for the first time since 1892. Wilson had 435 electoral votes; Roosevelt, 88 (Michigan, Minnesota, Pennsylvania, South Dakota, Washington, and 11 of California's 13); and Taft 8, (Utah, Vermont).[8] Wilson polled 6,296,547 popular votes, to 4,126,020 for Roosevelt and 3,486,720 for Taft. This made Wilson a minority President; but it would be a mistake to assume that he would have lost if he had had only one major opponent. In the two-party battle of 1910 the Democrats had won a majority in the House and had elected governors in several Republican states. The tide had not changed in 1912, and Wilson was to be victorious in 1916 when conditions were much less favorable.

[7] Milwaukee had a Socialist mayor and a Socialist Congressman, Emil Seidel and Victor Berger, elected in 1910. In 1912 it was estimated that 1,141 Socialists held elective offices in the nation.

[8] Vice President Sherman, running with Taft, died on October 30. The eight Republican electors cast their Vice Presidential votes for Nicholas Murray Butler.

The surprising increase in the Socialist vote from 420,820 in 1908 to 897,011 gave clear proof of the country's swing to the left. The liberalism of Roosevelt and Wilson kept the Debs total from being greater. The Prohibition vote, which had been around 250,000 for two campaigns, dropped to 209,923 in 1912. Reimer, Socialist Labor, had 29,079.

The new Congress was Democratic: the Senate 50 to 44, not counting one Progressive and one vacancy; the House 291 to 144. Of the 144, only about 15 were Progressives though many others had been elected with Progressive assistance. The situation was much the same in the various state legislatures, thus placing the new party under a serious handicap. With few officeholders and almost no patronage, it was not in a good position to establish itself as a major party. But much depended on what happened to the Democrats under Wilson's leadership.

1916

Wilson provided a type of leadership for the Democratic Congress that seemed to hark back to Jefferson. The strong-willed President had to his credit by October, 1914, a notable group of progressive laws dealing with tariff, banking, and trusts. But the problems that followed the outbreak of World War I dwarfed all domestic issues, and the progressive movement lost its momentum. His handling of neutral rights drew the fire of German-Americans and Irish-Americans at one extreme and ardent sympathizers with the Allies such as Roosevelt at the other. His tardiness in advocating military preparedness measures was a further count against him.

Republicans and Progressives began to draw together in 1914, and the Progressive vote fell off badly. Roosevelt, now concerned about war problems and national defense, was willing to return to his old allegiance if a suitable candidate were offered for 1916. The usual flock of favorite sons, mostly undistinguished conservatives, appeared on the scene but not one of them seemed to fit the situation. A man was needed who was not involved in the battle of 1912, who had not offended Roosevelt, and who had a record that was

completely blank on controversial issues. Justice Charles
E. Hughes, a member of the Supreme Court since 1910 and
a former governor of New York, was the answer. He preserved a sphinx-like silence but important leaders took care
of his interests. When the convention met at Chicago on
June 7, it was Hughes against the field.

The Republican platform assailed Wilson's foreign policy
as one of "shifty expedients" and "phrase making" and
promised an honest neutrality and the protection of American rights, but did not clarify the party's position on these
points. It criticized Wilson's policy toward business and
offered a strong national defense plank.

The Progressive party was holding its convention in Chicago at the same time, and a committee conferred with a
Republican committee as to candidates, but no agreement
could be reached.

The Republican convention proceeded to ballot and nominated Hughes on the third trial. Former Vice President
Fairbanks was named to run with him. Derisive Democrats
suggested "Win with Whiskers" as a slogan, referring to the
hirsute adornments of both candidates.

The Progressive convention delegates, who had been held
in restraint by George W. Perkins and other compromisers,
broke loose and nominated Roosevelt with John M. Parker
of Louisiana as his running mate. Roosevelt's reply was a
conditional refusal. His final decision would be determined
by the attitude of Hughes on the vital questions of the day.
The convention adjourned in an atmosphere of bitter resentment, leaving the party's future course to the determination of its national committee. When, after a conference with
Hughes, Roosevelt announced his definite withdrawal, the
Progressive national committee voted against a separate
ticket.

The Democratic convention, meeting at St. Louis on June
14, was a ratifying rather than a nominating body. Wilson
was renominated with one dissenting vote and Vice President Marshall by acclamation. The platform recited the accomplishments of the administration, favored preparedness,
had a strongly worded Americanism plank, and indorsed

woman suffrage by state action. The delegates yelled loudest and longest when speakers stressed the peace theme. A significant statement in the platform praising Wilson's diplomatic victories ended with the words "and kept us out of war."

Hughes, asserting his prerogative as the party's nominee, selected as campaign chairman William R. Willcox of New York City, a man not well known to party leaders. Cornelius N. Bliss, Jr., served as treasurer of the national committee. Wilson displaced William F. McCombs with Vance McCormick of Pennsylvania as chairman of the Democratic national committee, while Henry Morgenthau looked after finances and Robert W. Woolley directed publicity. On the whole the Democratic campaign was handled much better than the Republican, although it was not so well financed.

Hughes was one of the country's finest legal minds, but the task assigned to him was an impossible one. A man of force and sincerity, he was not gifted in equivocating; but any other course would cost votes. His dilemma on the major issues of foreign policy was a cruel one. He had to criticize Wilson's handling of Mexican difficulties and his failure to compel respect for American rights at sea. This provoked Democratic charges that Hughes's more vigorous policy might lead to wars with Mexico and Germany, which, of course, he must disprove. German-Americans and many pacifists believed that Wilson had dealt too harshly with Germany; the friends of the Allies, as represented by Roosevelt, charged him with spinelessness. Hughes had to satisfy both groups. The Democrats could insist that Wilson had preserved peace; no one knew what Hughes might do. On preparedness the Republican candidate was more effective, for Wilson had been tardy in advocating defense measures. But his conversion and the steps taken satisfied most voters. Americans were not military-minded, and in some quarters the Hughes-Roosevelt position smelled of the militarism charged against the Kaiser.

Among domestic questions, only the tariff offered a safe issue, for Wilson's accomplishments in other respects were hard to attack. But a war boom had ended the recession of 1914, and Republican warnings of bread lines to come under the Underwood Tariff fell flat. Hughes blundered in criticizing the Adamson Act to authorize an eight-hour day for railway trainmen, enacted in September, 1916, at Wilson's suggestion to avert a nation-wide rail strike. Without opposing the eight-hour day in principle, he assailed Wilson for submitting to a pressure group. His forthright stand was taken in speeches in Ohio, headquarters of the Railway Brotherhoods. Organized labor, already suspicious of Hughes, swung sharply to Wilson, and Ohio proved to be a crucial state.

An inadvertent blunder probably cost him the vote of California. Here Governor Hiram Johnson, Roosevelt's running mate in 1912, was a candidate for the Republican nomination for United States Senator and was bitterly opposed by an Old Guard faction headed by National Committeeman William H. Crocker. Johnson of course was supporting Hughes and, as governor, might have been expected to preside at a Hughes meeting or confer with the candidate when he arrived in California in August. Crocker, however, made all the arrangements and kept the two men apart, even though at one time they were in the same hotel. This unnecessary snub was repaid in full when Johnson won the senatorial nomination and was elected in November by 300,000 votes, while Hughes lost the state by 3,773. Like the Reverend Mr. Burchard in 1884, Crocker achieved the unenviable distinction of defeating his own candidate. But Hughes ought to have realized the dynamite in the situation and made it a point to conciliate Johnson.

Despite the bogging down of the Hughes campaign shown by the decline in betting odds from two to one to ten to seven, the Republicans expected to win. The return of the Progressives, and German-American and Irish-American resentments toward Wilson, seemed to insure Democratic defeat.

But the strategy of the Democrats was to view the East as lost and center their efforts on the states west of Pennsylvania. They had two powerful appeals. One was Wilson's progressive accomplishments. Progressives who put principles ahead of loyalty to Roosevelt came trooping into the Wilson camp, especially west of the Mississippi.

The other appeal was, "He kept us out of war," one of the most effective slogans ever used in a campaign. It did tremendous damage to Hughes away from the eastern seaboard, particularly in farming sections with pacifist and isolationist leanings, and in the woman suffrage states of the West. Roosevelt became a Democratic asset in this connection. His belligerent utterances were quoted and coupled with a statement of Hughes that he and Roosevelt were in complete accord. A pre-election Democratic paid advertisement carried this appeal:

> You are working, not fighting!
> Alive and happy, not cannon-fodder!
> Wilson and peace with honor?
>   Or
> Hughes with Roosevelt and war.

This must have been galling to Roosevelt, who was not happy in his support of the "bearded iceberg" and was reported to have remarked that Hughes was the kind of man who would vote for Wilson.

Wilson, with Congress in session all summer, could not campaign then. Later he yielded to party leaders and spoke at Omaha, Indianapolis, Chicago, and Cincinnati, key points in Democratic strategy. Speeches at Buffalo and New York City just before the election were concessions to the feeling that New York must not be abandoned without a struggle. A great parade headed by Sheriff Alfred E. Smith preceded the final rally at Madison Square Garden, where thousands, unable to get in, clamored for a sight of the President. The enthusiasm was metropolitan only; the state voted for Hughes.

The campaign closed with the Democratic candidate much stronger than at the beginning but with Wall Street still betting on Hughes. The returns up to midnight, November 7, bore out this view. Even the Democratic papers in the East conceded defeat. As the returns from the Middle West came in with only Ohio for Wilson, the President privately admitted to a feeling of relief that the great burden of office had been lifted from him. A great Democratic "victory" banquet given by Henry Morgenthau for party leaders and cabinet members at the Biltmore Hotel in New York that night was a "morgue-like" affair while rejoicing Republicans serenaded Hughes at the Astor with two bands. Toward morning, as word came from the West, doubt succeeded certainty. Minnesota and California were the last to report, and not until Thursday afternoon was it known that Wilson had the latter state. This elected him, regardless of Minnesota, which finally went to Hughes by a plurality of fewer than four hundred votes.

Wilson had 277 electoral votes, Hughes 254. The popular vote was in Wilson's favor, 9,127,695 to 8,533,507.[9] The new House of Representatives was almost evenly divided between Republicans and Democrats, while the new Senate was Democratic by ten votes, instead of the former sixteen. Clearly it was a Wilson rather than a Democratic party victory. His liberalism and his avoidance of war received a vote of confidence. Other factors were incidental. Among them were the failure of the Republicans to get a solid German-American vote, the poor strategy of Hughes and his managers, the swashbuckling of Roosevelt, the effect of the Adamson Law, the apparent swing of the Mormon voters of Utah and neighboring states to Wilson, the peculiar California situation, and the support given to Wilson by the woman suffrage states of the West.

The alignment was singularly like that of 1896 with one or two significant exceptions. Wilson had the solid South and the border states except Delaware and West Virginia (which gave Hughes 7 of its 8 votes); all the trans-Mississippi West except Oregon, Minnesota, South Dakota, and Iowa; and Ohio and New Hampshire east of the Mississippi. Hughes

---

[9] The minor parties were as follows: Benson, Socialist, 585,113; Hanly, Prohibition, 220,506; Reimer, Socialist Labor, 13,403. The sharp decline in the Socialist vote was due probably to the party's extreme antiwar position, which was confused in the popular mind with pro-Germanism, and to the attractions of Wilsonian liberalism for many radicals and pacifists.

had the remaining area from New England westward to South Dakota, including the great industrial and older farming sections. He carried substantially the McKinley states of 1896 with two fatal exceptions, California and Ohio.

Hughes and the Republicans in a sense were fortunate in defeat. The Democrats had to bear the chief responsibility for American entry into the war. If Hughes had won, he could scarcely have avoided doing what Wilson did in 1917. Yet the Democrats then could have thrust upon him and his party the blame for what followed. It might have given the war a partisan aspect and engulfed the Republicans in the great revulsion of 1920. Luck was really with them in 1916, for to the successful peace candidate fell the momentous decision to make war.

CHAPTER IX

REPUBLICAN ASCENDANCY

1920–1932

1920

WHEN GERMANY's unrestricted submarine warfare brought the United States into the war, politics, it was said, had been adjourned for the war. But the political truce did not last. Already badly strained, it broke down in 1918 when Wilson appealed to the country for a Democratic Congress. The election gave both Houses to the Republicans. This weakened Wilson's hand in the diplomatic game at Paris and in his own country when he asked for approval of the Treaty of Versailles. The Senate's rejection of the treaty containing the League of Nations, in part because of Wilson's refusal to accept reservations or make concessions, made the League an issue in the Presidential election. His physical breakdown left his party leaderless as the campaign of 1920 approached.

Difficult economic and social readjustments and a general postwar disillusionment provided grist for the Republican mill when the party's delegates assembled at Chicago, June 8–12, 1920. Henry Cabot Lodge, Wilson's chief opponent in the battle over the League of Nations, was both temporary and permanent chairman, and Senatorial colleagues held key positions. The platform assailed Wilson and his works, but it took a vague, meaningless plank on the League of Nations to keep moderates and irreconcilables from staging a floor fight.

Three candidates had conducted extensive campaigns for delegates: General Leonard Wood, Governor Frank Lowden of Illinois, and Senator Hiram Johnson of California. The heavy spending of Wood and Lowden became liabilities, and Johnson was an extreme isolationist on the League of Nations. Several favorite sons, seeing a deadlock in prospect, set up their lightning rods. Among the better known were Governor Calvin Coolidge of Massachusetts and Senator Warren G. Harding of Ohio. The latter's campaign manager, Harry M. Daugherty, predicted that the nomination would be decided for a deadlocked convention by a little group in a smoke-filled hotel room "about eleven minutes after two o'clock" in the morning, and his candidate would be the lucky man.

On the first ballot Wood, Lowden, and Johnson led in that order, but after four ballots Lodge adjourned the convention until the next morning. That night, a long conference, or succession of conferences, did the work. Lodge and his Senatorial confreres looked over the field and decided that Harding was the man. He possessed a pleasing personality, a handsome figure, was not assertive, and would work well with Congressional leaders.

Next day, the deadlock ran on for a few ballots while Lowden passed Wood; then the shift toward Harding began. He received the nomination on the tenth ballot on Saturday afternoon.

The delegates gagged at the Senatorial clique's choice of Senator Irvine Lenroot of Wisconsin for Vice President and nominated Governor Calvin Coolidge of Massachusetts, who was *persona non grata* to Lodge but was acclaimed for his role in putting down a Boston police strike.

The Democrats assembled at San Francisco on June 28 and passed a Wilsonian platform which indorsed his course on the League of Nations and defended his conduct of the war. William G. McAdoo, recently resigned as Secretary of the Treasury, and Attorney General A. Mitchell Palmer of Pennsylvania, "Red-hunter" extraordinary, were the leading candidates, but Governor James M. Cox of Ohio was more available as he carried no Wilson administration burdens.

Several local favorites had delegate support. It took forty-four ballots before the deadlock ended with Cox's nomination. The Vice Presidential choice was made quickly. New York seemed to require representation on the ticket, and Cox suggested Franklin D. Roosevelt, Assistant Secretary of the Navy, who was named by acclamation. Charles Murphy, Tammany boss, did not care for Roosevelt but let Cox have his way.

The Republican campaign as managed by the efficient and tireless national chairman. Will H. Hays of Indiana, was a model of vote-catching banality. "Americanism" and "Getting back to normalcy" constituted its sum and substance. The first—which no one has ever been able to define—implied that Wilson had put the rest of the world ahead of his own country. The Republicans would reverse this. The second nostalgically promised a return to some less troubled past, though no one could be sure just when Americans had lived in a state of "normalcy." At least Harding was the ideal candidate to present this dose of soothing syrup to an angry and disillusioned electorate. Modest, unassuming, given to making speeches that consisted of "an army of pompous phrases moving across the landscape in search of an idea," he seemed to the typical good resident of small town and countryside to be a man who understood the ways of his fellow men and would work with them to find solutions for their problems. Except for a few carefully prepared major speeches which skillful ghost writers provided, he campaigned from his front porch at Marion, Ohio, uttering pleasantries to visiting delegations after the McKinley pattern but less studied, more informal, more human.

One problem stumped Harding and almost baffled his speech writers. This was the League of Nations. He had voted for the League with the Lodge reservations attached, and this position was supported by Hughes, Taft, Root, Hoover, and other party bigwigs in varying degrees. But the Borah-Johnson irreconcilables had blood in their eyes and demanded repudiation of the League. Harding tried to emulate the vagueness of the platform; but the task proved to be far too great for his powers of circumlocution, and George

Harvey and Richard Washburn Child came to the rescue. The result was a long and involved speech in which the candidate seemed to favor a world court of justice and an "association" of nations for conference in place of the Wilsonian League. Even these vague proposals were not to be final, for he promised to consult "the most experienced minds of this country" before presenting his plans to other nations. Late in the campaign, still confused, the candidate seemed to wobble more to the isolationist side, though thirty-one distinguished Republicans signed a public appeal urging his election as the only way to bring the United States into "an effective league."

A 1923 magazine article, written with White House approval, stated that Harding had never had any intention of having the United States enter the League of Nations. Apparently he had convictions and was merely concealing them during the campaign.

Lesser Republican speakers, unable to follow their leader along the tight wire, felt free to flay Wilson's League as a superstate dangerous to American sovereignty. Voters of Irish, German, and Italian ancestry, hostile to the Treaty of Versailles for various reasons, joined in the clamor against American involvement. In the upper Mississippi valley, where the peace appeal had worked for the Democrats in 1916, isolationism was now rampant.

Cox put up a brave battle against heavy odds. Soon after the nomination he and his running mate, Franklin D. Roosevelt, called upon the pathetic figure in the White House and assured him they would stand with him on the League. As Cox had not been involved in the Senate battle, such a pledge seemed to be inexpedient; but he refused to be a trimmer. Then he went on the stump, speaking in all parts of the country. He attempted to revive the progressivism of the prewar days, in which he had played a notable part in his home state; but the country was in no mood for reform. George White, Democratic national chairman, was hampered by finances and apathy in building up an effective organization. The Democratic national committee spent $1,470,000 compared with the Republican $5,417,000; but no amount of money could have saved Cox. The swing was to the right.

In this campaign appeared the first large-scale attempt to poll the electorate in a Presidential election. The *Literary Digest*, a well known weekly devoted to presenting newspaper opinion in digest form, undertook the task through millions of postcards. Its methods overemphasized middle-class sentiment, but this was not evident when the Republican trend was so general.

The whispering that sometimes disgraces a Presidential campaign appeared in 1920. The most sensational story was the allegation that Harding had Negro blood. Circulars purporting to prove it by affidavits and a family tree appeared mysteriously on doorsteps and even in the mails. The authorship could not be clearly established. It had an Ohio origin but was widely circulated shortly before the election.

On November 2 a tidal wave engulfed the Democratic party. Harding carried the entire North and West including Oklahoma; the border states of the South except Kentucky; and Tennessee from the Solid South—its first lapse from Democratic orthodoxy since 1872. He had 404 electoral votes to Cox's 127. The popular vote was divided as follows: Harding 16,153,115; Cox, 9,133,092; Debs, Socialist, 915,490; Christensen, Farmer-Labor, 265,229; Watkins, Prohibition, 189,339; Cox, Socialist Labor, 30,594. With more than 60 per cent of the total vote and a plurality of 7,000,000, Harding shattered all records. In the new House of Representatives, more than 300 of the 435 members were Republicans. In the Senate 59 were Republicans, and only 37 Democrats.

In 1920, it has been said, the voters voted their resentments. Champ Clark, defeated after twenty-eight years in Congress from Missouri, snarled one word at a newspaperman who asked the cause of the landslide: "Wilson!" It was not the broken man in the White House that the voters were repudiating but Wilson as the symbol of things they wanted to forget. The intoxication of patriotic sacrifices for high ideals and the exhilaration of war prosperity were over. The year 1920 was the morning after. The world was out of joint, and the American people, in their disillusionment, sought a victim. The election was not, as Wilson had hoped, a "great and solemn referendum" on the League. Without the League as a factor, the result would have been much the same. Americans were homesick for the hopeful, sane, and secure world of 1914. Perhaps an average man like Harding could restore that "normalcy." But the President-elect was looking beyond that. He wanted to go back to McKinley.

1924

Harding's administration followed a generally conservative and isolationist course, but the nation had not reached the port of normalcy when he died suddenly while on a western trip and left the burdens of his office to Calvin Coolidge.

Two Senate investigations exposed former Secretary of the Interior Albert B. Fall as corruptly involved with two large oil producers and revealed some dubious activities of an Ohio Gang close to Attorney General Daugherty. Coolidge saw that prosecutions were instituted in the oil cases and asked for Daugherty's resignation. The Ohio Gang had already departed. With the Harding inheritance disposed of and business booming, the Republican nomination of 1924 came to the shrewd, silent, Yankee politician with only a dissenting murmur from a band of Wisconsin LaFollette irregulars.

Cleveland's first national convention, opening on June 10, was a cut-and-dried affair. Economy and tax reduction were emphasized in the platform, which was also anti-League of Nations and pro-World Court. Corruption was passed over as affecting both parties, and punishment of the guilty was demanded, but the platform condemned attempts to besmirch the innocent and undermine confidence in the government. This was a slap at nosey investigators.

Senator Borah refused to be considered for Vice President, and former Governor Lowden of Illinois was nominated. He declined the honor, and General Charles G. ("Hell'n Maria")

Dawes, also of Illinois, banker and author of a reparations plan for defeated Germany, was then nominated.

The Democrats spoiled whatever chance they had to make use of the Harding scandals by staging a bitter cat-and-dog fight at their national convention, held in Madison Square Garden in New York on June 24. The eastern Democrats, largely urban, wet, and Catholic, were aligned against their brethren of the more rural, dry, Protestant hinterlands.

The revived Ku Klux Klan, antiforeign, anti-Catholic, anti-Jewish, and anti-Negro, had infiltrated the Democratic party in many parts of the South and West and exerted its influence over a considerable bloc of delegates. When the platform was reported, a bitter battle developed over the question of denouncing the Klan by name or by implication. The advocates of the milder plank won by a narrow margin, but the cleavage continued into the struggle for the nomination. Governor Alfred E. Smith of New York represented the anti-prohibition, Catholic East, William G. McAdoo of California the dry Protestant West, although the situation was complicated by the presence of a considerable number of favorite son candidates and some potential dark horses who waited for the leaders to destroy each other.

McAdoo was well in the lead and hoped to reach a majority after which he expected the Smith forces would concede the two-thirds. He was unsuccessful and the struggle dragged on through 103 ballots. In sheer weariness the convention finally accepted John W. Davis, nominally of West Virginia, a conservative lawyer, who had been ambassador to Great Britain, and who practiced in New York City. The violent partisanship of the galleries for Smith angered the McAdoo partisans and helped prolong the deadlock. Proposals were made to hold closed sessions and even to move the convention to Kansas City.

Governor Charles W. Bryan of Nebraska, brother of William Jennings Bryan, was nominated for Vice President.

The convention had lasted from June 24 to July 9, and its proceedings had been covered by radio, which did not help the public image of the Democrats.

Dissatisfied liberals, seeing an opportunity for a farmer-labor movement, turned to Senator Robert M. La Follette, who had at last decided to break with the Republican party. A gathering of farmer, labor, and liberal groups at Cleveland on July 4 named him for President and Burton K. Wheeler, Democratic Senator from Montana who had conducted the Daugherty investigation, for Vice President. The platform, prepared by La Follette, declared that the great issue before the people was the control of government and industry by private monopoly. It indorsed public ownership of the nation's water power, important natural resources, and railroads, and favored constitutional amendments to permit Congress to re-enact a law over a judicial veto and to provide for popular election of federal judges, abolition of injunctions in labor disputes, direct nomination and election of Presidents, a popular referendum on declarations of war, outlawry of war, and a drastic reduction of armaments.

The Conference for Progressive Political Action, active since 1922, launched the La Follette candidacy, and it had the support of the American Federation of Labor, the railroad brotherhoods, the Socialist party, and other left-wing farmer and labor groups, as well as intellectuals of liberal stamp as represented by the *New Republic* and the *Nation*. La Follette and Wheeler made an active campaign; but there was no party organization and little money back of them, and labor did not prove to be of much assistance. Their chief hope was to carry enough states in the upper Mississippi valley, where farmer discontent centered, to throw the election to the House.

The Republicans, blessed with a campaign fund of more than $4,000,000, a popular candidate, an able manager and organizer in the person of William M. Butler, and a return of prosperity—even farm prices went up in 1924—had no very serious problems. A fear that La Follette's strength in the farm states might prevent an electoral majority led the party leaders to center their attack on the independent candidate. They played up his economic radicalism and his proposal to take away the judicial veto of the Supreme Court in order to frighten conservatives into voting for Coolidge rather than Davis, thus making certain that the election would not go to the House. Prosperity and satisfaction with the status quo made Republican success almost certain in any case. Had Harding lived, the exposures of corruption might have been awkward to meet; but with Coolidge in office the situation was completely changed. The slogan "Keep Cool with Coolidge" expressed the sentiments of a majority of the electorate.

The Democrats, having used up their energies at the convention, had none left for the campaign. Clem Shaver of West Virginia became national chairman at Davis's request, but he was not well known to party leaders and was hampered by lack of funds and by organization problems. Expenditures were about $1,100,000. Davis went on the stump and made able speeches assailing Republican corruption, but could not overcome Democratic lethargy or draw Republican fire. Labor was cold toward the Wall Street lawyer, and the Bryan West refused to be stirred by the speeches of the aging Commoner. The Klan question drifted into the background and had slight effect on the election. Prohibition had become a matter of law enforcement, and both major parties, of course, gave it lip service.

The *Literary Digest* poll predicted a Coolidge victory, and the prediction was more than verified in November. Coolidge had 382 electoral votes; Davis, 136; La Follette, 13 (Wisconsin). West Virginia, Kentucky, Missouri, Maryland, and Delaware followed the lead of the entire North and West in going Republican. Only the South (including Oklahoma) was Democratic. Coolidge's popular vote was 15,719,921; Davis had 8,386,704; La Follette, 4,832,532. Several minor-party candidates polled insignificant votes.

The outcome was less sweeping than in 1920 but still decisive enough. Both houses of Congress were Republican by safe majorities. La Follette had run second in eleven western states. He had been favored by those farmers who were not satisfied with Coolidge prosperity, and his antiwar stand had not been forgotten in German communities. In California and the Pacific Northwest, thousands of liberal Democrats preferred him to Davis. East of the Mississippi, liberal, labor and socialist support accounted for a heavy urban vote. But admiration for the Wisconsin veteran and disgust with the old parties could not, of themselves, create a new party. The basic groundwork of local organization was not laid, and the Progressive movement of 1924 passed into history.

This campaign marked the last stumping appearances of two old warriors of liberalism, La Follette and Bryan. Both died in 1925. La Follette bequeathed his Wisconsin organization and his principles to his sons, but Bryan had all but blotted out the memory of his battles against plutocracy by his later crusades against the liquor traffic and the teaching of evolution.

1928

Coolidge had his difficulties with Congress in his second term, but his renomination seemed certain, for the stock market was booming and his personal popularity was still great. Quite suddenly, on August 3, 1927, he announced from his summer residence in the Black Hills of South Dakota, "I do not choose to run for President in 1928."

This opened the way for Secretary of Commerce Herbert Hoover, who had long been making plans, and soon his personal organization was engaged in a delegate hunt. The "Great Engineer" had as his assets his achievements as director of Belgian relief and later as food administrator in World War I, and the special administrative tasks he had carried out while Secretary of Commerce. He lacked Coolidge's blessing, but only a mediocre crop of favorite sons opposed him, and the nomination was practically settled when the Republican convention began its sessions at Kansas City on June 12. His only threat, a "Draft Coolidge" movement, had made no headway.

Farm discontent was becoming a problem, and the vagueness of the plank in the platform caused a floor fight, but the attempt to amend it was defeated overwhelmingly. The drys were satisfied with a plank declaring for vigorous enforcement of the Eighteenth Amendment. Earlier, Hoover had referred to prohibition as "a great social and economic experiment, noble in motive and far-reaching in purpose." The rest of the platform recited the Harding-Coolidge accomplishments and promised to continue along the same lines.

It took only one ballot to make Hoover the party's choice. The nomination of Charles Curtis of Kansas, Senate floor leader, to run with him was also decided by a single ballot. Curtis had criticized Hoover as not a genuine Republican, but Borah had insisted that the Kansas veteran be chosen.

The Democrats were now ready for Alfred E. Smith of New York. Son of Irish immigrant parents, newsboy, clerk in a fish market, and holder of minor political offices, Smith had emerged from his Tammany cocoon to become an important figure in his state and to win the governorship in 1918. Defeated for reelection by the Harding landslide, he was returned to the office in 1922 for three more terms. Backed by certain wealthy eastern Democrats and by city-controlled state organizations, Smith was able to overcome the handicaps of his Catholic faith, his anti-prohibition stand, and his Tammany upbringing, and to ride toward the nomination in 1928 with only some local favorites in his path.

The convention opened on June 26 at Houston, drawn there by the money and efforts of Jesse Jones and the desire of the Smith men to appease the South.

Prohibition troubled the platform makers but they ended up with a plank criticizing the Republican record and promising an honest effort to enforce the Eighteenth Amendment. The farm relief and tariff planks did not differ sharply from the Republican efforts. For the third time Franklin D. Roosevelt, who in 1924 had called Smith the "Happy Warrior," presented his name to a Democratic convention, and this time success crowned his effort. Smith was ten votes short of the required two-thirds on the only roll call, and changes quickly put him across. Next day, Senator Joseph T. Robinson of Arkansas, permanent chairman of the convention, became the choice for Vice President. He was a dry, a Protestant, and a southerner. Smith startled the convention in its closing moments with a telegram reiterating his belief in "fundamental changes in the present provisions for national prohibition." The drys regarded this virtual repudiation of the platform pledge as a challenge in the coming campaign.

The minor parties presented candidates as usual, but only Norman Thomas, named by the Socialists, was in a position to cut into the major party vote. A man of high intelligence and fine character and a forceful speaker, he had naturally inherited the mantle of Debs and could appeal to dissatisfied liberals; but, as the campaign went on, most of these turned to Smith, and Thomas had a disappointingly small vote.

The Republican organization was quickly set up. Dr. Hubert Work of Colorado resigned as Secretary of the Interior to be national chairman and Joseph R. Nutt of Ohio was treasurer. Jeremiah Milbank, a New York banker, served as contact man with Wall Street. A huge campaign fund was raised, and the national committee spent more than $6,000,000, a record-breaking total; but the general prosperity made collecting money less difficult than in some other campaigns.

Hoover's acceptance speech, delivered in the stadium of Leland Stanford University, played up Republican accomplishments and the prosperity issue. In this and later speeches he talked optimistically of the coming abolition of poverty and want, praised rugged individualism, and opposed state socialism. His radio addresses, solid, humorless, and often boring, reiterated his basically conservative tenets.

Charles E. Hughes in the East and Senator Borah in the midlands displayed more voter appeal than the candidate. Hughes stuck to prosperity and Republican achievements in the East where prohibition was unpopular. Borah, the bellwether of the Republican progressives, used prohibition, farm relief, and Tammany Hall in the depressed farm belt and did much to allay farmer discontent. Only Senator Norris, the veteran Nebraska progressive, and the La Follette group in Wisconsin refused to follow him. Norris, satisfied with Smith's stand on government operation of hydroelectric power at Muscle Shoals, bolted Hoover in a speech which also paid his respects to the religious intolerance that was engulfing all other issues.

Smith was his party's most dynamic figure and its best campaigner. After a set acceptance speech at Albany on August 22, he took to the road and covered a large part of the country with major addresses. Radio enabled him to reach a nation-wide audience without exhausting his voice in short speeches at a series of train stops. Disdaining careful preparation, he spoke from notes scrawled (but well organized) on the backs of envelopes. Each speech was confined to a particular subject, designed for a particular locality: for example, farm relief at Omaha; prohibition at Milwaukee; religious intolerance at Oklahoma City. His captivating personality, his ready wit, his pungent expressions, and his brown derby won the visible audiences and stamped him as one of the most colorful campaign speakers in the history of American politics. An old popular song, "The Sidewalks of New York," was revived to add the final touch. Not one serious slip did he commit through his free, extemporaneous method of speech. Unfortunately, he was less successful over the radio—or "raddio," as he called it. His voice had a rasping quality, and listeners caught occasional grammatical lapses while missing the appeal of his personality.

Smith's campaign was the best financed in Democratic annals. John J. Raskob of Delaware, lately a Republican but a personal friend of the Democratic nominee, managed it. An official of General Motors and a millionaire, he gained business support for the party; but he lost some votes, for he was both Catholic and wet. Senator Peter G. Gerry of Rhode Island helped direct the political strategy. James W. Gerard, ambassador to Germany under Wilson, was treasurer of the national committee. A Wall Street banker, Herbert H. Lehman, acted as chairman of the finance committee and was aided by Jesse Jones of Texas. This set-up enabled the national committee to collect and spend $5,342,000. But clearly the election was not determined by the size of the war chests. Had Raskob spent twice what he did, the result would have been much the same. The Democrats were faced with an impossible problem.

Boiled down to its lowest terms, the difficulty was twofold: to combat the prosperity appeal, and to overcome the triple objections to Smith, namely, his "wetness," his religion, and his Tammany associations. In the wet East, when Smith attempted to appeal to antiprohibition feeling, he was confronted with the prosperity argument. In the farm belt, when he pointed to the depressed condition of the farmer and virtually indorsed the McNary-Haugen plan, Borah answered with charges of "wetness" and Tammany and promises that Hoover, the miracle man, would come nearer to solving the farm problem than the inexperienced city politician. Thus prosperity served the Republicans where it existed; where it fell short, emotional appeals to bigotry and prejudice took its place.

In the Democratic South the Republicans kept in the background and let the anti-Smith Democrats, or "Hoovercrats," fight their battle. The real force in the anti-Smith movement was Bishop James Cannon, Jr., of the Methodist Episcopal Church South, who appealed to his large following to vote against rum, Romanism, and Tammany, and helped organize the rural South for Hoover. A certain Colonel Horace Mann operated in the background with funds from Republican sources. The Anti-Saloon League, the Woman's Christian Temperance Union, the Ku Klux Klan, and other dry or Catholic-baiting organizations joined in the hue and cry.

Though Smith boldly met the religious issue in his Oklahoma City speech and attempted to bring his accusers into the open, he could do little to combat the "whispering" which made the campaign one of the dirtiest in American history. Tales went around of Catholic projects to bring the Pope to the United States to reside if Smith were elected, and pictures of the governor at the entrance of the new Holland Tunnel under the Hudson were circulated in the rural South with the amazing explanation that the tunnel was to be extended under the Atlantic to the basement of the Vatican! A story was fabricated that Smith was so drunk on a certain public appearance that it took two men to support him, though different versions made the occasion of this lapse vary considerably. Evidence pointed to a common source for this invention but denials of authorship met his efforts to run it down.

In the East liberals without party affiliation who had followed La Follette in 1924 tended to swing to Smith, as he clarified his views by his speeches in contrast with Hoover's more evasive but generally conservative attitude. The *Nation* and the *New Republic* and Professor John Dewey spoke for this group. The Scripps-Howard League of independent newspapers expressed a preference for Hoover at the start of the campaign but grew more lukewarm toward the close, though nominally for him. Labor, to judge from the expressions of its leaders, was divided though Smith seemed to have more indorsements.

On November 6 this bitter campaign ended in another great Republican victory. Hoover had the East with two exceptions, the entire West, the border South, and Texas, Florida, North Carolina, Tennessee, and Virginia from the old "Solid South." He had 444 electoral votes; Smith had 87, carrying but eight states: Massachusetts and Rhode Island, where his antiprohibition stand and his religion were assets, and South Carolina, Georgia, Alabama, Mississippi, Louisiana, and Arkansas. Even New York was lost by more than 100,000 votes. He had persuaded Franklin D. Roosevelt to help the Democratic cause by running for governor. The latter surprised by carrying the state in the face of the tremendous Republican sweep.

The popular vote was nearly 8,000,000 above that of 1924. Hoover received 21,437,277; Smith, 15,007,698. The vote of the minor parties was unusually small. The Socialist vote for Thomas was but 265,583, the poorest showing since 1900.[1] Smith had the consolation of knowing that he had polled the largest vote ever given to a Democratic candidate, and that, despite the electoral vote, he had run far better than Cox in 1920 or Davis in 1924. He had received a large urban vote, carrying New York, Boston, Cleveland, St.

[1] The others were as follows: Foster, Workers', 46,896; Reynolds, Socialist Labor, 21,585; Varney, Prohibitionist, 20,101; Webb, Farmer-Labor, 6,390.

Louis and San Francisco, and running well in other large cities. A dry Protestant candidate would have held the southern electoral votes but would have done far worse than Smith in the East and probably but little better in the West. No Democrat could possibly have won, and none but Smith could have gained such a large popular support.

The Democrats could thank their lucky stars for the defeat of 1928. Had they won, the Great Depression would have descended upon them as relentlessly as it did upon Hoover, and the Republican dogma that prosperity was a G.O.P. monopoly would have become so established in the popular mind that no Democrat could have overcome it for another generation. The Great Engineer was the unfortunate man in 1928, not his defeated opponent. The Happy Warrior would not have remained happy very long in the White House after 1929.

1932

The stock market crash of October, 1929, and the spread of the Great Depression changed the political picture, as depressions always do. Hoover's acceptance of the high Smoot-Hawley Tariff and his reluctance to use federal power to meet the emergency caused liberals in his party to turn against him. When he did act, as in setting up the Reconstruction Finance Corporation and in providing federal loans to the states for relief purposes, his critics charged that his measures were always too little and too late. Yet neither progressives nor old-line party regulars, who had never cared for him, attempted to prevent his renomination.

The 1932 Republican convention met at Chicago on June 14 in an artificially cooled new stadium. It proved to be a spiritless affair. A floor battle over the prohibition issue created the only excitement. The Hoover administration offered an evasive plank which proposed to submit to the people a substitute for the Eighteenth Amendment that would seem to return control of the liquor traffic to the states but under some kind of federal supervision. A dissenting minority report favored outright repeal. The administration won a sharply contested floor battle. The other planks of the platform were largely defenses of the Hoover record. The continuance of the depression was attributed to events in Europe.

Hoover was renominated with 1,126 1/2 votes to 13 for Senator Blaine of Wisconsin and 10 1/2 for four others. There was some opposition to the renomination of Vice President Curtis, but he was only 19 1/4 votes short of a majority on the roll call, and Pennsylvania then put him over the line.

The optimistic Democrats had been smelling victory since their mid-term successes of 1930, which included capture of the House of Representatives. Candidates were numerous enough but Governor Franklin D. Roosevelt, two-term governor of New York, took an early lead. His campaign manager, big genial James A. Farley, established friendly contacts with hundreds of local leaders all over the West and South. Speaker John N. Garner, who added California to his Texas support, some favorite sons, and a dark horse or two, such as Newton D. Baker of Ohio, did not seem able to stop the Roosevelt band wagon until Al Smith entered the race. He had broken with Roosevelt for personal reasons and became his strongest opponent, rounding up a considerable bloc of eastern delegates.

The convention opened at Chicago on June 27 and soon was engaged in a battle over the permanent chairmanship. The Roosevelt forces won, electing Senator Thomas J. Walsh of Montana over Jouett Shouse, choice of the national committee controlled by the Smith-Raskob leadership of 1928, by a vote of 626 to 528. The platform recommended outright repeal of the Eighteenth Amendment. It favored reduction in expenditures, a balanced budget, a revenue tariff and reciprocal trade agreements, and an extension of federal action along a number of lines to meet depression problems, particularly unemployment. The vague farm plank included extension of cooperatives and control of crop surpluses, among other proposed remedies. Of broader appeal were promises to enforce anti-trust laws and to regulate more effectively public utilities, holding companies, and the stock market. The overtones of a resurgent liberalism were present in the platform, and it challenged Hoover's rugged individualism.

The first ballot gave Roosevelt 666 1/4; Smith, 201 3/4; Garner, 90 1/4; seven others lesser numbers. Adjournment came after three ballots with Roosevelt 88 votes short of the required two-thirds. Next day Garner consented to take second place, California and Texas shifted to Roosevelt, and he had the nomination with 945 votes. Garner became his running mate without opposition.

On the final day the victor broke precedent by flying to Chicago and accepting the nomination in person. He pledged himself to a new deal for the American people with the nation listening on the radio.

Depressions produce a bumper crop of protest parties and extremist movements, some of which never get beyond the name stage. In 1932 twenty-one different parties had their names on the ballots in various states, and several others claimed an existence that was not in evidence on Election Day. In the end none of the new movements reached the strength of the older third parties, all of whom offered candidates as usual.

Of the others that did not expire before Election Day, Coin Harvey's "Liberty" party made the best showing. Harvey, forgotten since 1896, raised the inflationist banner again, but few flocked to it. However, he had a larger total than that once famous leader of the jobless of the nineties, General Jacob S. Coxey of Massillon, Ohio. Coxey, candidate of a Farmer-Labor remnant, did not get on the ballot in most of the states. Some other protest parties were confined to a single state.

The Democratic campaign was well planned and well managed. James A. Farley naturally became national chairman and handled affairs from his New York headquarters directly through the state organizations, without special regional or branch headquarters. Charles Michelson took care of publicity. An efficient corps of assistants worked with Farley, and the "brain trust"—experts selected for their knowledge of public problems but lacking in political experience—came on the scene to advise the candidate and help him in the preparation of important addresses. The charter members were Raymond Moley, Rexford G. Tugwell, and Adolf A. Berle, Jr., all from Columbia University, and Justice Samuel I. Rosenman. According to Moley, the group was concerned exclusively with policy-planning and had nothing to do with campaign management or tactics. Roosevelt's major speeches were prepared from materials compiled and interpreted by this "brain trust." That a candidate should seek guidance from unbiased experts on difficult problems, chiefly economic in character, was indeed an innovation in a political campaign. Unlike Harding, Roosevelt did not recite what others had written. He used the ideas of others but, according to Charles Michelson, was a better phrase-maker than anybody around him.

Roosevelt conducted a vigorous offensive, with twenty-seven major addresses from coast to coast. His purpose was not only to give the lie to whispers about his physical condition but, more important, to play the role of a New Deal Messiah, particularly in the midwestern farm belt where riots against mortgage foreclosures and forced sales indicated the temper of farm voters.

His sympathetic approach attracted George N. Peek, Henry A. Wallace, and other farm leaders to his camp and was a factor in the bolt of Senators Norris, Hiram Johnson, Bronson Cutting of New Mexico, and Robert M. La Follette, Jr. Norris was more interested in his friendliness toward public ownership of electric power. Borah preserved a sullen silence toward both candidates.

In the East the conservative Smith-Raskob wing of the party had to be conciliated. Roosevelt and Smith cooperated in obtaining the nomination of Herbert Lehman for governor of New York, and then the man with the brown derby went on the stump to make antiprohibition speeches. Tammany also fell in line, and the urban East seemed united behind Roosevelt.

The Republican organization was headed by Everett Sanders, former Indiana Congressman and secretary to President Coolidge. As in 1928, Joseph R. Nutt and Jeremiah

Milbank handled finances. Hoover had intended to make only three or four set speeches, but alarming reports of Republican defections—Maine went Democratic in September —forced him to take the stump. In ten major speeches and many brief talks at train stops he exhibited a sturdy fighting spirit, in contrast to his ignoring of Smith in 1928. Despite fears of his advisers, he was treated everywhere with respect, except in Detroit, where there were some catcalls and boos from the sidewalks.

Republicans hoped that the depression would begin to lift and prosperity peep around the corner in time to save them, but Fortune refused to favor them this time. There was left only the argument that things would be worse if the Democrats won. "Grass will grow in the streets of a hundred cities," warned Hoover in his final speech in a moment of emotional strain unusual with him. But the old fear argument had lost its potency. With better psychology his opponent was offering the more abundant life to the forgotten man.

Neither party was blessed with a huge campaign chest. The Republicans as usual were better off, but the depression had reduced some of their chief sources of revenue. At one time Hoover had to take personal direction of the job of collecting funds to stave off a financial breakdown. About $2,900,000 was spent, against receipts of $2,650,000. The Democrats collected $2,379,000 and spent $2,246,000, without allowance for a large deficit incurred in the preceding four years. Both national committees continued heavily in debt after the campaign was over.

Radio was a more powerful factor in 1932 than in 1928. The major speeches of both candidates and many broadcasts by lesser figures reached millions of listeners and challenged the significance of newspapers and other forms of publicity. The direct appeal of candidates to voters sitting in their homes and unmoved by crowd psychology compelled greater care in the preparation of speeches and a special technique in presentation. Here the Democrats showed to advantage. The heavy, monotonous seriousness of Hoover's speeches made listening an effort. Roosevelt, by contrast, was at his best when heard over the air. The deep mellow tones of his voice, a cheerful warmth of personality, and a skill in interjecting light, humorous touches into his speeches made his broadcasts the most effective type of propaganda the Democrats used.

The result was almost foreordained. Republican money, organization, and propaganda could not meet the deadly realities of the Great Depression. The difference between the two candidates was not so much in specific issues as in methods of approach. Hoover stood on his record and could promise little more than continuance along the same lines. Roosevelt, critical of the President's conservatism, could offer an open mind and a willingness to try new paths. The country had soured on Hoover, and felt that any change would be for the better.

On November 8 the Republicans went down to a crushing defeat. Roosevelt had 472 electoral votes; Hoover, 59. Pennsylvania, Delaware, Maine, New Hampshire, Vermont, and Connecticut constituted the Republican total. In the popular vote Roosevelt had a plurality of more than 7,000,000.[2] The Democrats had more than 70 per cent of the House and a margin of twenty-two votes in the Senate. Such Old Guard leaders as Watson of Indiana, Smoot of Utah, and Moses of New Hampshire were defeated. As in 1920 the voters had voted their resentments; but this time the Republicans were the victims. The Socialist vote approached the total Debs had received in 1920; but on the whole the minor parties made a poor showing for a depression year. The discontented had chosen the Roosevelt road, which offered some hope of immediate relief, rather than unfamiliar third-party bypaths and blind alleys. It remained for the Democrats to prove that they had made no mistake.

[2] Roosevelt, 22,829,501; Hoover, 15,760,684; Thomas, Socialist, 884,649; Foster, Communist, 103,253; Upshaw, Prohibition, 81,-872; Harvey, Liberty, 53,247; Reynolds, Socialist Labor, 34,043; Coxey, Farmer-Labor, 7,431.

CHAPTER X

ROOSEVELT AGAIN
AND AGAIN AND AGAIN

1936–1944

1936

THE NEW DEAL crash program of 1933–34, combining recovery and reform, seemed to be moving in all directions at once. Temporary expedients and more basic measures ground out of the legislative mill at an amazing speed. Roosevelt's personal popularity seemed to be undiminished as the end of his term approached, but millions were still unemployed, lavish expeditures had not restored prosperity, and conservatives were worried about the continuing expansion of the powers of the federal government. The Republicans began to see the clouds lifting a little. Perhaps they could initiate a popular revulsion against the New Deal.

The chief Republican problem was to find a suitable candidate. The defeats of 1932 and 1934 had cost the party heavily in governorships and Senate seats. Senators Arthur H. Vandenberg of Michigan and Charles McNary of Oregon and Governor Alfred M. Landon of Kansas were the best of an unpromising lot. Landon had withstood the Democratic sweep, had once followed Theodore Roosevelt and was mildly progressive, and as an oil producer had an appeal to businessmen. A group of Kansas friends, John D. M. Hamilton, Roy A. Roberts of the *Kansas City Star*, and William Allen White, provided backing and publicity, and the Hearst papers soon chimed in. Colonel Frank Knox, publisher of the *Chicago Daily News,* a former Bull Mooser, also entered the race but aroused no popular enthusiasm. Belatedly Borah decided to run, but the regulars would not consider him.

The Landon backers came to the national convention at Cleveland on June 9 with the nomination sewed up. Before the balloting half a dozen nominal favorite sons released their delegates. Landon was nominated with 918 votes to Borah's 19. Colonel Knox received the Vice Presidential nomination after Senator Vandenberg refused to be considered. The platform was a long denunciation of the New Deal but made some concessions to reform in its farm aid, labor, and old-age security provisions. John D. M. Hamilton became national chairman.

The Democratic convention met at Philadelphia in the Municipal Auditorium, June 23–27, 1936. It was a ratifying affair, as platform and candidates were predetermined. The most significant action was the abrogation of the century-old two-thirds rule. The platform was a recital of administration accomplishments. It derided Republican proposals to solve national problems through state action, promised to use federal legislation within the Constitution, but if this proved impossible, to propose a "clarifying amendment."

Roosevelt and Garner were renominated, and Roosevelt accepted the nomination at Franklin Field that evening before an assemblage of one hundred thousand people. His denunciation of "economic royalists" sounded the keynote of the campaign.

On June 19, Congressman William Lemke of North Dakota, a nominal Republican but an agrarian radical, announced his Presidential candidacy on a "Union Party" ticket. He received the indorsement of three minor prophets of discontent: Reverend Gerald L. K. Smith, self-proclaimed leader of a Share-the-Wealth Movement started by Senator Huey P. Long of Louisiana, who had made himself virtual dictator of that state when he was assassinated; Father Charles Coughlin, a Detroit Catholic priest with a large radio following which he tried to organize into a Union for Social Justice; and Dr. Francis E. Townsend, whose proposal for pensions of two hundred dollars a month for the retired dependent elderly had produced thousands of Townsend clubs. This troika pulled in somewhat different directions, and did not agree on a platform, although they gave their support to Lemke.

The older minor parties had candidates as usual. The Communists embarrassed the Democrats by following the "party line"—later changed—of "a united front against Fascism," meaning the Republicans.

Landon's acceptance speech, at Topeka on July 23 before 50,000 persons, was preceded by a picturesque pageant of frontier days, emblematic of the candidate's background; and an enthusiastic and apparently united party approved of the general tenor of his remarks. But the pageant, not the candidate, provided the color. He appeared as a sincere, uninspiring conservative, rather than as the wielder of the sword of Theodore Roosevelt. It remained for the Republicans to prove that the country needed his type, an average man of substantial virtues without Coolidge's narrowness or Franklin Roosevelt's dangerous "charm."

The campaign soon revealed that the country was dividing less along traditional party lines and more according to economic groups than at any time since 1896. The leaders of the American Federation of Labor and its new rival, the Committee for Industrial Organization, supported Roosevelt. In the political field their support was made effective by an organization known as Labor's Nonpartisan League. John L. Lewis, though not the official head, was its real organizer. The farmers, less united in sentiment, seemed to be still favorable to the New Deal in the great grain-growing regions, once Republican strongholds. The La Follettes, Norris, the Minnesota Farmer-Laborites, and other western progressives cooperated with the Democrats on the Presidential ticket, while Senators Borah and McNary campaigned for themselves, not for Landon. Thus the party of Roosevelt appeared as a farmer-labor combination, as Bryan had attempted to make it in 1896, and as it had been in Jackson's day, though the labor partner then was a pygmy compared with 1936.

Backing the Republican cause was big business as represented by the Liberty League, the National Association of Manufacturers, and other organizations, numerically small but financially powerful. There was general expectation among Republicans that the smaller businessmen and the professional groups—the upper middle class—would be with them as in the past. Dislike and fear of New Deal spending and regimentation were evident here. The conservatism of the party also drew Democratic allies, unable to stomach New Deal liberalism. These conservatives, calling themselves "Jeffersonian Democrats," included such impressive names as John W. Davis, Alfred E. Smith, James A. Reed of Missouri, Bainbridge Colby (Wilson's Secretary of State), and former Governor Joseph B. Ely of Massachusetts. Unfortunately for the Republicans, these figures were hardly more than museum pieces, imposing to gaze upon but useless as vote getters. In fact, the Toryism of the Republicans cost them far more votes through defections on the left than were gained from recruiting on the right.

The Republican management seemed to be liberally supplied with funds, though it ended the campaign with a budget badly out of balance. It spent nearly $9,000,000—a new record for campaign expenditures. This did not include sums raised and spent by the Liberty League and by state committees. Such names as Hearst, Guggenheim, Rockefeller, Du Pont, Pew, and Vanderbilt among Republican contributors indicate the party's financial backing.

Yet money alone could not solve the problem. A strategy had to be devised to recover the populous East and Middle West, long Republican but rendered doubtful by the popularity of the New Deal with labor and farmer. Relying upon the past conservatism of this area, the Republican general staff began a vigorous assault upon the New Deal and all its works. Criticisms of its spending policy, its farm-relief measures, its attitude toward business, its currency program, its disregard of the Constitution, and Roosevelt's violation of his platform of 1932 filled Republican newspapers, were the meat of hundreds of speeches, and reached millions of voters over the air waves. These attacks were made more pointed by charges that the New Deal was collectivistic and even Communistic.

Toward the close of the campaign a concerted attempt was made to use the Social Security Act against Roosevelt. To alarm wage earners, the act was assailed as a "pay reduction" measure. Many employers assisted the Republican cause with explanations designed to influence their employees. Some used bulletins in factories and slips in pay envelopes, reminiscent of the tactics of 1896. The net effect was to sharpen the class alignment, and make labor more resentful toward such pressure and more pro-Roosevelt than before.

The Republican organization functioned badly. Chairman Hamilton, inexperienced in national politics but filled with enthusiasm for his task, found the state and local organizations in bad shape, their morale broken by the succession of defeats since 1930. The national chairman, assuming the role of a traveling salesman, went around the country making the acquaintance of local leaders, stirring them to action, and delivering speeches for Landon at the same time. The national headquarters at Chicago became a huge propaganda machine manned by supersalesmen, and pouring forth every possible type of publicity for the Republican cause. Much of this was wasted because of bad management and bungling tactics.

Chairman Farley's Democratic machine reached its peak in 1936. Fortified by victory and the possession of offices, and stimulated by the chairman's unceasing vigilance, the Democratic organizations, national, state, and local, left nothing to chance. Numerous reports from party workers to the New York headquarters, tabulated, checked, and analyzed by Emil Hurja, gave the national chairman a clear picture of the battle at every stage and enabled him to adapt his tactics to the immediate situation.

The hostility of big business reduced the number of large contributors and compelled the Democrats to rely upon a larger number of small gifts than in the past. Half a million individuals gave to the Democratic campaign fund, more than a third of the total amount being accounted for by gifts of less than $100. Labor organizations—a hitherto untapped source of funds—were heavy contributors. A new device, continued after 1936, was the holding of Jackson Day dinners all over the country on January 8, with tickets selling as high as $100 a plate but graded down to fit the pocketbooks of the faithful who attended in the provinces.[1] The campaign expenditures by the national committee amounted to $5,194,000. Like the Republicans, the Democrats had the assistance of auxiliary organizations whose outlays added materially to the total cost.

The Democratic strategy was not cautiously defensive but a vigorous assault on the forces of reaction. The "economic royalists" and "Tories" behind Landon, "the straw man," received the major brunt of the attack. The support given by Hoover, Hearst, former Governor Smith, and the Liberty League was offered as concrete evidence of the reactionary character of the opposition.

But the strongest argument in the Democratic repertory was the contrast between 1932 and 1936. Even conceding that the glittering prosperity of the 1920's had not returned, they argued that conditions had improved immeasurably under Roosevelt, that old abuses had been removed and confidence had been restored, and that farmer, laborer, and businessman were better off. Against this the Republican cry that the Constitution and the American way of life were in danger fell flat.

Both candidates took the stump. They centered their attention on the Middle West but appeared also in the East, and Landon made a foray to the Pacific coast. Roosevelt aroused far greater mass enthusiasm. At Chicago five miles of streets were almost impassable for the Presidential car, and a hundred thousand people packed the stadium to hear him. His oratorical cleverness and his role of crusader against plutocracy made him the greatest political attraction since

[1] Another device, much criticized, was the sale of the *Book of the Democratic Convention*, with the President's autograph, at $100 or more per copy. Its sale was continued after the campaign to help pay off the national committee's deficit.

Theodore Roosevelt and Bryan had charged and counter-charged. Landon, utterly lacking in magnetism and mediocre as a speaker, did not appear to advantage on the stump; and he was further handicapped by a poor radio voice.

The power of radio to overcome unfavorable newspaper publicity was clearly shown in this campaign. No candidate since Bryan in 1896 had had to fight such a powerful array of newspapers as confronted Roosevelt. To the normal Republican journalistic preponderance outside the South were added the Hearst chain, the *Baltimore Sun*, and the *St. Louis Post-Dispatch*. In the fifteen largest cities the newspaper alignment was 71 per cent for Landon, as measured by circulation figures. In Chicago it was eight to one in his favor, but Roosevelt's majority was almost two to one. The press, with its savage editorial denunciations of the New Deal—comparable to the anti-Bryan violence of 1896—its warped news stories, and its misleading headlines, played a rather sorry part in the campaign.

The whispering, or under-cover, campaign that has so often disgraced American politics appeared chiefly in the form of stories about the President's sanity. In 1932 it was his physical condition; in 1936, his mental state. It was "whispered" at country clubs and across bridge tables that his mind had been affected by his siege of infantile paralysis; and medical authorities were cited to prove that his symptoms foreshadowed mental collapse. The divorces in the Roosevelt family and Mrs. Roosevelt's manifold activities offended the sensibilities of middle-class Roosevelt haters and were used as propaganda wherever possible. Among the overly well fed the most astonishing reason offered for opposing the President was that he was a traitor to his "class."

The various polls, with one notable exception, pointed toward a Roosevelt victory. But the huge postcard poll of the *Literary Digest*, so successful in its prophecies in the past, indicated a large Landon electoral majority. Its failure to give due weight to the different groups and classes in the voting population was its undoing. On the other hand the careful "sampling" methods of the American Institute of Public Opinion, headed by Dr. George Gallup, and similar techniques used by *Fortune* magazine and by Archibald M. Crossley were completely vindicated by the result in November. They underestimated the size of the Roosevelt victory, as did all the polls and the major prophets except Chairman Farley. With Emil Hurja's figures before him, he created amusement among Republicans by extravagantly claiming all the electoral votes for Roosevelt except those of Maine and Vermont.

On November 3 he was found to be exactly right. Roosevelt had 523 electoral votes; Landon, 8 (Maine and Vermont). Not since Monroe had a winner come so near to a clean sweep. Roosevelt's share of the popular vote, 60.8 per cent, was slightly over Harding's in 1920; and his plurality was the largest ever recorded, over eleven million votes.[2] Lemke's poor showing indicated the end of the Union party. Father Coughlin's German and Irish Catholic isolationists had provided much of his support. The Townsendites and Huey Long's old following had gone elsewhere. The other minor parties likewise had fared badly. The Socialist vote was the smallest since 1900.

The House had 333 Democratic members out of the total membership of 435; the Senate, 75 Democrats out of 96; and a host of Democratic candidates for state and local offices rode to victory on Roosevelt's coattails. In 1932 the verdict had been anti-Hoover; in 1936 it was pro-Roosevelt. The New Deal's good works had built up a powerful farmer-labor-Negro coalition and had cut heavily into Republican middle-income strength. Urban solidarity for Roosevelt was without precedent. The Democratic tide had receded somewhat in the trans-Mississippi West, and nationally the Republicans carried more counties than in 1932. But the loss of the cities was fatal. Labor, whether of native or of immigrant stock, voted its economic interests.

The result was a complete repudiation of the Toryism that had governed the Republican party's strategy despite the new leadership. The old myths and the old slogans had failed

[2] Roosevelt had 27,757,333; Landon, 16,684,231; Lemke, Union, 892,267; Thomas, Socialist, 187,833; Browder, Communist, 80,171; Colvin, Prohibition, 37,677; Aiken, Socialist Labor, 12,829.

to convince. Standing by the Constitution, defending the American way of life, and calling New Dealers Communists would not supply food for the unemployed, higher farm prices for debt-burdened agrarians, or security for the wage-earners. So the masses of voters had seemed to reason. No Republican could have defeated Roosevelt, but a more intelligent leadership in the years before 1936 might have averted the complete debacle. This was the lesson for 1940. The emaciated frame of the Grand Old Party needed both vitamins and calories.

1940

The mid-term elections of 1938 were the first indications of a Republican resurgence. Roosevelt's attempt to add justices to the Supreme Court to give it a more liberal composition—termed "court packing"—had been defeated in Congress by a revolt of conservative Democrats. His prestige suffered another setback when he went on the stump in an effort to defeat for renomination certain leading conservative Democrats and was slapped down by the voters. A business recession and an epidemic of sit-down strikes were more important issues in the elections of 1938, which gave the Republicans control of eighteen states and raised their membership in the House of Representatives from 89 to 170 as against 262 Democrats.

But World War II began in September, 1939, and foreign problems soon overshadowed domestic issues. Roosevelt's policy of all-out aid for England short of war, after the fall of France, and immediate rearmament divided the Republicans as their national convention opened at Philadelphia on June 24, 1940. Many agreed with his position, but an isolationist group accused him of "warmongering," with a third term as his objective. A platform battle in committee produced a compromise which promised adequate national defense and aid to "all peoples fighting for liberty," provided it was not in violation of international law or inconsistent with our own defense requirements. The domestic planks of the platform were more forward-looking than the proposals of 1936, but continued to emphasize state action over federal.

Unlike 1936, there was no shortage of candidates. Senator Robert A. Taft of Ohio and District Attorney Thomas E. Dewey of New York City emerged from the elections of 1938 to begin a rivalry that was to last until the former's death. Vandenberg, McNary, and other favorite sons were entries, but a latecomer, until recently a Democrat, Wendell Willkie, Indiana-born and formerly of Ohio, a utilities lawyer, who had become the head of Commonwealth and Southern Corporation, was a more dangerous contender. A big, tousel-headed man, forty-eight years old, he had a dynamic personality, a wisecracking sense of humor, supreme self-confidence, and an appeal to business and professional men that politician candidates lacked. A group of so-called amateurs led by Oren Root, Jr., and Russell Davenport, editor of *Fortune* magazine, circulated literature, sent out petitions, and evoked a last minute barrage of letters, telegrams, and declarations for this newcomer. His gallery support in the convention suggested that the Willkie supporters had been well taken care of in the distribution of tickets. Delegates pledged to other candidates resented this pressure and threatened to form a coalition for a true-blue Republican.

On the first ballot Dewey led with 360, Taft had 189, Willkie, 105; eleven others divided the rest of the thousand votes. Dewey's support began to disintegrate, the favorite sons faded out, a coalition failed to materialize, and the contest became a Willkie-Taft battle. It ended with the maverick winning over the regular on the sixth ballot.

Second place went to Senator Charles McNary of Oregon, whose western residence, post as floor leader, and friendliness to New Deal measures made him a good choice.

That the 1,094 Democratic delegates who assembled at Chicago on July 15 would nominate Roosevelt for a third term was a foregone conclusion, unless he refused to be drafted. He had failed to groom a successor, city bosses needed his coattails, and the rank-and-file sentiment for him was overwhelming. Without knowing Roosevelt's intentions, Vice President Garner and Postmaster General

Farley announced their candidacies, and two or three others, such as Senator Wheeler of Montana, acted as polarizers of anti-Roosevelt sentiment. If Roosevelt had withdrawn, Secretary of State Cordell Hull might have been nominated.

The Chicago convention, like the Republican gathering, had to devise a watered-down compromise on foreign affairs to appease isolationists. It pledged the party against participation in foreign wars except in case of attack and promised aid to liberty-loving peoples attacked by aggressors, in much the same language as its Republican counterpart. The New Deal's accomplishments were praised with special emphasis on its public power policies, a thrust at Willkie's utilities connections.

Although Roosevelt had sent a message to the convention, read by Chairman Barkley, freeing all delegates to vote for any candidate, the balloting gave him 946 13/30 votes; Farley, 72 9/10; Garner, 61; Tydings, 9 1/2; Cordell Hull, 5 2/3. A battle over the Vice Presidency developed when word was passed that Secretary of Agriculture Henry Wallace was Roosevelt's choice. Old-line regulars, who regarded Wallace as a star-gazing idealist, turned to Speaker William B. Bankhead who received 328 2/3 votes to Wallace's 627 7/10, with scattered votes for some others. Roosevelt accepted immediately in a calming radio address, declaring that the world crisis had forcel personal considerations into the background in his decision to run again.

Willkie's acceptance speech, delivered on August 17 before a huge crowd at his old home in Elwood, Indiana, shocked right-wing Republicans. He accepted the major objectives of the Roosevelt foreign and domestic policies and confined his criticisms chiefly to methods. He advocated an economy of production as opposed to one of scarcity, which he charged upon the New Deal, without calling for the repeal of any significant New Deal measure. On foreign policy he rejected isolationism and promised to "outdistance Hitler in any contest he chooses."

On the whole, Willkie's strategy was sound. The Toryism of 1936 would not be repeated in 1940; nor would he accept the equally fatal position of the isolationists, which would have opened the way to Democratic charges of appeasement and Hitlerism. His courageous indorsement of the pending selective service law, opposed by the majority of Republicans in Congress, was a case in point. Ambiguous silence or open opposition would have pleased the party regulars, but he refused to compromise with his convictions. Thus the issue was eliminated from the campaign.

Willkie also indicated his intention of controlling the management of his campaign by relegating Chairman Hamilton of the national committee to a post of executive secretary and placing in the chairmanship Joseph W. Martin, Jr., who had presided over the convention. Martin's task was not easy. The untamed candidate often ignored the professionals and listened to the amateurs, and the campaign broth had too many cooks. Raising funds was turned over to a leading industrialist, Tom M. Girdler, head of Republic Steel Corporation, who had the confidence of business but had an anti-labor record that was a source of embarrassment in the campaign. Willkie announced at the outset that his campaign expenditures would be kept strictly within the $3,000,000 limit prescribed by the new Hatch Act.

The first speech was on September 17 at Coffeyville, Kansas, where Willkie had once taught school. The "battle of America" was his theme—the battle to save democracy at home against concentration of power in one man. Then followed as arduous a campaign as any since Bryan's famous stumping tours. Covering thirty-four states, he traveled an estimated 30,000 miles by rail, air, and automobile to deliver 540 speeches. Perhaps 12,000,000 people turned out to see and hear him. His deep voice grew strained and husky, but he never spared it. He was the despair of his throat specialist, for he held forth in his private car between platform appearances. His inexperience in politics cropped out sometimes in indiscreet statements that had to be qualified or explained away afterward. But his unfailing good humor, his abundant vitality, and his vigorous style of speech were increasingly effective in arousing enthusiasm as the campaign progressed and he developed greater adeptness in presenting his case. Over the radio he was a better speaker than

Landon; but a sloppiness of diction and a clumsiness of phrasing reduced the effectiveness of his appeal somewhat.

The Republican organization was assisted by several auxiliary groups, separately financed, the most important being the "Associated Willkie Clubs" and the "Democrats for Willkie." Thousands of "amateurs" gave their services to Willkie Clubs to prepare and mail literature, telephone to voters, and perform other political labors usually left to the professionals. Middle-class housewives, discovering a sudden interest in politics, worked in relays at the telephones in Willkie headquarters to warn women voters about the dangers of war and the third term. The "Mothers of America," financed by the Republican national committee, presented emotional radio appeals on behalf of Willkie and peace.

In some of the more doubtful states local Republican organizations raised and spent large sums, ostensibly for state and local tickets, thus evading the limitations of the Hatch Act. In Pennsylvania, for example, a survey after the election revealed that the Republicans had spent $2,500,000 through state and local organizations and volunteer clubs, an astonishing amount even for a state accustomed to freehanded spending in primaries and elections. Wide use of every form of political advertising and propaganda testified to the size of the Republican party's war chest and the elaborateness of the Willkie set-up.

Meanwhile, the Democrats were having their troubles. The coldness of many regulars toward the New Deal element made the problem of a successor to Farley as national chairman an awkward one. But Roosevelt found a reasonably satisfactory solution. He chose Edward J. Flynn of New York, a successful lawyer of independent means and for years boss of the Bronx. He had long been close to both Roosevelt and Farley, who was to continue as state chairman. Thus it was hoped that the soreness in evidence at Chicago might be removed. Flynn lacked his predecessor's wide acquaintance among politicians of the hinterland, and did not essay the role of traveling salesman; but he managed the campaign competently from his New York headquarters. In any case, the grand strategy was in the hands of Roosevelt.

That some conservative Democrats would repudiate the New Deal leadership seemed to be certain, and with the no-third-term tradition as a convenient bridge, a long procession was soon crossing over to the Willkie camp. The wisdom of naming a former Democrat as Republican standard-bearer seemed to be amply justified; but observers pointed out that nearly all of the more prominent bolters were either former "greats" or lame ducks who had lost influence in the party. Among them were former Governors Smith of New York, White of Ohio, and Ely of Massachusetts, former Senator Reed of Missouri, former Representative John J. O'Connor of New York, and Senator Edward R. Burke of Nebraska, who had just been defeated for renomination. Such Senate conservatives as Glass and Byrd and Tydings, and the isolationists Wheeler of Montana and Bennett Champ Clark of Missouri silently acquiesced in the Roosevelt candidacy, Clark even giving a half-hearted indorsement of the national ticket in a belated radio speech. Vice President Garner neither spoke nor voted.

As a partial offset to conservative defections a group of liberals set up a committee of "Independent Voters for Roosevelt." The veteran progressive, Norris of Nebraska, and Mayor La Guardia of New York were the leaders, with Thomas G. Corcoran the chief organizer. Willkie's headship of a great utilities holding company and his battle with the Tennessee Valley Authority made him anything but satisfactory to Norris and the friends of public power. Mayor La Guardia, Fusionist opponent of Tammany, threw his fiery energy into the Roosevelt cause. The American Labor party of New York also indorsed the President. In Wisconsin, Robert M. La Follette, Jr., who had cooled toward the administration and was opposing its foreign policy, ran for reelection to the Senate with his state Progressive party's backing. Fighting for his political life against a Republican trend, he decided for Roosevelt on domestic issues and won the backing of liberal Democrats. Dorothy Thompson, influential woman columnist, who had been critical of the New Deal, supported Roosevelt on foreign policy.

The President in his acceptance speech had indicated the

line of argument to be followed in the campaign, but the brunt of the battle was to be left to the Vice Presidential candidate. Wallace centered his attention on the doubtful farm belt; but the growing enthusiasm aroused by Willkie required that the Democrats play their trump card, and so Roosevelt went before the voters to inspect national defense projects from Maine to Virginia and west to Dayton, Ohio. Though his brief remarks were in a nonpartisan key, huge crowds turned out at all stops to cheer him. Republican newspapers frothed at this further evidence of Rooseveltian hypocrisy.

In the closing days of the campaign the President threw off all disguise and made five major political addresses in key cities of the East and the Middle West. His entry into the campaign did much to restore Democratic morale, which had been shaken somewhat by the Willkie trend of some of the polls and by the tremendous barrage of Republican propaganda.

Magnifying Roosevelt's refusal to respect the no-third-term tradition into an assault upon constitutional government, Republican newspapers and orators proclaimed that dictatorship was imminent and democracy itself in dire peril. Willkie himself solemnly declared that if the administration was restored to power for a third term, "our democratic system will not outlast another four years." Obsessed with dislike of the man in the White House, Republicans forgot that they would have rejoiced if Calvin Coolidge had consented to stand for another term in 1928, and that in their ranks were many old-timers who had done their best to put Theodore Roosevelt in the White House for a third term in 1912. Several Democratic Senators and the Progressive La Follette found themselves compelled to eat their own words, as they had supported a resolution against a third term in 1928.

The Democrats met the third-term argument with much talk about the grave emergency and the dangers of swapping horses "until we reach the clear sure footing ahead"— as Roosevelt phrased it in his Cleveland speech. Hurling back at his critics the dictatorship cry, he attacked the "unholy alliance" of Communists and "Girdlers" who were trying to weaken democracy in America and "to destroy the free man's faith in his own cause." The Democrats invoked Washington's authority to offset Republican quotations of Jefferson's familiar anti-third-term sentiments. Had not the Father of His Country once written that he saw no reason for "precluding ourselves from the services of any man, who on some great emergency shall be deemed universally most capable of serving the public"? Yet the third-term issue was a difficult obstacle for the Democrats to hurdle. Americans are pronounced traditionalists in their political thinking, and the Republicans were defending an old tradition. Their appeal was simple and emotional and irrational, and therefore all the more difficult to combat.

In the closing stages of the campaign the Republican offensive centered on the war issue and the closely related problem of national defense. Willkie had indorsed the Roosevelt policy of all possible aid to the democracies, and favored immediate rearmament and the compulsory military service law. Both candidates declared that they would not send American boys to Europe to fight except in defense of American liberty. Republican propaganda, however, charged that Roosevelt was the war candidate, and used the air waves and the newspapers to appeal to the mothers of America to save their boys from slaughter on foreign battlefields by voting Republican. Roosevelt partisans denied that he was a warmonger and countercharged that leading Republicans were isolationists and Hitler appeasers. As to national defense, the pot called the kettle black by pointing to the spots on its record.

A dramatic incident of the campaign was John L. Lewis's radio address on October 25 urging labor to vote for Willkie and pledging himself to retire from the headship of the C.I.O. if Roosevelt won. He charged that the Democratic party had broken faith with labor, that Roosevelt was aiming at war and dictatorship, that the administration had failed by every test, and that Willkie's election was imperative to the country's welfare.

Lewis's plea won support from some left-wing leaders in

the C.I.O. including Harry Bridges, under fire as a Communist; but the heads of the larger unions generally repudiated his stand and reaffirmed their support of Roosevelt. Most of the leaders of the rival American Federation of Labor, then bitterly hostile to Lewis, were already strongly pro-Roosevelt. The presence of Tom Girdler, Ernest T. Weir, and other antiunion industrialists in the Willkie camp detracted from the effectiveness of the Lewis appeal to labor.

Minor parties received slight support from labor and farmer in 1940. The crazy-quilt Union party of 1936 had not survived. Father Coughlin tried to take his following over to Willkie; but his support was regarded as a liability. The Republican candidate denounced racial and religious intolerance and offered cold comfort to budding Fascist groups. The Socialist party convention at Washington in April adopted a strongly isolationist and antiwar platform, opposing even economic aid to any belligerent. Norman Thomas was again its nominee.

The Communist party, weakened in membership and even more in prestige by the Stalin-Hitler pact of 1939, offered Earl Browder for President. It declared against any participation in the "imperialist war," opposed military preparations, and in general followed the party line laid down from Moscow. Browder, sentenced to prison for misuse of a passport, was out on bail; but his campaign activities were sharply circumscribed.

The Socialist Labor and Prohibition parties also nominated candidates but attracted little attention and few votes.

The polls, scientific and otherwise, which attempted to predict the result, were in such sharp disagreement that even veteran political analysts were bewildered. The American Institute of Public Opinion—the Gallup poll—issued a final statement on the eve of the election giving Roosevelt 198 electoral votes, Willkie 59, but leaving 274 doubtful! Roosevelt, it conceded, might have 52 per cent of the total popular vote, but because of the heavy concentration of Democratic strength in the South this might not mean electoral success. *Fortune* magazine's survey gave Roosevelt 55.2 per cent of the popular vote but admitted that Willkie might

squeeze through with an electoral majority. Two other nation-wide samplers of opinion predicted a decisive Willkie
victory. Chairman Flynn's claim of 427 votes for Roosevelt
seemed to be the customary exaggeration of a party manager.

But the verdict on November 5 went beyond even Flynn's
expectations. Roosevelt had 449 electoral votes to Willkie's
82. The Dakotas, Nebraska, Kansas, Iowa, Colorado, Indiana, Michigan, Maine, and Vermont constituted the Willkie
total. Roosevelt's popular vote was 27,313,041, Willkie's
22,348,480.[3] The victor's 54.7 per cent of the popular vote
was lower than it had been in 1932 (57.4) and 1936 (60.8).
The Democrats added slightly to their House majority but
lost three Senate seats.

Willkie ran better in the western wheat and corn states
than anywhere else. His persuasive philosophy of an expanding economy, with farm subsidies if needed, struck the right
note. Farmers, unhappy over government restrictions even
with benefit payments, complained about laborers loafing on
the W.P.A. while farm workers were hard to get, were
alarmed at continuing Treasury deficits, and, especially in
German-American localities, suspected Roosevelt of maneuvering to involve the nation in the war.

But the Democrats retained most of their urban support.
Republican charges that reliefers decided the election ("You
can't beat Santa Claus") were apparently refuted by the
equally heavy Roosevelt vote of employed labor. Prolabor
policies and various New Deal benefits weighed heavily
with the city voters. The swing of Polish-American, Jewish,
and other anti-Hitler elements to Roosevelt overcame losses
among voters of German and Italian ancestry, where emotions overruled economics.

The role of the press came in for much comment. Roosevelt lost the *New York Times*, the Cleveland *Plain Dealer*,
the Scripps-Howard chain, and other supporters of 1936,
while some nominally Democratic organs were lukewarm.

[3] Minor party totals were: Thomas, Socialist, 116,410; Babson,
Prohibition, 58,708; Browder, Communist, 46,529; Aiken, Socialist
Labor, 14,892.

Yet in the face of a heavy Republican journalistic preponderance, he had carried every city of more than 400,000 population except Cincinnati, sometimes without a single friendly newspaper. Was it radio? or popular feeling that urban journalism, having evolved into a few big business corporations, reflected its corporation character? Or was Roosevelt too overshadowing to be much affected by editorial arrows or editorial praise?

1944

Administration measures providing aid for England had to overcome isolationist opposition, but Pearl Harbor closed the mouths of administration critics. As in 1917, politics was adjourned. The mid-term elections of 1942 aroused slight interest and political analysts predicted little change in the composition of Congress. They were wrong. The Republicans gained ten seats in the Senate and forty-seven in the House, which they almost captured. The war machine was slow in getting under way. Criticisms of men and measures, of wartime restrictions, of price controls and labor policies, took their toll of the party in power. It was like 1862.

In the new Congress a bloc of southern conservatives led by Senator Harry S. Byrd of Virginia formed a coalition with the Republicans and modified or rejected administration proposals on the domestic front while supporting war measures. A battle over authorizing a federal ballot for soldier voting ended in a compromise measure. It permitted a federal ballot to be used for absentee voters in the armed services who had not received a state ballot, provided the governor of the state certified that it might be used in his state. It was permitted in some twenty states in the election of 1944.

One effect of the election of 1942 was the organization by C.I.O. leaders of a Political Action Committee in July, 1943, with Sidney Hillman in charge, to get labor to the polls through organization and propaganda at the household level. It soon showed its power in state primaries, even in the conservative South. The P.A.C. was a virtual Democratic auxiliary.

The elections of 1942 provided the Republicans with three governor possibilities for 1944: Dewey of New York, John W. Bricker of Ohio, and Harold E. Stassen of Minnesota. Bricker and Stassen had been re-elected. Dewey refused to announce his candidacy but delegates pledged to him were generally successful in state primaries. A movement for General MacArthur never got beyond the talking stage. Wendell Willkie, criticized by isolationists and the more orthodox Republicans for his internationalism and his increasingly liberal viewpoint, announced his candidacy and rashly entered the Wisconsin primary in the isolationist Middle West. Dewey defeated him there, and his withdrawal followed. Poor showings in two primaries practically eliminated Stassen, then in the Navy.

Bricker, replacing Taft as Ohio's choice, was well liked by party regulars as an old-fashioned Republican of the McKinley type, but Dewey was better known and had primary successes to his credit.

The national convention, held in Chicago, June 26–28, was a harmonious affair. Hoover appeared in his role of prophet of gloom, and Mrs. Clare Boothe Luce ran the emotional gamut with her creations, "G. I. Joe" and "G. I. Jim." The platform committed the party to a prosecution of the war to total victory and promised responsible participation by the United States in "postwar cooperative organization" to maintain peace. Bricker withdrew before the balloting, and the ticket became Dewey and Bricker. One MacArthur vote kept Dewey from unanimity. The New York governor flew to Chicago and accepted in a speech assailing incompetence in the administration composed of "stubborn men grown old and tired and quarrelsome in office."

For the Democrats Roosevelt was the only choice, and he agreed to accept a fourth nomination. The delegates came to Chicago on June 19 and adopted a platform upholding the party's record in peace and in war. The Democrats did not copy the fair employment practices and anti-poll tax proposals that were in the Republican statement of promises. On the ballot for President southern conservative opposition provided 89 votes for Senator Byrd of Virginia to Roosevelt's 1,086.

Roosevelt had given Vice President Wallace the kiss of death by expressing a preference for him but a readiness to let the convention decide. A letter to National Chairman Robert E. Hannegan approved Senator Harry S Truman or Supreme Court Justice William O. Douglas for second place. It took two ballots for the northern state machines and southern conservatives to make Truman the winner over Wallace, backed by a liberal-labor group.

Both campaigns were managed by newcomers; but they were not amateurs. Democratic Chairman Robert E. Hannegan had lined up the organization leaders in the Vice Presidential battle at Chicago, and he worked with them in the campaign. Hillman, Murray, and the labor group continued the P.A.C. but allied with it a "National Citizens Political Action Committee" appealing to liberals of all shades and not limited in its spending by the Smith-Connally Act. The P.A.C.'s most effective work was in getting the labor vote to the polls. A series of simple leaflets, prepared by writers and artists at its New York headquarters, appealed to the workers to register and vote. Some of these abandoned any pretense of nonpartisanship, and one, entitled "Lest We Forget," contained a photograph of an unemployed man selling apples in front of a "Hoover Club" in 1932, with an inset showing a large red apple and a picture of Dewey conferring with Hoover. Nearly 10,000,000 such leaflets and pamphlets went out every week in the closing stages of the campaign to C.I.O. unions and through their 14,000 locals to the members. Clubs, speeches, radio programs, and even doorbell ringing helped arouse labor from the lethargy of high wages and war prosperity. Democratic organization leaders welcomed the P.A.C. as an ally and worked with it.

Herbert Brownell, Jr., manager of Dewey's campaign for governor, handled his pre-convention campaign with assistance from Edwin F. Jaeckle, New York state chairman, and J. Russel Sprague, national committeeman from New York. These three continued to direct the national campaign, Brownell heading the national committee. John Foster Dulles was Dewey's adviser on foreign policy. This grandson of a Secretary of State had had considerable diplomatic experience in his earlier years, and his law practice had had international connections. Republican contacts with the business world were maintained through James S. Kemper, chairman of the finance committee and a former president of the United States Chamber of Commerce, who had shown marked isolationist sympathies.

The moneybags of business were opened to the Republicans as in 1936 and 1940. The legal limitation of national campaign expenditures to $3,000,000 did not prevent heavy contributions to state campaigns and independent organizations. The totals, according to the Senate Campaign Expenditures Committee, almost equaled the record level of 1936. The United Republican Finance Committee for Metropolitan New York collected $1,629,451 and spent $1,260,593; the Pennsylvania Republican Finance Committee, $1,252,-700 and $939,934. The P.A.C.'s receipts for the entire country were $1,405,120; its expenditures, $1,327,775. The Du Pont and Pew families together gave more than $200,000 to the Republican chest. The Democrats collected $22,000 from the Marshall Fields and $20,680 from the Andrew J. Higgins family of New Orleans. The Republicans spent nearly twice as much as the Democrats, with expenses of local candidates not reported to the Senate committee.

The campaign opened late and was comparatively brief. Much depended, as in 1864, on the military situation. A summer of victories in France was followed by an autumn stalemate but with ultimate allied victory not too far off. This was probably more favorable to Roosevelt than to Dewey. It was no time to swap horses.

Dewey's speechmaking began at Philadelphia on September 9, and covered a large part of the country outside the South. He made no platform appearances, kept secret the exact train route on his western swing, and aimed his brief, well phrased speeches at the radio rather than the visible audiences. His general themes were a more efficient administration, an end to the quarreling and bickering of the "tired old men," better relations with Congress, a durable peace settlement, and jobs for all through the stimulation of private enterprise. He assailed the administration for inadequate preparedness, for burdening labor, agriculture, and business with unnecessary and conflicting restrictions, for planning to keep men in military service to prevent unemployment, and for consorting with Communists.

The last charge was the basis for an eleventh-hour fear campaign. Sidney Hillman of the P.A.C. was linked with Earl Browder, Communist leader, as "Hillman, Browder, and Co.," a Communist conspiracy controlling the P.A.C. The attacks upon Hillman as "foreign-born" and "Russian-born" came close to anti-Semitism, as when a leading New York newspaper referred to his "rabbinical education." The admonition, "Clear it with Sidney," was the favorite Republican slur, for Roosevelt had allegedly made this remark with regard to the Democratic Vice Presidential nomination before the Chicago convention. It became a stock gibe in Republican campaign speeches, and Hearst newspapers had "Sidney" limerick contests. This concentrated assault on an important labor leader, with its scarcely veiled Ku-Kluxism, gave Roosevelt the opportunity in his final speech to slash at the Republicans as enemies of the foreign-born, and gave the P.A.C. a publicity that probably helped it in getting lethargic labor to come to the polls.

Roosevelt limited his campaign to two dinner addresses and three public speeches, all broadcast, and three special radio talks. Rumors about ill health seemed to be disproved by the vigor of his campaigning.

On foreign policy the two candidates were close together. Both upheld the Dumbarton Oaks plan for a world security organization, and both favored empowering the American representative on a security council to act in an emergency to enforce peace. But Dewey was embarrassed in his criticisms by his party's record on defense and foreign policy and by the isolationism of a considerable segment. Though he courageously repudiated the candidacy of Hamilton Fish for reelection to Congress from New York, he had to accept the support of the *Chicago Tribune* and its middle western satellite papers and to indorse his party's candidates generally, despite their deviations from his stands on major policies.

On October 8 Wendell Willkie died suddenly without revealing how he intended to vote. Some of his Republican and independent sympathizers announced for Roosevelt. These included Russell Davenport, his 1940 pre-convention manager, Bartley C. Crum, head of the California Willkie Committee, Gifford Pinchot of Pennsylvania, Daniel A. Poling, nationaly known Baptist minister, and Walter Lippmann, columnist. A surprise bolter was Senator Ball of Minnesota, a Stassen supporter at the Republican convention. Although the newspaper preponderance was heavy for Dewey, two independent newspapers that had been hostile in 1940, the *St. Louis Post-Dispatch* and the *New York Times*, favored Roosevelt.

As in Roosevelt's earlier campaigns, the Democrats depended on radio to offset newspaper hostility; but Dewey's deep voice and clear diction made him the strongest opponent the old Democratic master of air technique had faced.

The two second-place nominees concentrated on doubtful areas. Bricker thundered at bureaucrats and "Hillman, Browder, and Co.," and worked to keep the party regulars in line. Truman's plain, uninspired speeches were helpful in appeasing the Democratic disgruntled. Henry Wallace also stumped for the ticket and was especially effective with the Negro voters.

Political forecasters and professional takers of polls had a hard time. The size of the soldier vote, the number of disfranchised migratory workers, and the apparently narrow margins between the candidates in the large states forced them to hedge their predictions with many qualifications, so that they had slight value. The usual conclusion was that Roosevelt had a narrow popular lead, but the electoral vote might go otherwise. Unusually heavy registration in several large cities dampened Republican hopes somewhat.

The early returns of November 7 indicated another Roosevelt sweep, which became greater as the urban vote was reported. The electoral landslide—432 to 99—represented a popular plurality of approximately 3,600,000 votes in a total vote of 47,976,670. Despite the fact that several millions in the armed services had not been able to vote, the total was surprisingly near the 1940 vote of 49,900,418. The percentages of the popular vote were 53.4 (25,612,610) for Roosevelt and 45.9 (22,017,617) for Dewey.[4]

Dewey carried Ohio, Wisconsin, and Wyoming, which had gone for Roosevelt in 1940. He lost Michigan, which Willkie had carried, but won the other Willkie states: Maine, Vermont, Indiana, Iowa, the Dakotas, Kansas, Nebraska, and Colorado. Both houses of Congress were Democratic by substantial margins.

The soldier vote was not a decisive factor. In the few states that tabulated it separately it was more heavily pro-Roosevelt than the civilian vote, giving point to the earlier fears of some Republicans that a uniform federal ballot would work to their disadvantage. The Republican radio appeal, "End the war quicker with Dewey and Bricker," may have influenced civilian voters, but soldiers on the fighting fronts had little interest in poltics, and many who could have voted did not.

The fundamental explanation of Roosevelt's fourth victory was the war. The majority felt that it was too great a risk to drop the pilot. "Without a doubt the desire to play it safe was the determining factor in the election," stated a leading Republican newspaper. "Roosevelt's leadership represented a known quantity which had every prospect of going on to victory." "He would have won," commented another, "if we had never heard of the P.A.C. and if Dewey had received the solid Republican vote."

[4] Minor parties polled 0.7 per cent of the total: Thomas, Socialist, 79,003; Watson, Prohibition, 74,779; Teichert, Socialist Labor, 45,191; others (mostly bolting Democrats), 147,470.

CHAPTER XI

TRUMAN AND EISENHOWER

1948–1956

1948

HARRY S TRUMAN, made President by Roosevelt's sudden death, was as unprepared for the heavy burdens of his office as most Vice Presidents in the past. But the former Missouri Senator, whose start in politics had come from the support of Boss Pendergast of Kansas City but who had won a respected place in the Senate, soon made it evident that he was not lacking in the qualifications for leadership.

Truman was successful in continuing the bi-partisan foreign policy of his predecessor, supported, as it was, by Senator Vandenberg who held the majority of Republicans in line. But when he pressed for action on the domestic front, he was checkmated by the old conservative coalition. Postwar readjustments and difficulties, as in 1919–20, turned the voters against the party in power, and the Republicans captured control of Congress in 1946 with promises to "end controls, confusion, corruption, Communism."

Truman was able to secure approval of the Marshall Plan to aid European economic recovery, but the new Congress refused to act on his recommendations for social welfare measures and passed over his veto the Taft-Hartley Act restricting labor unions. Truman called the Eightieth Congress the worst in American history. This became his campaign theme in 1948.

Governor Dewey, triumphantly re-elected in 1946 and not

badly damaged by his wartime loss to Roosevelt, led Republican Presidential possibilities in public opinion polls. Senator Taft was the early choice of party regulars. Harold E. Stassen of Minnesota appealed to the more liberal elements and the younger voters. Governor Earl Warren of California was popular on the Pacific Coast; Senator Vandenberg was open to a "draft" in case of a deadlock; and General MacArthur was willing to accept any public duty. General Dwight D. Eisenhower issued an unequivocal refusal to run.

Stassen showed surprising strength in the Wisconsin and Nebraska primaries and forced Dewey to campaign intensively in Oregon. The latter won an impressive victory there. Stassen also failed against Taft in Ohio and was relegated to third place.

An enthusiastic horde of Republicans converged on Philadelphia on June 21 to nominate "the next President," while millions on the eastern seaboard watched through the miracle of television. Speeches from party notables included, again, Mrs. Claire Boothe Luce and Herbert Hoover in their respective roles. The platform was internationalist, and generally innocuous on domestic issues. It included a strong civil rights plank, upheld the Taft-Hartley restrictive labor law, and cautiously favored federal aid for slum clearance and low-rent housing.

It took seven hours of oratory, parading, and carnival revelry to dispose of the nominations. The first ballot gave Dewey, 434; Taft, 224; Stassen, 157; Vandenberg, 62; Warren, 59; and there were half a dozen others. Dewey gained on the second, and before the third the opposition caved in and gave him a unanimous nomination. A carefully organized blitz had done the work.

Governor Warren reluctantly agreed to run for Vice President with the understanding that the office should have more authority than in the past.

Democratic prospects seemed to be so hopeless that a concerted movement developed to put aside Truman for General Eisenhower. The latter settled the matter with a positive refusal, and only some die-hard southerners continued to oppose Truman's nomination. The convention met at Philadelphia on July 12, and heard such a rousing speech from Senator Alben W. Barkley as temporary chairman that he became everybody's choice for Vice President.

A floor battle developed over the civil rights plank offered by the resolutions committee. Attempts by southerners to weaken it were defeated, but Mayor Hubert Humphrey of Minneapolis objected to it as too vague and led the fight for a stronger statement. His amendment carried by a vote of 651 1/2 to 582 1/2. It called upon Congress to guarantee the principles of equal political participation, equal opportunity of employment, the right of security of person, and equal treatment in the armed services. Other planks upheld President Truman's chief recommendations to Congress: measures to control inflation, housing and education programs, national health insurance, repeal of the Taft-Hartley Act, and retention of price supports for farm products.

The ballot for President gave Truman 947 1/2; Senator Richard Russell of Georgia, 263; Paul V. McNutt, 1/2. Barkley had no opposition for Vice President. President Truman, in his militant acceptance speech, announced that he was calling "that worst Eightieth Congress" into special session to give the Republicans a chance to carry out their platform pledges.

Two more conventions named candidates that month. The anti-Truman southerners, denying that they were bolters, met at Birmingham on July 17 and nominated Governor J. Strom Thurmond of South Carolina for President and Governor Fielding L. Wright of Mississippi for Vice President on a state-rights and anti-race-equality platform. In spite of appeals to the emotions and prejudices of the white South, these sectionalists—called Dixiecrats—drew in few nationally important southern Democrats. But the bolters had control of the state organizations in several states and could compel the regular Democratic Presidential electors to support Thurmond. This would force the Truman electors to run as independents with slight chance of success. The Dixiecrats aimed to defeat Truman, even though Dewey's civil rights position was just as unsatisfactory.

While the Dixiecrats preempted the extreme right, a new party appeared on the left—not a wing of seceding Democrats but a hybrid of radicals and non-party liberals of all shades of opinion. In December, 1947, Henry Wallace had accepted the invitation of a group called the Progressive Citizens of America to run for President. A national convention, meeting at Philadelphia on July 22, organized the Progressive party and nominated Wallace and Senator Glen Taylor of Idaho as its candidates. Wallace appeared at a great mass meeting at Shibe Park to accept the nomination on a platform that attacked the Marshall Plan, called for disarmament and the destruction of atomic-bomb stockpiles, and demanded equality of treatment for all minority groups. It was a gathering, in large part, of idealistic young voters who, gazing through the tinted glasses of peace and equal rights and alarmed at the cold war and the revival of the draft, could not see the Communist pattern of the platform and the skillful management of the party-liners in the convention's proceedings. Early in August a Communist party convention indorsed Wallace and adopted a platform very similar to that of the Progressive party.

Congress, called into special session by Truman, refused to act on most of his program. The Republican majority denounced his action as a political move—which it was—and adjourned after passing weak housing and anti-inflation bills that were hardly more than gestures for campaign purposes. The cast-iron conservatism of the House leadership played into Truman's hands. He could now go on the stump and repeat his charges against the Eightieth Congress with even more emphasis.

But Truman's plight seemed to be hopeless. The Dixiecrats were certain to win some southern electoral votes. Wallace would cut into Democratic strength in New York and possibly other states of the East and the Middle West. If Dewey polled the normal Republican vote he would move into the White House. And there was no evidence that the Republican trend of 1946 had been reversed. As a result, the Democratic leadership fell into a defeatist lethargy, and Truman and a few loyal supporters had to bear the brunt of the campaigning. The national chairman, J. Howard McGrath, was confronted with a lack of funds and a disorganized party, and had one of the most difficult tasks a campaign manager had ever faced.

Truman, undaunted by the odds against him, traveled 31,000 miles in a "whistle-stop" campaign and spoke to some 6,000,000 people. He hammered away at the record of the Eightieth Congress, blaming it for price and rent rises and the housing shortage (an appeal to salaried workers and veterans) and for the Taft-Hartley Act (an appeal to labor). For farmers, he pointed to years of prosperity under Democratic rule and warned of the dangers of an end of price supports if the Republicans won. For the conservation-minded West, he emphasized the benefits of a liberal federal policy and the threats to reclamation projects from Congressional cuts in appropriations. Thus he offered both performance and promise. Late in the campaign, he shifted to the civil rights issue in speeches in the East and the Middle West where large minority groups—Negroes, Jews, foreign-born—were tempted by the Wallace lure. This put a strain on southern Democrats, but traditional party loyalty had to take care of the Thurmond threat.

The President's speeches were homely, down-to-earth, hard-hitting talks of an average man aimed at the average man. A little group of faithful aides assisted him, and their planning belied the caustic comment of a newspaperman: "With Truman's staff, Robert E. Lee couldn't carry Virginia." All the working journalists were puzzled by the large crowds that turned out to see the President, and wondered at the apparent warmth of their greeting. But did this mean votes or merely admiration for a little guy who didn't know when he was licked?

On the Republican side the campaign was managed by the same efficient methods that had brought Dewey the nomination. Representative Hugh D. Scott, Jr., of Pennsylvania was national chairman, but Governor Dewey and his experienced general staff directed the strategy. Dewey's speeches stressed the need for an administration that would promote national unity and the cause of world peace. He promised to "work for peace through the United Nations and by every honorable means wherever the peace is threatened." At home, he would promote both social progress and individual freedom. He avoided concrete commitments which might create trouble in his own party and might prove embarrassing after election. His task, with victory seemingly assured, was not to win friends but to keep from alienating people. His deep voice, excellent for radio, poured out polished, faultless sentences, correctly inflected and uttered with a confident assurance that carried conviction. Truman appeared as an inept fumbler beside him; but the Republican candidate's speeches seemed to flow over his audiences, not into them. He seemed to be the cool, cautious champion; Truman, the fighting challenger. Dewey chose to let his wild-swinging opponent defeat himself, rather than to take chances by trading punches; but it made the campaign singularly dull. Dewey was a machine with a cellophane cover, said one observant critic.

In the South the Dixiecrats conducted a vigorous campaign. They controlled the state committees in Alabama, Mississippi, South Carolina, and Louisiana, where their electors ran as the regular Democratic candidates. In Alabama the ballot listed no Truman electors. In other parts of the South Thurmond-Wright electoral candidates ran as independents and threatened to give Virginia, Florida, and Tennessee to the Republicans. Loyal Truman Democrats believed that the Southern Rights movement had financial support from northern business interests with southern connections, and that state rights, rebel yells, and Yankee dollars worked in harmony for Republican victory.

Henry Wallace provided the thunder on the left. His invasion of the South to preach equal rights produced some acts of rowdiness where it defied Jim Crow regulations, but his political importance was in the urban sections of the East and the Middle West. Wherever his name appeared on the ballot, it lessened Democratic chances of victory. Likewise, it pointed up the Communist issue for the major parties. The Un-American Activities Committee of the House of Representatives, under Republican control, unearthed sufficient evidence of Communist espionage and other operations to create a good deal of concern, and Republican speakers made much of Communist infiltration. Dewey, however, opposed outlawry of the Communist party. Truman criticized the inquisitorial methods of the investigators and called their allegations "a red herring" to divert attention from more important matters. Wallace's candidacy actually did the Democrats a good turn. It attracted radicals of all shades and freed Truman of the taint of their support. But there were fears that he would need these votes to win the close states.

All the leading polls, the political analysts, and the important newspapers predicted a Dewey victory, though some conceded that Truman's fighting campaign had stirred lagging Democratic spirits, and that control of the next Senate was in doubt. The cautious *New York Times*, on the basis of reports of its correspondents, gave Dewey 305 electoral votes, Truman 105, and Thurmond 38, with 43 votes doubtful. The President himself forecast in mid-October: Truman, 229 votes; Dewey, 109; Thurmond, 8; doubtful, 189.

On the night of November 2 the early returns put Truman in the lead, but Republican headquarters remained optimistic. These were urban votes that would be nullified by later returns from rural districts. Quite the reverse happened. Truman's popular lead increased as the western states reported, but there was uncertainty about the electoral votes. The election might go to the House. Not until 11:14 A.M. on Wednesday, after California and Ohio had gone into the Truman column, did Dewey concede defeat. The electoral results were 303 votes for Truman, 189 for Dewey, 39 for Thurmond. Dewey had carried Maine, New Hampshire, Vermont, Connecticut, New York, Pennsylvania, New Jersey, Maryland, and Delaware in the East, Michigan and Indiana in the Middle West, North Dakota, South Dakota, Nebraska, and Kansas in the farm belt, and Oregon on the Pacific coast. Thurmond had South Carolina, Alabama, Mississippi, and Louisiana, and one Tennessee elector who violated his Truman pledge. Truman carried the remaining twenty-eight states.

The states from Ohio westward and the upper South provided most of his votes, but the surprising thing was the wide distribution of his strength. But for the Wallace candidacy he might have carried New York, Michigan, and Maryland; and Thurmond certainly cost him 39 electoral votes in the South. Dewey's percentage of the popular vote (45.1) was a little under that in 1944 (45.9). Truman had 49.6 per cent; the minor parties, 5.3 per cent.[1]

Various explanations were offered for the incredible result: farm prosperity and farmer distrust of Easterner Dewey; labor's weight in the cities; Truman's whistle-stop campaign, stressing the record of the Eightieth Congress; Dewey's failure to come to grips with the issues; Republican overconfidence and consequent failure to get out a full vote; an unusually strong crop of Democratic candidates for the Senate and for state governorships, which aided the national ticket; the failure of Thurmond and Wallace to do what the pollsters had predicted.

The most heartening thing about the election was the stubborn independence of the voting majority in defying the band-wagon psychology created by polls, newspaper opinion, and the near-unanimous verdict of the political pundits. These samplers of opinion were quite crestfallen, and the laughter over their discomfiture tempered the disappointment of the defeated. Never again would an election be regarded as settled until the votes were counted.

1952

Most of Truman's Fair Deal program was swept down the drain by the bi-partisan alliance in Congress, but, again, his major foreign policy objectives were being attained when

[1] The popular vote was as follows: Truman, 24,179,345; Dewey, 21,991,291; Thurmond, 1,176,125; Wallace, 1,157,326; Thomas, Socialist, 139,572; Watson, Prohibitionist, 103,900; Teichert, Socialist Labor, 29,241; Dobbs, Socialist Workers, 13,614.

the outbreak of war in Korea saddled the administration with a set of liabilities so potent that Republican hopes rose to a new high by 1952. Exposures of shady deals and influence peddling in some of the departments were an unexpected boon to the Republicans. "Mink coats," "deep freezers," and "five per centers" hit the headlines to provide grist for the Republican propaganda mill.

Senator Taft, re-elected to the Senate by a landslide in 1950, felt that his turn had come at last. All over the land party wheelhorses, courthouse politicos, isolationists, Asia Firsters, small-town and country conservatives, lined up votes for the man who would not be a "Me Too" candidate. Except for New England, Taft was strongest where the party was well-entrenched—in much of the Middle West—and where it was weakest—in the southern states.

But liberal and internationalist Republicans feared that a man who had been an isolationist, a defender of Senator Joseph McCarthy's witch-hunting, a critic of organized labor, and an unrelenting conservative would drive away liberals and independents and lose the large doubtful states. The anti-Taft forces had to find an outstanding figure to oppose "Mr. Republican."

The problem was solved when, early in 1952, a "Draft Eisenhower" movement persuaded the popular military leader of World War II to permit his name to be entered in the New Hampshire primary. Senator Henry Cabot Lodge headed the Eisenhower forces. They could count on financial backing from big business sources and friendly publicity from metropolitan newspapers and the large news weeklies. Eisenhower won in New Hampshire, but results were indecisive elsewhere with the candidacies of Stassen and Governor Warren complicating matters. Eisenhower resigned as NATO commander, returned home to campaign actively, and made surprising headway by being himself.

When the national convention opened at Chicago in International Amphitheater on July 7, 1952, Taft led in pledged delegates but the uncommitted, the Stassen and Warren blocs, and some seventy contested seats held the balance of power.

The fate of the contested seats from three southern states, it seemed, would decide control of the convention. The Taft men lost on a preliminary vote over temporary seats, but won in the credentials committee. The convention, however, rejected the committee report and the Eisenhower delegates were seated. The mounting bitterness between the opposing forces harked back to 1912.

The platform attracted little attention. It attacked Communism and corruption in the government, leaned strongly toward states rights, and promised to end "the negative, futile and immoral policy of containment."

The votes on the contested seats had indicated that unpledged Michigan and Pennsylvania and the Warren-Stassen votes were anti-Taft. The single ballot gave Eisenhower 595 votes, (9 short of a majority) and changes quickly nominated him. The Eisenhower high command selected Senator Richard M. Nixon of California, thirty-nine years old, to run with him. Nixon had played a part in a House committee's exposure of Alger Hiss, and his nomination pointed up the Communism-in-government issue. But it denied the Taft minority a customary consolation prize.

Truman's decision not to run again opened the way for a Democratic free-for-all battle. Senator Estes Kefauver, who had headed a special Senate committee to investigate crime, won some early primary victories. His reform record and his coonskin cap made the lanky Tennessean a popular figure, but neither the Truman administration nor southern conservatives accepted him. The latter backed Senator Richard Russell of Georgia.

Among favorite sons were W. Averell Harriman of New York, a Roosevelt-Truman loyalist who had held several administrative posts, Senator Robert S. Kerr, a wealthy Oklahoma oil man, and Vice President Alben Barkley, whose seventy-four years were a serious obstacle.

More available was Governor Adlai Stevenson of Illinois, grandson of a Vice President, who had held responsible posts with the Navy and State departments, had run ahead of Truman in Illinois in 1948, and had made a good record as governor. But Stevenson refused to run and discouraged a draft movement, preferring to try for reelection as governor.

The Democratic convention opened in Chicago, two weeks after the Republican conclave, in the same International Amphitheater. The platform virtually repeated the civil rights plank of 1948, defended the Truman policies, and promised the farmer ninety per cent of parity and labor the repeal of the Taft-Hartley Act. Stevenson's brief and witty address of welcome gave the draft movement a strong impetus, but more important was the swing of important state leaders to the reluctant candidate.

The first ballot gave Kefauver 340 votes, Stevenson 273, Russell 268, and several others smaller numbers. The two leaders gained on the second ballot, but on the third a general shift to Stevenson nominated him. His acceptance speech has become a classic in convention oratory.

Next day, the convention nominated for Vice President Stevenson's choice, Senator John J. Sparkman of Alabama, a southern moderate who had fought the Dixiecrats.

In the Republican camp Arthur Summerfield, who had swung unpledged Michigan to Eisenhower at Chicago, became national chairman and campaign manager. Governor Sherman Adams of New Hampshire was personal adviser to the candidate. A Citizens Committee for Eisenhower, which had worked for his nomination, continued its separate organization and aimed its propaganda at independents and Democrats. Stevenson chose Stephen A. Mitchell, a Chicago lawyer whose experience was more legal than political, but who brought new blood into the organization, and Wilson W. Wyatt of Kentucky, a founder of the liberal Americans for Democratic Action, to handle his campaign, with Mitchell as national chairman. Both had had experience in Washington positions. Sinclair Weeks handled finances for the Republicans, Beardsley Ruml for the Democrats.

The big Republican problem was Taft's attitude. The boos that had greeted Eisenhower when he called at Taft headquarters just after the nomination indicated the feelings of the Taft men. Taft himself formally indorsed the nominee, then left for his summer home in Quebec. Apparently he was prepared to sit out the campaign, and his devoted following might do likewise. They regarded Eisenhower as the tool of the "Dewey people" and another "Me, too" candidate. Not since the Taft-Roosevelt feud of 1912 had there been such fratricidal strife in the party. Eisenhower moved to heal the breach by inviting Taft to his home on Morningside Heights. They conferred on September 12, and a manifesto written by Taft was accepted with only slight changes by the candidate and made public. It committed him to the orthodox (to Taft) position on all major points, except for some "differences of degree" on foreign policy, and promised equality of treatment for Taft supporters as to offices.

This "surrender," as Democratic critics termed it, brought the Ohio Senator into the fold; his lieutenants went to work, and party unity seemed to be assured. Eisenhower appeared with Senators Jenner in Indiana and McCarthy in Wisconsin, though Jenner had called his old mentor and friend, General George C. Marshall, "a front for traitors" and "a living lie," and McCarthy had been equally harsh. Possibly, Eisenhower was thinking that he would need support from the Taft wing, so powerful in Congress, if he won in November. In any case, Republican nominees for office received pats on the back wherever the head of the ticket appeared.

Stevenson's troubles lay southward. There the conservatives were unhappy over the civil rights issue, and Texas, Louisiana, and Florida had a special grievance—Truman's vetoes of bills giving title of offshore lands to the states. The candidate refused to back away from his platform. Referring to civil rights, he told a Richmond (Va.) audience: "I should justly earn your contempt if I talked one way in the South and another way elsewhere." Later, in Texas, he upheld federal control of offshore lands and damned himself with the oil interests and with state-rights men generally.

These issues and the widespread dislike of southern conservatives for the Truman administration caused bolting to Eisenhower that was like the Hoovercrat revolt against Alfred E. Smith in 1928. Governors Byrnes of South Carolina, Kennon of Louisiana, and Shivers of Texas led the rebels, while Senator Byrd of Virginia criticized Stevenson without announcing for Eisenhower. Most members of Congress were loyal, but many gave the ticket lukewarm support. Several important newspapers led by the *Atlanta Journal* came out for Eisenhower. The loyalty pledge of the Democratic national convention was observed everywhere, and Stevenson electors ran as Democrats. To avoid the Republican imprint, Eisenhower Democrats offered independent electoral tickets in South Carolina and Mississippi. Eisenhower campaigned vigorously in the South and drew large crowds. And sentimental southerners did not forget that he was born in Texas.

Using train and plane, the two rivals displayed their bald heads all over the continent. Important addresses in key cities were televised. This meant a different speech for each occasion, and a corps of skilled phrasemakers supplied much of the ammunition. This was particularly necessary in Eisenhower's case. Not well informed on domestic questions, nor blessed with the gift of eloquence, and inexperienced before the television camera, he had much to learn about campaign spellbinding. But his technique improved under coaching, and his audiences liked him for his sincerity, his humanness, his informal presence and folksy ways. They were not too concerned about what his advisers put into his set speeches. In his whistle-stop appearances, when he talked in familiar, if hackneyed, terms about his middle-of-the-road philosophy with Mamie waving at the cheering throngs, he was at his best. He was not a good partisan, he had no grudges, he chose to attack the "administration" rather than Truman, and his Communism, Korea, and corruption lacked personal devils. Yet, while he had trouble acting like a strong party man, he belonged in the Republican party. Fundamentally, he was a conservative.

Stevenson was a surprising discovery to most Americans. This not very impressive man with a receding hair line and a slightly paunchy middle immediately moved into the front rank of American political orators of all time. He had a good voice, but his speeches read even better than they sounded. He had a gift for the telling phrase, a probing wit, a keen mentality, and a challenging, if troubled, idealism that sometimes emerged in passages of moving eloquence. The intellectuals that had enlisted with F. D. R. in the depression years, but had found themselves pushed aside by the "cronies" under Truman, thronged into the Stevenson camp, for they saw him as one of their own kind. But these "eggheads" were not all gain. In the climate of anti-intellectualism engendered by fears of Communist infiltration and McCarthy accusations, many voters confused loyalty with conformity and suspected men who thought too much. The Wisconsin Senator went on the air to smear Stevenson and his personal staff, and Senator Nixon echoed McCarthy that Stevenson had never expressed one word of indignation at Alger Hiss's treachery. Leftists were not to be trusted.

While Ike was a world figure, the Democratic candidate was virtually unknown when nominated. Even at the campaign's end, he was still, to many voters, an uncomfortable type of party leader. He was almost too clever, too witty, too abstruse. Ike's platitudes and homilies, they understood and accepted. More important, the supreme commander of World War II seemed to be better equipped to end the stalemated Korean War. His master stroke of the campaign, suggested by a shrewd journalist, was the eleventh-hour announcement that, if elected, he would go to Korea in person. Stevenson, carrying the weight of Truman's Korea burdens, could only reply that Moscow, not Seoul, held the key to peace.

The most dramatic development of the campaign involved Nixon, the Republican choice for Vice President. In late September, the *New York Post* featured a story that, as Senator, he had been subsidized by a secret fund set up by California millionaires. Nixon, then campaigning in the West, admitted that the fund had existed, but asserted that it had been used for purely political expenses and involved him in no obligations to his benefactors. The fund treasurer opened its books, which revealed expenditures of about $18,000 in a year and a half for such expenses as trips to California, printing and mimeographing, and radio and television appearances. The dubious ethics of a public career financed by men of wealth, the size of the fund, and the concealment of its existence seemed to provide the Democrats with an answer to the Republican reiteration of "mink coats" and "deep freezers," symbols of exposures at Washington. Republican newspapers, in alarm, debated whether Nixon should be dropped from the ticket; Eisenhower and his advisers were equally perturbed, but final action was held up until the California Senator had offered his defense on television.

That defense saved his public career. Skillfully shifting from the fund issue, where he was vulnerable, to a defense of his reputation for honesty and integrity, he related the history of his personal finances from youth on. It was the story of the honest poor boy's rise to fame through his own efforts with no ill-gotten gains to smooth his path. His wife (who was with him), her "respectable Republican cloth coat" (not mink), and their children's dog were brought into his affecting story. He invited his listeners to send their opinions to the Republican National Committee, which would decide his case. The result was a deluge of approving messages, and he went East to be greeted by Eisenhower as a man of courage and honor who had been subjected to "a very unfair and vicious attack." Democratic critics called his performance "ham acting" and "a financial strip tease," but he had emerged as a popular hero.

The Republicans kept pounding away at their trinity of Democratic failures: blunders in foreign policy, the "mess" in Washington, the Communist danger within. Other issues were peripheral, but all fitted the slogan, "It's time for a change." As the party of the outs, they could promise much and specify little. The hard-pressed Democrats had to defend and condone—an admission that all was not well. And so they turned to a weapon that had worked well in the past, and proclaimed that good times would end if the Republicans won. Prosperity and the social gains of the New Deal were in danger. "Don't let them take it away" and "You never had it so good" were their war cries. This was effective enough to cause the Republicans to promise that nothing would be taken away; things would only be made better. For instance, Eisenhower told the Minnesota farmers that they were entitled to 100 per cent of parity instead of the Democratic

90 per cent, and in New England he promised full employment and an extension of social security.

Public opinion polls indicated an Eisenhower victory, as the trend everywhere was strongly in his favor; but the percentage of undecided was still large enough to hold the balance in many states, and pollsters, after having burned their fingers in 1948, were duly cautious. That Eisenhower seemed to be much stronger than his party was a safe conclusion.

They were too cautious this time. It was an Eisenhower, if not a Republican, landslide. With a total of 442 electoral votes, he had the entire North and West; Virginia, Tennessee, Florida, and Texas in the South; and Maryland and Missouri in the border area. Stevenson, with only 89 electoral votes, carried the rest of the South and Kentucky and West Virginia—nine states in all. Eisenhower had surpassed Truman in 1948 and Roosevelt in 1944, and was two votes short of Hoover's total of electors in 1928. He had repeated Hoover's victories in the South, except for North Carolina. His popular vote was 33,936,234 (55.1 per cent) to Stevenson's 27,314,992 (44.4 per cent). The record total vote was 61,550,918. In contrast to 1948, the minor parties were unimportant.[2]

The country had voted overwhelmingly for Eisenhower but hesitatingly for his party. His coattails did not carry into office the usual proportion of Congressional and local candidates. In the House were 221 Republicans, 213 Democrats, and 1 independent; in the Senate, 48 Republicans, 47 Democrats, and Wayne Morse, Oregon Republican who had bolted and was now an independent. His vote enabled the Republicans to organize the Upper House. The defeat of three extreme isolationist Senators, and the fact that McCarthy of Wisconsin, Jenner of Indiana, Bricker of Ohio, and Malone of Nevada ran far behind Eisenhower indicated

[2] The older third-party votes were as follows: Vincent Hallinan, Progressive, 140,023; Stuart Hamblen, Prohibition, 72,949; Eric Hass, Socialist Labor (Industrial Government in some states), 30,267; Darlington Hoopes, Socialist, 20,203. Other splinter parties had smaller totals.

that many independents and Democrats had liked Ike but rejected his party.

Eisenhower's victory was a vote of confidence in the man himself but also in his party's somewhat fictionized picture of him, which assured troubled Americans that he had the answers to all the nation's problems. His appeal was like Harding's return to normalcy. Korean bloodshed, tax burdens, inflation, subversives, corruption—all would yield to the skill of the soldier statesman, and happier days would return.

1956

Matters of special significance for the Republican party in Eisenhower's first term include the death of Senator Taft and the choice of William F. Knowland of California to succeed him as Senate floor leader, the disposal of McCarthyism by a Senate resolution censuring the irresponsible Wisconsin investigator, the ending of hostilities in Korea, and a Democratic recovery in the mid-term elections of 1954, caused in part by corn and wheat belt dissatisfaction with Secretary of Agriculture Ezra Benson's farm policy, and a mild business recession. The Democrats won control of both Houses and seven close states elected Democratic governors, although Eisenhower and Nixon campaigned actively. Nixon's arraignment of the Democratic party for harboring Communists and subversives—he denied calling it the party of treason—made him political enemy number one for loyal Democrats.

In the Democratic camp a second nomination had been more or less conceded to Adlai Stevenson until Senator Kefauver, contesting the primaries, won in New Hampshire and Minnesota with his handshaking tactics. But Stevenson rebounded to defeat the Tennessean in Florida, Oregon, and California. State organizations in convention states also chose delegates hostile to Kefauver. On August 1 he withdrew in Stevenson's favor, though he had bagged 165 delegates.

On August 13, the Democrats assembled again at Chicago. Averell Harriman, elected governor of New York in 1954, had become a candidate but was not taken very seriously until former President Truman came out for him and arrived in Chicago to help his cause. Several favorite sons then became active. Mrs. Eleanor Roosevelt, a convention favorite, was in the Stevenson camp, and a skilled Philadephia professional, James A. Finnegan, was his manager. Stevenson's lines held firm, and the roll call nominated him when Pennsylvania was reached. The final count gave him 905 1/2 to Harriman's 210, with seven others dividing the rest of the 1,372 votes.

Stevenson left the Vice Presidential choice to the convention, and a night of wild politicking followed. Senators Hubert Humphrey of Minnesota, John F. Kennedy of Massachusetts, Kefauver and Albert Gore of Tennessee, and Mayor Robert Wagner of New York went the rounds of state delegations hunting for votes. On the first ballot Kefauver led with Kennedy, Gore, Wagner, and Humphrey following in that order. On the next trial a southern group, hostile to liberal Kefauver, joined with easterners to back Catholic Kennedy, but last-minute changes from Humphrey and Gore saved Kefauver.

The platform attacked, deplored, and viewed with alarm Eisenhower policies at home and abroad and offered a program similar to that of 1952 for farmer and laborer. On civil rights it accepted recent Supreme Court decisions on desegregation but "rejected all proposals for the use of force to interfere with the orderly determination of these matters by the courts." A more liberal minority report was defeated, with Truman speaking for the majority version.

Republicans feared for a time that Eisenhower's health might be a barrier to his renomination. He suffered a heart attack in 1955 and underwent an emergency operation after an attack of ileitis a year later. But his recovery was fairly rapid, and the Republican convention, when it opened at San Francisco's Cow Palace on August 23, was a unanimity affair.

Vice President Nixon's renomination was as certain as his chief's, although Harold Stassen tried to promote a boom for Governor Christian Herter of Massachusetts. Herter's response was to make the nominating speech for Nixon, and Stassen was booed whenever he appeared in public. Both the victors of 1952 were nominated by acclamation.

The platform contained a civil liberties plank which favored carrying out the Supreme Court's decision on desegregation with "all deliberate speed" but not by using force. The farm plank indorsed Secretary of Agriculture Benson's "versatile flexible program." The foreign policy section upheld collective security, a strong United Nations, aid for under-developed countries, and other features of the Eisenhower-Dulles policies. There was no concession to isolationism. Eisenhower, in his acceptance speech, even held out the hope of a peaceful coexistence with a more conciliatory Communist world.

Stevenson appointed James A. Finnegan, his pre-convention strategist, as his campaign manager with Paul Butler continuing as chairman of the national committee. A separate organization, the Volunteers for Stevenson-Kefauver, was designed to operate outside the party fence. It tapped the enthusiasm and energy of the younger voters.

In early September the Democratic nominees attended a series of regional meetings with party leaders and state and local candidates to coordinate the different levels of the campaign. To offset the personal popularity of Eisenhower, Stevenson needed to activate party loyalties and to make common cause with strong local vote-getters—coattails in reverse, it was dubbed. Nine eastern and middle western states had elected Democratic governors since 1952. Their aid and the voting pull of popular candidates for the Senate might swing close states. Kefauver was to center his efforts in the western farm belt where he had never lost a primary, where the rural voters liked his homespun personality. After joining with Stevenson in the television opening of the campaign at Harrisburg, Pennsylvania, he embarked on his canvass of the common man.

The Democratic campaign was given a sudden lift on September 10 when traditionally Republican Maine reelected its popular Democratic governor, Edmund S. Muskie, and for the first time in twenty-two years sent a Democrat to

Congress from one of its three districts. Maine had been an uncertain barometer in past Presidential elections, but the size of the Democratic victory there could not be overlooked in the crystal balls of the forecasters.

Stevenson set out to show himself to as many voters and to shake as many hands as possible. He directed his talks at ordinary folk, ever suspicious of highbrow candidates with flashing rapiers. Consequently, he was less witty, more down-to-earth than in 1952. Major addresses were televised. From friendly quarters came occasional expressions of disappointment that he was not projecting his speeches well, that his perfectionist concern with the text did not include its delivery, which sometimes left the impression that he was still pondering over his sentences. His technique improved toward the end but his appeal was rational, not emotional. Yet he had attracted a devoted personal following centering in the Volunteers for Stevenson who too often had to take over registration drives, circulation of campaign literature, telephone canvassing, and other tasks when party organizations were dragging their feet or pushing only local candidates.

The Republican campaign, directed by Leonard W. Hall, national chairman since 1953, was planned to start late, use Nixon for heavy barnstorming, and call upon Eisenhower only for a token trip or two to demonstrate his physical fitness. But the Maine outcome, the early burst of Democratic energy, disaffection in the Republican farm belt, and pleas for the use of his coattails by hard-pressed Senatorial candidates—several of them his personal selections—drew the President into making some half a dozen forays that reached nearly all of the key states. But for the Near East crisis, he would have spent most of the final week on the trail. He drew larger crowds than Stevenson and helped mightily to restore party morale.

The Republican appeal added peace and prosperity to "We Like Ike." The administration had ended the Korean War and had stabilized prosperity without war and inflation. "America is happier than it was four years ago," said Eisenhower again and again, and crowd responses to his

smiling face and confident voice made his discussi /
issues almost a waste of time.

The Democrats answered that the prosperity was inhe.
that Stalin's death had made possible the Korean truce, a
Democrats in Congress had done more for Ike than his ov
party. Stevenson tried to draw his opponent into debates o.
specific policies but had only limited success. His problem
was to find vote-getting issues and to break through Nixon,
Dulles, Benson, and the rest of the White House cordon to
battle with the chief himself. Foreign policy, farm problems,
national defense, conservation, aid for public schools, and
the broader questions of Eisenhower's past conception of
his office and his fitness for future leadership, with Vice
President Nixon's role a major consideration, all were legiti-
mate subjects for party debate, but the Democratic candidate
could not stir a complacent electorate. Attacks on the Dulles
foreign policy were shrugged off so long as the nation was
at peace. Farmers were dissatisfied, but, outside certain
western drought areas, not distressed, and the Democratic
offer of 90 per cent parity was viewed with mixed feelings,
even by the considerable number who disliked Secretary
Benson's flexible price supports and his soil conservation plan.

Stevenson threw national defense into the campaign hopper
by suggesting the possibility of an end to the draft system,
and later by proposing that the United States offer to join
with Russia in stopping hydrogen bomb tests. Both proposi-
tions met with Republican charges that they would weaken
national defense, and Eisenhower's stand carried special
weight here, though the proposed ban on bomb tests did
provoke discussion and disagreement among scientists as to
the health hazards involved in repeated testing.

"Give-away" charges leveled at the administration's part-
nership policy toward power projects had some effect in the
Pacific Northwest and entered into the defeat of former
Secretary of the Interior Douglas McKay by Senator Wayne
Morse for the Senate seat from Oregon. The fact that in
Congress a number of Democrats had voted with Republi-
cans on the Hell's Canyon, school-aid, and natural-gas regula-

tion bills made it difficult for Stevenson to use these issues, about which few of his listeners were well informed or felt much concern, in any case.

The Democratic candidate put the greatest emphasis on the failure of Eisenhower to provide strong leadership. The President, he charged, "has never had the inclination and now lacks the energy for full-time work at the world's toughest job." A man whose age and state of health were serious voter considerations became a more doubtful risk, Democrats argued, when the Republican Vice Presidential choice was evaluated. Kefauver was expected to carry more than his weight, Nixon less than his. No Republican name called forth such roars of boos at Democratic rallies. The "hatchet man" tactics of past campaigns and his popularity with right-wing Republicans made "this man of many masks" (Stevenson's characterization) the one personal devil all Democrats could assail.

The Vice President's answer was to conduct a campaign to sell a "new Nixon." His speeches dealt with the accomplishments of the administration—"the best four years of our lives"—and the commanding stature of the President. Skilfully intermingling statistics with praise and pleas, he answered Democratic charges by comparing the records of Eisenhower and Truman, and the merits of Ike and Adlai. The slashing partisanship of 1952 and 1954 was missing and personal attacks upon him were not answered in kind. While he disappointed the McCarthy following by ignoring the Communist issue, the new Nixon filled more effectively the role of the second in command. His strenuous barnstorming—42,000 miles—was a model of efficient management. He consulted with local leaders, eulogized local candidates, fitted his remarks to his audiences, and was especially effective in appealing to women and young voters. At his side was Mrs. Pat Nixon with an appeal of her own. Yet, to the end of the campaign, Democrats saw only the horns of the old Nixon.

One issue was not emphasized on the national level—segregation in the schools. Eisenhower insisted that it made no difference whether or not he indorsed the Supreme Court decision, that the question must be handled on a state and local basis, that his record in the army and as President spoke for itself. Stevenson upheld the Supreme Court but agreed with his party's platform in rejecting the use of force to interfere with the orderly determination of such matters by the courts. Senator Eastland of Mississippi, an active segregationist and chairman of the Senate Judiciary Committee, was an embarrassment to northern Democrats, for Republicans charged that he would block all civil rights legislation with the support of other southern Democrats. Congressman Adam Clayton Powell, Jr., of New York, a Negro Democratic leader, after an interview with the President, announced that he was supporting him. Several Negro newspapers and a number of prominent professional men were reported as turning to the Republicans.

Organized labor—now the united AFL-CIO—through its executive council voted to indorse Stevenson, although 8 of the 22 members were against any indorsements. Walter Reuther, head of the United Automobile Workers, led the Stevenson forces and was the most active labor leader in the campaign both for the national ticket and for other candidates. In states where labor indorsed senatorial or gubernatorial candidates, as in Michigan and the Pacific Northwest, doorbell ringing by union workers increased Democratic registration and insured a heavy vote.

Secretary of Labor James P. Mitchell, popular in labor circles, worked strenuously to convince the rank and file that the administration was friendly to labor and that southern Democrats would, if Congress was Democratic, block pro-labor and social welfare measures. The peace-prosperity theme was used in urging workingmen to discard their old distrust of the Republican party.

With no burning issues to stir a complacent electorate, Stevenson and Kefauver could not overlook the old battle cry that the Republicans favored big business, the Democrats were for the little people. "It is time to take the government away from General Motors and give it back to Joe Smith," declared Stevenson. Eisenhower defended his appointees from the business world as men who had demonstrated administrative fitness. His party, he said, supported social welfare measures but would do for the people only what they could not well do for themselves; the Democrats would guide and direct from Washington.

In the final two weeks of this lethargic contest American voters were shaken out of their complacency by the news of a bloody revolt against Communism in Hungary, which required Russian tanks to suppress, and an Israeli invasion of Egypt followed immediately by Anglo-French military intervention at the Suez Canal. The American government supported the United Nations in condemning aggression in both areas and this course did not draw direct partisan fire. But Stevenson, who had been attacking the Dulles "brinkmanship" policy for its failure to checkmate Communism, its lack of direction, its rose-tinted view of the world's problems, now saw in these eruptions "the total bankruptcy of the administration's foreign policy." "The NATO alliance is crumbling," he charged, "the Middle East is in shambles"; Communism had benefited, and the United States had been cut off from its old friends.

Eisenhower, in the one speech he made after the Suez crisis, discussed only the broad principles of American policies. He said that he was undisturbed by "the strident voices of those who seem to be seeking to turn world events to political profit"—his only reference to his critic. The election was too near for these explosions abroad to have much effect on the voters. Their minds were already made up.

The first returns on the night of November 6 pointed to an Eisenhower victory which soon became an avalanche surpassed only by the Roosevelt sweep of 1936. The President polled 457 electoral votes and 35,590,472 popular votes to Stevenson's 73 and 26,022,752.[3] One electoral vote went to Judge Walter B. Jones of Alabama from an Alabama elector who violated his party pledge.

Of the Eisenhower states of 1952, only Missouri shifted to Stevenson; but Kentucky, West Virginia, and Louisiana left the Democratic column, which consisted of only North

[3] Minor parties polled 413,684 votes, three-fourths of the total going to various state-rights tickets.

Carolina, South Carolina, Georgia, Alabama, Mississippi, Arkansas, and Missouri. The explanation was simple. The nation voted its confidence in an experienced leader whose administration had a peace-and-prosperity record, whose middle-of-the-road policies fitted the mood of the American people, and whose services, despite his age, seemed indispensable with external dangers mounting. Generally, except in the western farm belt and California, his margins were larger than in 1952. His best showings were in the urban East, where foreign problems mattered most, and in the South, where apparently a shift of Negro voters swelled his totals.

Nevertheless, the nation elected a Democratic Congress, the Senate 49 to 47, the House 234 to 201. Why Eisenhower's coattails pulled so badly was hard to understand in view of his pleas and his party's well-filled coffers. It was conjectured that party lines had come to mean little, that voters were picking candidates on their merits or personalities. One might more logically argue that Democrats had come to outnumber Republicans, that they tended to vote for party candidates for Congress and state offices, but that large numbers liked Ike and voted for him in spite of his party.

Viewed in its immediate aftermath, the election, then, was actually a vote for a bi-partisan administration—a perplexing verdict for believers in party or parliamentary government. The voters wanted peace and prosperity continued and this was their solution. They trusted Eisenhower to preserve the one, the Democrats to safeguard the other. In 1956 this seemed to make sense.

CHAPTER XII

KENNEDY AND NIXON

1960

CONGRESS BECAME more Democratic as a result of the mid-term elections of 1958. A sharp business recession, farmer disapproval of Secretary of Agriculture Benson's policies, and Republican sponsorship of anti-union, right-to-work laws in several states were factors in what was a near-debacle. Two Republicans withstood the Democratic sweep. Liberal, personable Nelson Rockefeller was elected governor of New York, and outspoken Senator Barry Goldwater, right wing Republican, was reelected from Arizona.

The civil rights issue was moving to the center of the stage. Negro organizations began to use economic boycotts, sit-in demonstrations, and other passive resistance tactics with some success to end discrimination in public transportation facilities and business places. Two civil rights acts of Congress did not greatly alter the voting situation in the South. President Eisenhower used federal troops in Little Rock, Arkansas, to enforce school desegregation when Governor Orval E. Faubus attempted to block Negro enrollment in a high school.

Relations with Russia deteriorated when an American reconnaissance plane was brought down on Russian soil. Fidel Castro, who had overthrown the corrupt Batista regime in Cuba with American approval, proceeded to set up a Communist-oriented dictatorship and created a situation that led to a break in diplomatic relations. The Cuban problem inevitably became a political issue.

Business recovery, a balanced budget, Ike's personal popularity, and the prospect for a battle royal in the Democratic party encouraged the Republicans as convention time approached.

The Democratic sweepstakes had four contenders, all members of the Senate: Lyndon B. Johnson of Texas, Hubert Humphrey of Minnesota, Stuart Symington of Missouri, and John F. Kennedy of Massachusetts. Johnson had been an outstanding success as Senate floor leader and had the support of Speaker Sam Rayburn, Texas, and much of the South, but northern liberals and labor were not ready to accept him. He avoided primary battles. Humphrey was acceptable to liberals but was a little too far left-of-center and too much the spokesman of the farm belt to appeal to large-state leaders.

Stuart Symington of Missouri had a record that was satisfactory to almost every segment of the party outside the South, but his reputation was confined chiefly to Washington and Missouri, and his personality lacked voter appeal. Kennedy, son of Joseph P. Kennedy, Roosevelt's isolationist ambassador to England before World War II, had as his assets family wealth, a Harvard education, a fine war record as a naval officer, and the authorship of a best-selling book. But his liabilities included his comparative youth—he was approaching forty-three—his lack of administrative experience, a not particularly outstanding Senate record, and a health problem resulting from a back injury and operations to correct it.

Both Kennedy and Humphrey had to demonstrate vote-getting ability by taking the primary route. Kennedy had no oppoisition in New Hampshire but battled with Humphrey for Wisconsin, which was in Humphrey's territory. He carried six of the ten districts and led on the state-wide vote, but it was charged that Catholic Republicans had voted in the Democratic primary for him. West Virginia on the edge of the Bible Belt was a better test. He met the anti-Catholic issue head-on and won decisively. Here his superior organization and use of television, and the necessary funds for both, played an important part. Humphrey's withdrawal followed his defeat. The remaining primaries, largely uncontested, gave the Kennedy cause a momentum that weakened the neutrality of the uncommitted large states. Deals were completed or under way, to be completed at convention time, for their votes.

Adlai Stevenson, out of the country for several weeks during the pre-convention struggle, refused to indorse any candidate and a movement to draft him showed vigorous signs of life.

The tide was running strongly for Kennedy when the Democratic delegates assembled in the new sports arena at Los Angeles on July 11. The Kennedy board of strategy had a superb organization headed by Robert Kennedy, the candidate's brother. Stevenson was the local crowd favorite, and his loyal following found ways to rule the galleries, but not to influence delegates. Lyndon Johnson, aided by Sam Rayburn, was putting on a desperation fight to stop Kennedy.

A good deal of preparatory work had been done on the platform before the convention met. Except for the customary southern attempts to amend the civil rights plank, it was adopted as presented. The platform declared for equal access to all areas of community life for all Americans. It called for federal action to insure the right to vote and favored a federal fair employment practices commission. The "Rights of Man" section comprised a broad program of public welfare measures. It charged the Eisenhower administration with a failure to promote the national economy and with an exaggerated concern over balancing the budget.

Nine candidates were put in nomination. Kennedy's victory was assured when Wyoming was reached. The roll call gave him 806 votes; Johnson, 409; Symington, 86; Stevenson, 79 1/2; others 140 1/2.

The big surprise of the convention came next day when Kennedy announced that Johnson was his choice for running mate. Why he chose Johnson and why Johnson accepted became problems for future historians. But it proved to be good politics.

Nixon seemingly was assured of the Republican nomination long before the convention met. For a while after his election as governor of New York, Nelson Rockefeller was regarded as a possible aspirant, but party sentiment ruled him out and he announced, late in 1959, that he would not be a candidate without, however, indorsing Nixon. Just before the convention met he criticized Nixon for not offering a more definite program, but a meeting of the two ironed out their differences. Nixon's approval of Rockefeller's stand on certain points angered the predominantly conservative platform committee but the majority gave in and rewrote the controversial planks.

The twenty-seventh Republican national convention opened in the Chicago International Amphitheatre on Monday, July 25, with its program planned in advance and carried out carefully. One of the highlights was the appearance of President Eisenhower who gave a review and defense of his administration.

The platform's civil rights plank was a little more general than the Democratic, but was satisfactory to the liberals and angered the southerners. The central theme of the Republican document was the danger of Communist imperialism and the need for responsible and mature leadership to meet it. Eisenhower had provided it; Nixon would continue it.

Nixon and Goldwater were put in nomination, but the latter withdrew and appealed to conservatives to follow Nixon. Ten Louisiana delegates insisted on voting for the idol of the right wing, after which the nomination was made unanimous. Nixon chose Henry Cabot Lodge, ambassador to the United Nations and former Senator, to run with him. Lodge's selection pointed up the issue of foreign affairs, which Nixon played up in his acceptance speech.

Senator Henry Jackson of Washington succeeded Paul Butler as Democratic national chairman, but the young Kennedy organization, much expanded, planned and directed the strategy. Lawrence F. O'Brien, chief Kennedy organizer in Massachusetts and in the primary states, became director of organization for the national committee. Byron ("Whizzer") White of Colorado, a past football all-star, looked after the National Citizens for Kennedy-Johnson, designed to operate outside the party lines. Closest to the candidate was his manager and brother, Robert F. Kennedy. Pierre Salinger, press secretary, Kenneth P. O'Donnell, in charge of scheduling, Theodore C. Sorenson, policy adviser and brain trust director, and Louis Harris, chief pollster, were other key figures. A squad of Harvard professors headed by Archibald F. Cox supplied materials for speeches, and made suggestions on policies.

The candidate, delayed by the fruitless summer session of Congress, took to the hustings on September 2, and opened the campaign formally at Detroit on Labor Day, September 5. Thereafter his jet plane carried him on a carefully planned but exhausting campaign that overlooked no section of the nation, although it did concentrate to a degree on the large key states of the East and Middle West.

Nixon had announced in his acceptance speech that he would begin his campaign at once, and that he would go into every one of the fifty states. His organization was also headed by a United States Senator as national chairman, Thruston B. Morton of Kentucky, a stanch Eisenhower supporter. Former Chairman Leonard Hall, who had managed Nixon's pre-convention campaign, and Robert Finch, a Los Angeles lawyer, played major roles in directing the Nixon strategy. Charles S. Rhyne headed the Volunteers for Nixon-Lodge. The National Committee created a special advertising agency, "Campaign Associates," with Carroll Newton and Edward A. Rogers in charge, to handle publicity. A brain trust of economic and governmental specialists included two Harvard professors. The Vice President believed that a campaign should build up gradually to reach a peak just before the election, and that too rigid planning was unwise, as it left no room for maneuver when circumstances might require it.

The climactic event of the campaign was a series of four television debates arranged by the three great national networks. The results were no Lincoln-Douglas classics. The rivals battled for points and displayed their skill in fast exchanges and sharp returns, with occasional misses. Performance overshadowed content.

Kennedy drew first blood, although he had been given the underdog rating. Various explanations were offered for Nixon's poor initial showing before the relentless TV camera —bad lighting, bad makeup (it was even charged that a Democrat had done the job), campaign weariness, the disconcerting self-possession of his supposedly immature rival, or some other less tangible factor. Whatever the reason, his past mastery of television seemed to have departed at the outset, and he appeared haggard, ill-at-ease, perspiring with nervousness, and on the defensive. Kennedy, more photogenic, projected to the viewers the image of a coolly confident, highly articulate, quick-witted antagonist who measured up to the requirements of national leadership. The immaturity charge lost its momentum.

Nixon was more like himself in the later debates, and scored effectively, especially in the area of foreign relations, but the effect of the first encounter could not be undone. People forgot the arguments, and remembered what they saw. This may have been the turning point of the campaign. After the first debate the Kennedy forces were buoyed up by favorable polls and the mounting size and enthusiasm of his crowds. Ten of eleven southern governors attending a conference fell in line and sent a telegram of congratulations.

On the campaign trail the two candidates, with much repetition, developed the major issues. Kennedy favored expanded federal action to deal with social and economic problems and to strengthen the American economy. Nixon held that federal power should be used only to stimulate private enterprise and to deal with situations where local solutions had failed.

On foreign relations Kennedy assailed the administration for following a policy of drift and stagnation which was not checking the inroads of Communism. Nixon defined the policy as one of peace without surrender of principle. On the question of the defense of the Chinese offshore islands of Quemoy and Matsu, charges and countercharges seemed to show that both candidates were occupying practically the same position. As to Cuba, Nixon charged that Kennedy was "dangerously irresponsible" in demanding more vigorous measures against Castro. Kennedy had called him "trigger happy" as to Quemoy and Matsu.

The religious issue was brought into the headlines when a hundred and fifty Protestant ministers and laymen held a secret meeting at Washington, called by Reverend Norman Vincent Peale, and listened to speeches on the dangers of Vatican control under a Catholic President. A manifesto of similar tenor was issued. Kennedy answered these "Citizens for Religious Freedom" in a notable speech before the Greater Houston Ministerial Association. He declared in favor of the absolute separation of church and state, and "against unconstitutional aid to parochial schools," and pledged himself to make decisions "without regard to outside religious pressures or dictates." Dr. Peale and his cohorts called Kennedy's Houston stand "complete, unequivocal and reassuring," and the Kennedy managers sent taped recordings of the Houston performance to all parts of the country. The upper air of the campaign was cleared for more vital issues, but there were lower levels where the miasma of ancient prejudices could not be dispelled.

While Kennedy was confronted by the religious problem, Nixon ran afoul of the race question. The strong civil rights plank of the Republican platform, largely his work, not only angered southern racists and conservatives, but was not used effectively to draw Negro support in the big nothern states. An incident involving the South's outstanding Negro leader, the Reverend Martin Luther King, gave Kennedy an opportunity that Nixon missed. Arrested for participating in a "sit-in" attempt in an Atlanta restaurant, King was sentenced in late October to serve a prison term at hard labor. Kennedy, advised of the situation by watchful members of his staff, telephoned Mrs. King to offer his sympathy and support, and next day his influence operated to help secure King's release on bail. His quick action, contrasted with Nixon's silence, accelerated a Negro swing to Kennedy, which may have accounted for Democratic victories in five or six states.

In the South, however, the major factor in combatting Republican appeal was the campaign activity of Lyndon

Johnson. He whistle-stopped his way across the old Confederacy on the L.B.J. Victory Special, "the grandson of a Confederate soldier," who talked the language of his listeners and who knew how to stir up the lagging loyalties of the party regulars who would get out the vote. His most effective work—and Speaker Rayburn assisted here—was done in Texas, twice carried by Eisenhower. The struggle was a bitter one. Late in the campaign the Vice Presidential candidate and Mrs. Johnson, entering a Dallas hotel for a public meeting, were booed, jostled, and shoved around by a group of well-dressed Nixon supporters. This treatment of a distinguished native son exceeded in political stupidity the acts of some Michigan irresponsibles who hurled eggs and tomatoes at the Nixon entourage, and a Milwaukee woman who threw a glass of whiskey into Kennedy's face. But only the Dallas episode backfired seriously in terms of votes.

Only in the final week did President Eisenhower take to the stump, although an earlier non-political tour was reminiscent of some of F. D. Roosevelt's subterfuges. The Nixon strategy was to build up the campaign to a grand finale with Eisenhower the great drawing card the last week. In metropolitan New York, accompanied by Nixon, and at Pittsburgh and Cleveland, the President extolled the merits of the experienced Republican candidates who could be depended upon to keep the peace and prevent inflation. He called Kennedy "this young genius" who lacked the knowledge, wisdom, and experience necessary for a President.

Earlier in the campaign Nixon had sought to dispel any impression that he was an apron-string candidate. He wanted to project the image of a leader who would stand broadly for the basic policies of the administration, but who was prepared to offer new programs where needed. But now, with the election a toss-up, the voters needed to be reminded that they still liked Ike, and that Nixon was Ike's choice. The President was warmly greeted by his usual large and enthusiastic crowds, but some hindsight Republican critics thought that Nixon waited too long to use him, and wasted his help in states that did not prove to be close.

Early returns on November 8 pointed toward a Kennedy sweep of the coastal East by large majorities. In the lower South he seemed to be holding much of the normal Democratic strength, although Virginia, Kentucky, and Tennessee were evidently repeating the defection of 1956, and unpledged electors were ahead in Mississippi and Alabama. But early talk of a Kennedy landslide subsided when the Middle West reported. Ohio and Wisconsin soon were conceded to Nixon—Kennedy's biggest disappointments—and the western argricultural states were almost solidly Republican. The election turned into one of the closest in American history. In four states—Illinois, Michigan, Minnesota, and California—early Kennedy leads were being whittled away by a heavy Republican non-urban vote. Nixon needed all four to win an electoral majority; Kennedy needed two. Mississippi's eight unpledged electors and Alabama's six (Kennedy had the remaining five) could play a decisive role if neither candidate had a majority.

Before noon on Wednesday, the four doubtful states fell into the Kennedy column, and Nixon formally conceded his defeat. Later, a surprisingly large number of absentee ballots in California, counted after the election, shifted his home state to Nixon. Little Hawaii's three votes were not finally determined for Kennedy until the electoral college was meeting. This made his total 303 electoral votes to Nixon's 219. Senator Byrd was the choice of the eight unpledged electors of Mississippi and the six of Alabama, and also of an Oklahoma Republican who defected from Nixon.

Republican charges of fraud in Texas and Illinois lacked sufficient evidence to warrant the prolonged court battles that would ensue if the official count were questioned. Kennedy's margin in Illinois was 8,858 votes, in Texas, 46,233.

By the tabulation of the clerk of the House of Representatives, Kennedy had 119,450 more popular votes than Nixon in a total of 68,836,385, a difference of one-tenth of 1 per cent. Other tabulations differ slightly from this. The mixed result in Alabama is the chief complicating factor. This was the closest voter verdict since 1880. Minor parties and unpledged electors accounted for enough popular votes to put both major party candidates below 50 per cent of the total.[1]

Both Houses of Congress were Democratic as expected, the Senate 64 to 36, the House 263 to 174. The Republicans had gained two Senators and twenty-one Representatives, and elections of state governors put fifteen Democrats and twelve Republicans in office, a net gain of one Republican.

Kennedy had swept the East, except for upper New England (Maine, New Hampshire, Vermont), divided the Middle West with Nixon, captured the lower South, except Florida and the unpledged electors of Mississippi and Alabama, lost the upper South (Virginia, Tennessee, and Kentucky), and carried only Nevada and New Mexico in the Great West north and west of Texas. Outside the South, it was largely urban America against small-town and rural America.

The victor's religion won back defecting Eisenhower Catholic Democrats but cost the candidate heavily in the rural Protestant areas, although the peace-prosperity appeal operated in favor of Eisenhower's heir in the old isolationist sections. In any case, the nation had elected a Catholic President and well over half of his votes had come from Protestants.

Campaign finances had become the most serious problem in party management. The rising costs of transportation, advertising, registration drives, polling, and other indispensables of an intensive struggle for votes made the campaign of 1960 the most expensive in history. On the national level the major parties spent over $25,000,000 as compared with a total of $17,200,000 in 1956. Unlike 1952 and 1956, the Democrats, if labor disbursements are included, spent slightly more than the Republicans nationally, although the former ended up with a huge deficit. Victory gave its customary stimulus to post-election fund raising, and saved the party's credit. If the expenditures at state and local levels are added,

[1] Scammon, *America at the Polls*, gives the following totals: Kennedy, 34,226,731; Nixon, 34,108,157; Louisiana independent electors, 169,572; Mississippi unpledged, 116,248; Haas, Socialist Labor, 47,522; Decker, Prohibition, 46,203; Faubus, National State Rights, 44,977; Dobbs, Socialist Workers, 40,165; others, lesser numbers.

the grand total has been estimated at $175,000,000. To meet such outlays, fund-raising dinners, large contributors, and state quotas, which passed the burden on to local organizations, were the chief sources, but these were in danger of being wrung dry by election day. A partial solution pointed toward some form of government subsidy.

The newspapers and the magazines of opinion, as in the past, displayed a heavy Republican editorial preponderance, but narrow partisanship in the form of slanted news stories and misleading headlines seemed to be less marked. The press in the many one-paper or one-ownership cities in the main recognized its responsibility to give equal space to and objective presentation of campaign activities of both parties. The working journalists who followed the campaign trail were charged by the Nixon staff with a Kennedy preference which, it was alleged, infiltrated their news stories. Certainly, the Kennedy entourage included a more sympathetic journalistic retinue, and the Democratic candidate achieved a rapport with press representatives that Nixon did not.

But contributing to the decline of newspaper editorial influence was the wide use of television. It provided candidates with direct contacts with the voters, who could see and hear them at close hand, and judge accordingly, if often irrationally. Kennedy demonstrated his maturity and increased his public stature by his television performances, particularly in the great debates. He believed that they made victory possible. Most political experts agreed with him.

CHAPTER XIII

L. B. J.

1964

PRESIDENT KENNEDY'S NEW FRONTIER made some limited advances, but the bi-partisan bloc of Republicans and southern Democrats operated much as it had in the Truman years, so far as domestic issues were concerned. He secured the creation of a Peace Corps of American volunteers for humanitarian and cultural work in the more backward nations and an Alliance for Progress to aid Latin American nations. Both were popular at home and abroad.

The "Bay of Pigs" fiasco, an attempted invasion of Cuba by anti-Castro exiles in April, 1961, which had American encouragement but insufficient American aid, gave the Republicans a promising issue for future use. But the edge was dulled by the President's success in getting Khrushchev to yield on the issue of constructing Russian missile bases in Cuba in October, 1962.

A strong conservative movement began to make considerable headway in the Republican party. Among the more extreme groups was the John Birch Society, founded by Robert H. W. Welch, Jr., a retired candy manufacturer, who called President Eisenhower a "dedicated, conscious agent of the Communist conspiracy." Operating in secret and well financed, it viewed Washington as a center of subversion and attacked the Supreme Court as Communistic because of its civil rights decisions, its banning of official religious exercises in the public schools, and its decision in Baker v. Carr requiring redistricting by state legislatures where apportionment of seats disregarded population. While many moderates were critical of the court, the Birch solution—"Impeach Chief Justice Earl Warren"—was copied only by rightist groups flocking to get into the promising financial waters of extremism.

In the mid-term elections the Republicans lost four Senate seats and added only four to their House minority, but they captured the governorships from the Democrats in Michigan, Ohio, and Pennsylvania, and Governor Rockefeller was re-elected in New York. These gains were partially offset by Nixon's defeat by Governor Edmund Brown in California. Of the newcomers, George Romney of Michigan, former head of American Motors, and William Scranton of Pennsylvania attracted attention as possibilities for 1964. Governor Rockefeller, an early favorite, now raised doubts about his availability by marrying a divorcée after a divorce from his first wife.

The most striking development in Republican ranks was a Goldwater boom. Frank and forthright in speech and actions, this son of a Jewish father and Protestant mother had become the voice of the booming Southwest with his simple conservative philosophy which found expression in his *The Conscience of A Conservative*. He opposed the whole fabric of the welfare state, questioned the final authority of the Supreme Court, would limit the scope of civil rights legislation, and held to a strongly nationalistic position on foreign policy, favoring an end of diplomatic relations with Iron Curtain countries and a hard line toward Castro in Cuba. A "draft Goldwater" movement headed by F. Clifton White of New York operated under cover for several months before coming out into the open in early 1963. The reluctant Arizona Senator finally accepted the fact that he was a candidate, and made a Phoenix friend, Denison Kitchell, his manager later in the year.

The Democrats were troubled by rising tensions over race relations in the South. The use of troops was required at the University of Mississippi to put down a riotous outbreak over the admission of a Negro student. Attorney General Robert Kennedy bore the brunt of criticism for this and other school desegregation actions. Governors George Wallace of Alabama, Ross Barnett of Mississippi, and other segregationist leaders planned to pre-empt the Democratic emblem for unpledged electoral tickets, wherever possible. Their aim was to capture the balance of power in the electoral college and throw the election to the House of Representatives.

President Kennedy secured Senate approval for a treaty with the Soviet Union banning atmospheric nuclear tests and gave administration approval to the sale of large quantities of surplus wheat to that nation. A tax-cut proposal was stalled by Senator Byrd, chairman of the Finance Committee.

On the business front Kennedy had come under fire for his policies, but a boom was getting under way in late 1963, no new crisis seemed to be impending with Iron Curtain countries, and the prospect was fair for the Kennedy ship to unfurl all its sails for a peace-and-prosperity campaign in 1964.

But the ship was never to sail. An assassin's bullet struck down the captain, and the grief and horror of the nation obliterated party lines. Even the voices of the extreme Kennedy haters were silenced, and their propaganda, ready for the coming campaign, became a liability.

Lyndon Johnson came to the Presidency with the best preparation of any Vice President suddenly elevated to the highest office. While not a member of the Kennedy inner circle, he had participated in the deliberations of the cabinet and the National Security Council, and had played an active part in other top-level matters, including the exploration of space. He had gone abroad as a good-will salesman for his country, and his range of greetings encompassed rulers and camel drivers.

The tall Texan, possessed of superabundant energy, self-assurance, a rather sharp temper, and an instinct for politics, lacked Kennedy's intellectual interests and gift of speech, but he was a skilled tactician in the art of the possible who operated best through personal contacts, and he had an unsurpassed knowledge of the men and methods of Capitol Hill. He had outgrown his Texas territorialism, and was strongly committed to civil rights legislation and other major Kennedy measures.

That he would be nominated at the 1964 Democratic national convention was taken for granted, presumably with a liberal from the East or Middle West as his running mate. But to win in November he needed to convince the urban Kennedy strongholds that he had no southern sectional spots on his national toga.

The new President, operating with a skilled hand in the legislative field he had ploughed so often, secured the passage of the long-delayed tax reduction measure and a stronger civil rights bill than the original Kennedy measure. A bi-partisan combination backed the civil rights bill with Senate Republican leader Everett Dirksen leading the conservatives of the midlands to its support after securing some clarifying amendments. Senator Goldwater was one of six Senate Republicans who voted against it. He called certain provisions unconstitutional and feared their enforcement would produce "a police state" and "an informer psychology." The Senate passed the bill on June 19. Goldwater was already well in the lead for the Republican Presidential nomination.

In the early spring the contest for the Republican prize had seemed invitingly open. The New Hampshire primary of March 10 produced a surprise result. A well-organized write-in campaign for Henry Cabot Lodge, ambassador to Viet Nam, put him ahead of Goldwater, Rockefeller, Nixon (also a write-in choice), Senator Margaret Chase Smith of Maine, and Harold Stassen.

Down to the California primary the Republican voters confused the experts with their own confusions. Candidates avoided direct primary battles where the results appeared doubtful, voters used write-ins frequently, and favorite son figureheads enabled some states to postpone commitments. In the convention states of the South and West Goldwater was capturing the delegates. Rockefeller won a surprising victory in the Oregon primary over Lodge, which practically eliminated the latter. Goldwater wisely had abandoned Oregon to his rivals. But contrary to pollster predictions he carried California over Rockefeller by a 68,350 margin in a total vote of 2,172,456. This meant eighty-six delegates. Later conventions, which included Texas, added enough, by his supporters' claims, to give him the 655 votes needed for the nomination.

Republican moderates, in alarm, looked to Eisenhower to encourage a stop-Goldwater movement, as the former President had made statements about the need for a candidate in the mainstream of Republican thinking. But when no help came from Eisenhower, Governor Scranton of Pennsylvania announced his intention to run and set about belatedly to win the uncommitted and the loosely committed delegates to his support. The forty-six-year-old prepossessing governor, who smiled easily and spoke fluently and with serious conviction, argued that Goldwater's votes and utterances were out of line with past Republican platforms. Could the party, he asked, "stand with one foot in the twentieth century and one in the nineteenth?"

Rockefeller, Romney, and Lodge were ready to help, and Lodge joined Scranton on a western delegate hunt, but the results were not encouraging.

The convention opened at San Francisco's Cow Palace on July 19 with National Chairman William Miller presiding. Governor Mark Hatfield of Oregon, in his keynote speech, emphasized the humanitarian heritage of the party. When he castigated extremists and lumped together the John Birch Society, the Ku Klux Klan, and the Communist party, there were ill-concealed murmurs of disapproval. Next day when Eisenhower spoke on the same general theme, an incidental reference to "sensation seeking columnists and commentators" produced a roar of approval and an eruption of fist shaking directed at the occupants of television booths and press seats. This showed the temper of the majority, convinced of the bias of eastern news media.

The platform committee had met the week before the convention opened to hear speakers for all manner of causes. The finished product did not suit the liberals. Senator Hugh

Scott of Pennsylvania, Scranton's manager, offered three amendments: a repudiation of extremists with the John Birch Society mentioned by name; a reassertion of Presidential control over nuclear weapons (not giving commanding officers in the field an option as to nuclear tactical weapons, as Goldwater had suggested); and a stronger statement for enforcement of the civil rights law. All were voted down, as were similar amendments offered by Governor Romney. But the most astonishing incident of the convention was the treatment of Rockefeller when he tried to speak for the first proposal. From the galleries came boos and hisses and cries of "We Want Barry," and Chairman Thruston Morton had great difficulty getting order for the grim-faced governor to speak for his allotted four minutes.

The platform on key points was a Goldwater textbook. Its central themes were the dangers to liberty at home from an expanding federal power, and the need for a dynamic strategy against Communism to secure victory for freedom "every place on earth." Democratic failures and weaknesses in both areas were cited at length. The touchy civil rights question was disposed of with a promise of full implementation of the Civil Rights Act of 1964 and continued opposition to discrimination, with the qualification that the elimination of such discrimination is "a matter of heart, conscience, and education, as well as of equal rights under law." Endorsement was given constitutional amendments to permit religious exercises in public places and to enable states having bicameral legislatures to apportion one house on a basis other than population.

At the Wednesday evening session, nominating speeches provided eight candidates. The customary demonstrations followed with most of the sound and fury for Goldwater. The one ballot gave Goldwater 883 votes; Scranton, 214; Rockefeller, 114; Romney, 41; Mrs. Margaret Chase Smith, 27; Walter Judd of Minnesota, 22; Hiram Fong of Hawaii, 5; and Lodge, who had withdrawn, 2. Scranton moved that the nomination be made unanimous.

The ticket was completed with the nomination of Congressman and National Chairman William Miller of New York for

Vice President. Although geographically and in religion—he was a Roman Catholic—he seemed to give balance to the ticket, Miller was a conservative, had slight strength in his home state, and was better known to party professionals than to the rank and file of party voters.

In his acceptance speech Goldwater offered no olive branch to the defeated. He reiterated his conservative creed and stirred his listeners with his challenging statement: "Extremism in defense of liberty is no vice . . . moderation in pursuit of justice is no virtue." The counterrevolution had been successful, and the Eastern Establishment had been toppled in the dust, even stamped upon.

The Goldwater forces took control of the Republican National Committee immediately after the convention. Dean Burch, a thirty-six-year-old Phoenix attorney who for several years had been a member of the Senator's Washington staff, became national chairman. Denison Kitchel, a Harvard-educated lawyer, was Goldwater's personal manager. A long-time friend, he had directed the pre-convention campaign but preferred to work in the background. The southern Goldwater forces were represented by John Grenier of Alabama, who ranked next to Burch in authority. Ralph Cordiner, former chairman of the board of General Electric, handled finances.

Old professionals such as former national chairman Leonard Hall of New York and Ohio state chairman Ray C. Bliss, were ignored as much as used for advisory purposes. The committee organization was staffed by the "Arizona Mafia" in all important positions. A new crowd was running the show, and the preliminary planning was done efficiently, on paper.

The Democratic national convention met at Atlantic City on August 24 with everything planned in advance by President Johnson, although he withheld the name of his running mate until the time came for nominations. Governor Wallace of Alabama had upset pre-convention harmony by entering the primaries in Wisconsin, Indiana, and Maryland against favorite son stand-ins for Johnson. He won no delegates but polled a considerable vote with his racist appeal, getting forty-three per cent in Maryland where white resentment against Negro militancy was especially strong.

The credentials committee was faced with the problem of two Mississippi delegations, a regularly elected one and a contesting "Freedom" group. The convention adopted a solution that gave seats to the regulars on the condition that the delegates take a pledge to support the ticket, and allotted two seats at large to the freedom claimants. Only four signed the loyality pledge, and the Freedom group rejected the compromise. The Alabama delegates were also asked to take a similar pledge, but only fourteen complied and were seated.

The lengthy platform promised "unflagging devotion to our commitments to freedom from Berlin to South Viet Nam," the further isolation of Castroism, and a continued resolve, under tested leadership, to use every resource to find the road to peace. On the domestic front it offered a broad federal program of social and economic welfare measures covering education, medicare, civil rights, the war on poverty, farm policies, urban improvement, and conservation. Labor was promised repeal of the Taft-Hartley Act. The Ku Klux Klan, the Communist Party, and the John Birch Society were condemned as extremist organizations. Thirty-eight citations from the platform of 1960 were followed by the accomplishments of the Kennedy-Johnson administration in each case.

The nominating session was a formality. President Johnson surprised everyone by coming to the convention, accompanied by his family, to announce that Senator Humphrey would be his running mate, which was no great surprise in itself. Senator Eugene McCarthy, also of Minnesota, had been regarded as the only other possible choice, with Robert Kennedy eliminated earlier by Johnson's politic decision not to take anyone from the cabinet. Kennedy was taken care of by an invitation from a New York group to run for the Senate from that state. Humphrey, a Middle Western liberal, had tempered his early crusading zeal into a more realistic willingness to work for the possible, had demonstrated his skill as party whip in the Senate, was a popular figure outside the lower South, and had no peer as a rapid-fire, extemporaneous speaker. Both Johnson and Humphrey were nominated by acclamation.

Tributes to three deceased party notables—John F. Kennedy, Mrs. Eleanor Roosevelt, and Sam Rayburn—and the acceptance speeches of the candidates came on the final day of the convention. The Atlantic City gathering had been a party jamboree, with a good time had by all, as the delegates had come merely to ratify.

Before beginning his campaign, Goldwater conferred with Republican notables including governors and gubernatorial candidates at Eisenhower's home. He tried to restore unity by clarifying his views on major issues to show that he was repudiating extremism of both the left and the right. Most of those present expressed approval of his explanations.

But the cleavage was too deep to be repaired in this fashion. Disaffection developed on a scale unequalled since the Bull Moose split of 1912. Among candidates who refused to indorse the Goldwater-Miller ticket were Senator Keating of New York and Governor Romney of Michigan, while several others, including Senator Hugh Scott of Pennsylvania, Robert Taft, candidate for the Senate from Ohio, and Charles H. Percy, running for governor in Illinois, conducted virtually independent campaigns. Senators Case of New Jersey, Kuchel of California, and Javits of New York, not up for re-election, withheld indorsement. Governor Rockefeller gave a nominal support to the ticket. Of the better-known figures only Nixon and Scranton went on the campaign trail.

In the South Governor Wallace dropped the idea of an independent candidacy but refrained from any indorsement to avoid embarrassing Goldwater, he said. He supported his unpledged electoral ticket. But in South Carolina Senator Strom Thurmond, a segregationist and a conservative, joined the Republican party.

Prominent Republican business and financial leaders and several Eisenhower officeholders, including four former cabinet members, took the bolters' path. The larger metropolitan pro-Republican and independent newspapers and periodicals were almost a unit in support of Johnson. In terms of circulation, the press was heavily anti-Goldwater, an unprecedented situation for a Republican candidate. Members of the working press in the Goldwater entourage were sometimes greeted with boos and insulting remarks. The Republican candidate, feeling that he had been the victim of misinterpretations of off-the-cuff remarks in the past, dispensed with formal press conferences and presented his case in prepared speeches and television appearances.

In one respect, the war of paperbacks, the Goldwater attackers far outdistanced the Johnson defenders in verbiage and venom. Right-wing organizations circulated thousands of copies of this hate literature, whose authors foot-noted one another to prove that the nation was in the clutches of a conspiracy of subversion, with the particular devils varying according to the speciality of the author.

Citizens' organizations appeared outside the regular party fences, aimed at bolters and independents. Citizens for Goldwater-Miller and National Citizens for Johnson and Humphrey led the procession, but auxiliaries and subdivisions for various professions and skills multiplied until the Republicans were accredited with thirty, the Democrats with twenty-eight, according to press reports. Here the advantage lay heavily with the Democrats, for the masses of Republican bolters could find congenial company in citizens' committees for Johnson, while Democratic bolters were lonesome outcasts, outside the South.

Goldwater opened his campaign formally on September 3 at Prescott, Arizona, the starting point for his two Senatorial campaigns. He attributed to the administration "the way of the regimented society," "the way of mobs in the streets," appeasement in foreign affairs, unilateral disarmament in the face of militant Communism, and a low tone of morality in the public service. He emphasized his own devotion to peace through strength. These themes he returned to repeatedly in later speeches with the need for morality in public life getting more and more attention toward the close of his campaign.

The slogan of the Republican campaign, "In Your Heart You Know He's Right," appeared in every kind of publicity put forth by the Goldwater supporters. It was easy to parody, and its interminable repetition possibly was a mistake.

The Democrats made sure that Goldwater's utterances before he became a candidate would return to plague him. He was called trigger happy because of his statement that the field commander might have the option of deciding when to use tactical atomic weapons, and the horrors of nuclear war were pictured in paid television propaganda. He was charged with hostility to social security because of a remark, before the New Hampshire primary, that it should be made voluntary, and he made matters worse by attacking medicare. A television picture of a social security card torn in two was an effective Democratic rejoinder. His vote against the Civil Rights Act of 1964 blotted out the memory of his support of the earlier acts. His campaign declarations against both forced segregation and forced integration appealed only to the South.

The issue of morality in government became Goldwater's strongest weapon. Two cases, both close to Johnson, came to light, Bobby Baker, Senate majority secretary and once a protégé of Johnson, had been forced to resign the preceding year while under investigation for possible conflicts of interest. The Rules Committee reported in July, 1964, that he was guilty of "gross improprieties" but left the question of law violations for the Justice Department to handle. Republicans charged that the report was a whitewash, that prominent Democrats were involved, and demanded that the Baker case be reopened. Unanswered questions about various Bobby Baker deals provided Republicans with excellent campaign ammunition.

Late in the campaign Walter Jenkins, long a confidential assistant to Johnson, was convicted on a morals charge. He was at once dismissed and placed in a hospital. The effects would have been more damaging but for startling news from abroad: Khrushchev had been deposed and Red China had detonated a nuclear bomb. The Jenkins affair was overshadowed by these developments, although not forgotten.

The Baker and Jenkins cases became Republican evidence of "a cloud over the White House" and "a mess in Washington." Immorality and loose standards at the top were trickling down to infect the nation, Goldwater asserted. But he rejected as racist a documentary film entitled "The Choice," which was designed to depict moral rot and violence in the streets. He refused to permit its use in the campaign.

The Democratic campaign management was headed by Chairman John Bailey, a professional who depended on professionals, but Johnson did his own planning; tactics and itineraries were changed on short notice. His personal control rested on groups of overlapping staff specialists—speech writers, television publicity men, campaign planners, directors of voter registration, citizens' committees, and minorities, and a flock of others. Several key members of the 1960 Kennedy team held important posts, notably Lawrence O'Brien and Kenneth O'Donnell.

The President began his campaign in Cadillac Square in Detroit on Labor Day. His theme then, and later, was national unity on a program of prosperity, justice, and peace. He set up the Great Society as his goal, with unemployment and poverty eliminated and equal opportunities for all. In the final weeks of the campaign he was on the stump almost as much as his rival and far excelled him in handshaking, crowd mingling, and folksy speeches. Although buoyed up by the favorable reports of the polls, he wanted to win by a landslide and set out to cover every section of the country. Critics dismissed his extemporaneous remarks largely as homilies and hokum, but he knew how to please the huge crowds and did not let some heckling, most evident in his own South, disturb his happy front. Both Mrs. Ladybird Johnson and Senator Humphrey had encountered some hostile treatment in tours of the race-conscious southern states.

Humphrey's long record as a battler for liberal causes and his membership in the Americans for Democratic Action labeled him as a Socialist in Republican propaganda and as a Communist in extreme rightist nomenclature. Miller, termed the hatchet man and the bantam gut fighter by hostile sources, confined his stumping chiefly to the smaller cities. Unlike the polyloquent Humphrey, he settled down to one basic speech which he could fit to different audiences with minor changes.

Smear tactics were used with little restraint on both sides, with hate more in evidence in extreme Republican propaganda and fear in Democratic. Bruce L. Felknor, executive director of the Fair Campaign Practices Committee, said that it was "the most vicious and bitter campaign I've ever seen, or for that matter, heard tell of."

The popular verdict on November 3 was more decisive than the Harding and Roosevelt landslides. Johnson received 43,129,484 popular votes to Goldwater's 27,178,188; in percentages 61.1 to 38.5.[1] The electoral votes were 486 and 52. Goldwater's electoral votes came from Arizona and five southern states—South Carolina, Georgia, Alabama, Mississippi, and Louisiana. The Senate was Democratic, 68 to 32; the House of Representatives, 295 to 140. In the governors' races the Republicans won only eight of twenty-five contests. Romney's success in Michigan kept him in the picture for 1968.

To defeat an incumbent riding a prosperity-peace horse has been proved an impossible task in the past, but the race would have been closer if a less vulnerable candidate had been named. An "echo" would certainly have run better than the "choice." At least the mortality percentages for lesser offices would have been reduced. The Goldwater record and bad strategy, which gambled too much on the white backlash, were the major causes of the debacle.

Goldwater's victories in the deep South added seven Republican members to the House of Representatives. These were elected as segregationists and only complicated matters for the party in the North. It was an anomalous situation for the party of Lincoln to have received nearly all of its electoral votes from the former Confederacy. Goldwater did not carry a state that had voted for Lincoln, Theodore Roosevelt, Hoover, or Eisenhower except Arizona in the last two cases and Louisiana in Eisenhower's second election.

The debacle produced an outburst of angry recriminations

[1] Minor parties and independent tickets polled 336,838 votes. Of these, the Alabama unpledged electors had 210,732 votes.

in Republican ranks. Goldwater loyalists blamed the defeat on the failure of the moderates to give the ticket united support and contended that their idol's conservative philosophy had been approved by twenty-seven million voters. Opponents countered that the majority of these were loyal Republican regulars who would vote for any party candidate, and that the swing to the right had driven away the moderates and the independents who had been so responsible for past Republican successes. The restoration of some degree of unity was the Republican goal and problem for the immediate future.

President Johnson, assured of the support of a liberal Congress, set about to reap the fruits of his great victory. The platform promises in the more important fields were carried out by a far-reaching program of legislation. But outbreaks of race violence in the cities, a prosperity that was expanding into inflation, and the persisting cloud of Viet Nam cast ominous shadows over the consensus achievement of 1964.

The effects of this national mood of uncertainty and discontent in these broad areas appeared in the mid-term elections of 1966. The old political axiom that unhappy voters take it out on the party in power operated in favor of the Republican "outs." They gained 47 seats in the House of Representatives and three in the Senate, and won eight additional governorships to bring their total to twenty-five, which included four of the five largest states.

Improving Republican prospects foreshadowed a sharp struggle for the Presidential prize at the convention of 1968. The early listing of possibilities included George Romney, returned to Michigan's governorship by a landslide, Charles Percy of Illinois, elected to the Senate over veteran liberal Paul Douglas, Ronald Reagan of California, former movie favorite, who had defeated Governor Edmund G. Brown, in his try for a third term, James A. Rhodes of Ohio, reelected governor by a wide margin, and Richard Nixon, who built up good will by campaigning in 1966 wherever Republican candidates could use his services. Governor Rockefeller of New York ruled himself out of contention, but his impressive victory for a third term in New York could not be overlooked. Only Reagan wore a conservative collar, although Nixon had made himself acceptable to the right wing.

In the Democratic ranks President Johnson seemed assured of a renomination, even though his escalation of the American military commitment in Viet Nam had come under fire from a segment of the liberals who had supported his domestic policies. The growing rift, much publicized, between the President and Senator Robert Kennedy seemed to be largely personal, but shades of differences over policies might be sharpened as tensions increased. Kennedy's aim seemed directed toward 1972.

In Alabama George Wallace, whose wife Lurleen had succeeded him as governor, was planning an independent candidacy for the Presidency if the party nominations did not conform to his state sovereignty views. This threatened to confuse further the party situation in the South where the Republicans had captured two governorships in 1966 and almost won a third—in Georgia—where the legislature voted in the Democratic contender in a contested outcome.

Democrats worried about the effects of the continuing involvement in Viet Nam and Johnson's decline in popular appeal. Republicans had to find a harmony formula to insure a united front in 1968. The venerable convention system and the creaking machinery of the electoral college, both much criticized, were still around to carry out, or possibly be used to circumvent, the wishes of the voters.

SELECTED BIBLIOGRAPHY

A MORE comprehensive bibliography, which is itself selective, is found in the author's *History of Presidential Elections* (2nd ed., New York, 1964). The following suggestions for further reading or for reference are intended to give the reader a sampling of the vast literature of past American politics. Space limitations rule out the extensive fields of biography, memoirs, and journals, and the many books dealing with the more restricted areas of party history, geographical, chronological, or topical in approach. Several recent books have been included that were not available when the parent volume was in preparation.

I. GENERAL ACCOUNTS OF NOMINATIONS, ELECTIONS, PARTIES

Binkley, Wilfred E., *American Political Parties: Their Natural History*. New York, 1947.

Burns, James MacGregor, *The Deadlock of Democracy: Four-Party Politics in America*. Englewood Cliffs, N. J., 1963.

Chambers, William N., *Political Parties in a New Nation: The American Experience, 1776–1809*. New York, 1963.

David, Paul T., Goldman, Ralph M., and Bain, Richard C., *The Politics of National Party Conventions*. Washington, D.C., 1960.

Eaton, Herbert, *Presidential Timber: A History of Nominating Conventions, 1868–1960*. New York, 1964.

Hatch, Louis C., *A History of the Vice-Presidency of the United States* (rev. and ed. Earl L. Shoup). Chicago, 1934.

Heard, Alexander, *The Costs of Democracy* (election expenses). Durham, N. C., 1960.

Hofstadter, Richard, *The Age of Reform: From Bryan to F.D.R.* New York, 1955.

Lorant, Stefan, *The Presidency: A Pictorial History of Presidential Elections, from Washington to Truman.* New York, 1951.

Lynch, William O., *Fifty Years of Party Warfare.* Indianapolis, 1931.

Mayer, George H., *The Republican Party, 1854–1964.* New York, 1964.

Moos, Malcolm, *The Republicans: A History of Their Party.* New York, 1956.

Pomper, Gerald, *Nominating the President: The Politics of Convention Choice.* Evanston, Ill., 1963.

Robinson, Edgar E., *The Evolution of American Political Parties.* New York, 1924.

Stanwood, Edward, *A History of the Presidency.* 2 vols., Boston, 1916.

Wilmerding, Lucius, Jr., *The Electoral College.* New Brunswick, 1958.

Young, Donald, *American Roulette: The History and Dilemma of the Vice Presidency.* New York, 1965.

II. REFERENCE WORKS

Bain, Richard C., *Convention Decisions and Voting Records.* Washington, D. C., 1960.

Burnham, W. Dean, *Presidential Ballots, 1836–1892.* Baltimore, 1955.

David, Paul T. (and others). Cited above.

Porter, Kirk H. and Johnson, Donald Bruce, eds. *National Party Platforms, 1840–1960.* Urbana, Ill., 1961. Supplement, 1964.

Robinson, Edgar E., *The Presidential Vote, 1896–1932.* Stanford University, Calif., 1934.

———, *They Voted for Roosevelt.* Stanford University, Calif., 1947.

Scammon, Richard, compiler, *America at the Polls.* Pittsburgh, 1965.

Stanwood, Edward. Cited above.

III. HISTORIES OF SOME SIGNIFICANT ELECTIONS

Bagby, Wesley M., *The Road to Normalcy: The Presidential Campaign and Election of 1920.* Baltimore, 1962.

Clancy, Herbert J., *The Presidential Election of 1880.* Chicago, 1958.

Gammon, Samuel R., Jr., *The Presidential Campaign of 1832.* Baltimore, 1922.

Glad, Paul W., *McKinley, Bryan, and the People.* Philadelphia, 1964.

Gunderson, Robert G., *The Log-Cabin Campaign.* Lexington, 1957.

Haworth, P. L., *The Hayes-Tilden Disputed Presidential Election of 1876.* Cleveland, 1906.

Knoles, George H., *The Presidential Campaign and Election of 1892.* Stanford University, Calif., 1942.

Luthin, Reinhard, *The First Lincoln Campaign.* Cambridge, Mass., 1944.

Moore, Edmund A., *A Catholic Runs for President: The Campaign of 1928.* New York, 1956.

Nichols, Roy F., *The Democratic Machine, 1850–1854.* New York, 1923.

Rimini, Robert V., *The Election of Andrew Jackson.* Philadelphia, 1963.

Thomas, H. C., *The Return of the Democratic Party to Power in 1884.* New York, 1919.

Thomson, Charles A. H., and Shattuck, Frances M., *The 1956 Presidential Campaign.* Washington, 1960.

White, Theodore H., *The Making of the President, 1960.* New York, 1961.

———, *The Making of the President, 1964.* New York, 1965.

Zornow, William F., *Lincoln and the Party Divided.* Norman, Oklahoma, 1954.

INDEX